SHOT FOR A WHITE-FACED DEER

~ ~ TO THOSE WHOSE LIFE AND LABOUR

I HAVE ENDEAVOURED TO DESCRIBE

IN THE PAGES OF THIS BOOK ~ ~

Shot For a
White-Faced Deer

LIFE AT THE NEW FOREST EDGE
1837 — 1914

Stephen Ings

First published in the United Kingdom in 2010
by The Hobnob Press, PO Box 1838, East Knoyle, Salisbury, SP3 6FA
www.hobnobpress.co.uk

British Library Cataloguing in Publication Data
A catalogue record for this book is available from the British Library

ISBN 978-1906978-00-6
Typeset in Scala 11/12.5pt. Typesetting and origination by John Chandler
Printed by Lightning Source

Contents

Acknowledgements		vi
List of Illustrations		vii
Prologue: Shot For a White-Faced Deer		ix
I	On the Forest Edge	1
II	Master and Man	10
III	The Labourer at Home	27
IV	Birth and Marriage	43
V	Deaths	59
VI	Outdoor Relief, Charity and Self Help	73
VII	The Workhouse – The Paupers' Daily Routine	91
VIII	The Workhouse – Education, Health and Changing Attitudes	104
IX	Work – Labour in The Fields	120
X	Work – The Artisan, The Shopkeeper and The Servant	130
XI	Nonconformity	144
XII	The Natural Result of the Spread of Education	157
XIII	Mobility	172
XIV	Transition	183
XV	From Peace to War	193
Epilogue		199
Notes		200
Index		206

Acknowledgements

I AM indebted to Rosemary Morris who typed the manuscript and whose help and support have been invaluable in producing the completed text, and to Mary Cook for her assistance in providing many of the illustrations.

List of Illustrations

Nomansland Green, before 1909	2
Gardeners and decorators employed at Melchet Court, c. 1912	11
Lockerley Hall, 1905	21
Cottages at Nomansland	31
St Peter's Church, Plaitford	67
Quavey Road, Redlynch, 1907	84
A fête on Lockerley Green, 1906	87
Lockerley Green, c. 1900	89
The New Forest Union Workhouse	93
Romsey Workhouse	119
The Street, Whiteparish, before the First World War	130
The bakery at Bramshaw, before 1913	137
'Fielder, Post Office, Bramshaw', 1906	139
West Tytherley Rectory	141
Landford Wood Mission Hall	150
Nomansland Green	156
Harry Churchill with pupils outside Landford National School, early 1870s	160
Melchet Court, 1904	170
The Shoe Inn and the former Sarum to Eling turnpike road	174

A Map of the district will be found on page xii

Prologue – Shot For a White-Faced Deer

IN 1899 a book entitled *The New Forest, Its Traditions, Inhabitants and Customs* included an account of a fatal accident that took place 'on the high ground above Nomansland', a hamlet partly in Wiltshire and partly in Hampshire that straddles the boundary of the New Forest. According to the book's authors, Rose C. de Crespigny and Horace Hutchinson, the accident occurred in the aftermath of the Deer Removal Act of 1851 (which called for the extermination of all the deer in the Forest) and at a time when the woods and enclosures 'resounded with rifle shots' as the animals were destroyed. One specimen was reported to be in the vicinity of Nomansland, and a keeper was sent to dispatch it. He stalked his quarry, 'although the white face was all that he could see', and shot it dead. Unhappily what he had mistaken for the face of a deer was that of a woman, and whilst de Crespigny and Hutchinson did not record what ensued, they did note that the scene of the fatality was still known as the place where the old woman was killed.

Eleven years after the appearance of *The New Forest, Its Traditions, Inhabitants and Customs*, a second account of the incident was included in a pamphlet entitled *Nomansland, A Village History*, written by Herbert Mann Livens.[1] According to Livens, the old woman was the victim of a 'poaching accident'. She had gone to collect sticks for match faggots, and as she stooped down to gather them in the autumn twilight, a keeper who 'mistook her cap for the target of a deer' shot and killed her. Livens obtained his material from the oldest inhabitants of the hamlet, and the account which he gave was evidently based on a different source from the one known to de Crespigny and Hutchison. Both must have circulated orally for decades before they were written down, but they contain so many circumstantial details that contemporary evidence of the incident should be readily located – yet none has been found.

Neither the shooting nor the inquest which would have followed it were reported in the *Salisbury Journal* in 1851, 1852 or 1853, although the paper carried the findings of inquest juries over a very wide area and de Crespigny and Hutchinson located the fatality 'on the Wiltshire side'. The burial registers for St Peter's Church, Bramshaw (where

Nomansland residents were usually interred, and where the incumbent from 1841 to 1861, the Rev. Mark Cooper, invariably noted any unusual aspects of death), are equally unforthcoming. Two women from the hamlet were buried in the churchyard in the autumn of 1851, but without any suggestion that either was the victim of a shooting accident.

Nor does Livens, many of whose informants had been born in Nomansland well before 1851, seem to have gathered any specific information about the old woman or the keeper who shot her. In other instances he was more precise. In a section of his pamphlet headed 'A Drinking Song' he wrote of Mrs Macey, who in the 1850s had been the shopkeeper and midwife and had also made lace. She had 'two sons, one of whom fell downstairs and broke his neck in the house he had built'. This is borne out by an entry in the Bramshaw burial register, although Livens omitted one detail which Mark Cooper (who seems to have used the registers to express his disapproval of the moral lapses of his parishioners) included: 'Edward Macey who according to coroner's inquest, falling downstairs when in liquor, died from the effects thereof. Nomansland 10.12.1855.'

John Wise, who wrote *The New Forest, Its History and Scenery* in 1862, complained that tradition killed the murderer instead of his victim: 'Here and there tradition may be true in a very general sense . . . but it is never particular in its dates and is ever in too much of a hurry to compare facts. Tradition, as often as not, kills the murderer instead of the murdered; and makes the man who built the place to have been born there.' Many of the details which give the accounts of the old woman's death such plausibility are likely to have been added as the story was told and retold, or were included when it was written down. (Horace Hutchinson may have assumed that the incident occurred after the Deer Removal Act, which was the subject of a whole chapter in his book *The New Forest*, which he published in 1904.) The factual basis for the tradition – if any – is probably lost. On the other hand, though, it is significant that the story circulated at all. If Livens heard the fatality described as a 'poaching accident', then it would have seemed grimly ironic to those who recounted it. Before 1851 a conviction for deer stealing carried a penalty of six months' imprisonment, and according to de Crespigny and Hutchinson many Foresters had served such a sentence in Winchester Prison. The suggestion that a keeper should have been engaged in poaching and, in the process, have shot an old woman rather than a deer, would have been greeted with sardonic amusement by those who heard it, reflecting a hostility to authority embodied in the office with which the cottagers had the most immediate contact.

At the same time Livens recalled an activity which evidently played a significant part in the Forester's domestic economy but has now largely passed from memory: match faggoting. Match faggots, a form of kindling wood, were sold in Salisbury for 10*d* a hundred.

Furthermore, the written versions of the tradition are reminders of the prudishness of the day. No British deer have white faces but fallow deer have two conspicuous white stripes on the rump which, like a rabbit's scut, are a warning of danger. Contemporary proprieties meant that de Crespigny and Hutchinson felt unable to indicate that even animals had hind-quarters, and compelled Livens to write vaguely that the woman's cap was mistaken for the target of a deer.

Part of what follows is based either on tradition or memory rather than more conventional and (to many authors) acceptable historical evidence. Tradition may not give a reliable, factual account of events but it can reflect the attitudes and experiences of those among whom it circulated; and whilst memory is notorious for its inaccuracies, it may provide insights and even evidence which are not otherwise available. Both are part of the unwritten history of the people, and as such are as important as the sources retained in archives and libraries – and just as worthy of preservation.

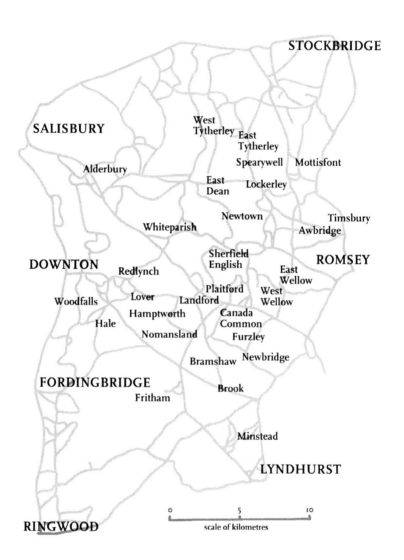

Chapter I
On the Forest Edge

O N Wednesday 8 September 1875 the Rev. Alfred Gay, the Rector of Plaitford, a village which was then in the south-eastern corner of Wiltshire,[1] buried one of his parishioners, Martha Hurst, a widow of fifty-eight. Having entered the name, abode and age of the deceased in the burial register and signed the entry as officiating minister he added a marginal note, 'Dropped down dead while milking her cow', a sentence which provided an unintentional insight into the circumstances of many cottagers living in and around the New Forest and beyond.

Plaitford, the parish of which Alfred Gay was incumbent from 1871 to 1899, had a population which included a high proportion of agricultural labourers but, as with other settlements, the number of labourers living in the village far exceeded the number with permanent positions on farms. Many of the labourers were squatters occupying mud walled dwellings built on common land. The Post Office Directory of 1848 described 'A scattered village consisting chiefly of a few miserable thatched houses situated on a common'.

In Nomansland, a hamlet which had begun to develop in the 1780s and was largely populated by labourers, all the cottages had been built on an area of vacant land situated just beyond the Forest boundary. H.M. Livens gave two accounts of the founding of the settlement. According to one the first inhabitant was a gypsy named Willett, but in the second it was John Shergold, who, having been evicted from a squatter dwelling in the village of Redlynch, erected a 'clotten shanty' on the site of the future hamlet, where his daughter Elizabeth was born in December 1784. Livens claimed that his oldest informants could remember 'clotten houses' which stood on plots afterwards occupied by mud-walled cottages. These were primitive huts comprising a conical framework of poles covered with turf and with an opening at the apex to allow the smoke to escape. By the late nineteenth and early twentieth centuries they were principally used as temporary shelters by charcoal burners or, as Edward Thomas found when cycling through Timsbury

Nomansland Green from a coloured postcard issued by F.G.O. Stuart, a Southampton photographer, before 1909.

near Romsey ahead of pouring rain and on the eve of the First World War, by hurdle-makers who covered their framework of poles with faggots rather than turves.[2] Whether the mud-walled dwellings erected by squatters in other villages were preceded by clotten houses is not known. Where they had been built on an estate they were often allowed to remain, provided that the occupiers paid a quit rent, a nominal sum that nonetheless asserted the landowner's title to the property. No record survives of the terms on which the cottagers held their dwellings on Plaitford Common, but whilst the Post Office Directory was unaware of any other holdings in 1848, George Matcham, a member of the local gentry, described the village in somewhat different terms nine years earlier: 'There are in the parish about 1,460 acres, the principal part of which, comprehending a farm of nearly three hundred acres and other small properties leased out for lives, belongs to the Earl of Ilchester.'[3]

Plaitford consisted of the ancient settlement which George Matcham described, comprising the Manor Farm and eight smaller holdings, and the squatter cottages to which the Post Office Directory had referred. All the small farms (the largest of which was only 33 acres in extent) were cultivated by the families who occupied them. These would nonetheless have required additional labour in busy seasons and so have provided spasmodic employment for some of the thirty-three agricultural workers listed in the census of 1871. Furthermore, whilst the bulk of the village was in the hands of an aristocratic landowner, the principal estates of the Earls of Ilchester were in Dorset and included

Abbotsbury and its Swannery. Plaitford and the small areas of two neighbouring parishes which had been acquired by the Fox Strangways[4] in the late seventeenth century was a backwater, evidence of which is provided by the references to 'small properties leased out of lives'. Life-holding was a form of tenure which was largely obsolete in the middle of the nineteenth century. A relic of feudalism, it involved tenants holding a property for the duration of the lives of (usually three) named individuals. When the last of these died the lease lapsed. In practice such life leases were often more secure than agreements drawn up for a set number of years. Life-holdings could be made for the lives of the occupiers themselves or of third parties, were often renewed and in some instances continued through several generations. Nonetheless they had been widely revoked in the eighteenth century and replaced by leases for a fixed period, frequently of twenty-one years, and their survival is indicative of the character of the communities in which they continued.

As with the squatter dwellings nothing is known of the terms of the life-holds in early Victorian Plaitford, but in an instance from another small community the details have survived. The hamlet of Newtown is on the edge of the much larger parish of Lockerley, near Romsey, and it was here, as late as 1843, that a life-hold was arranged between the nine trustees of a prospective Primitive Methodist chapel and the co-owners of a 'garden ground' or allotment. Under the lease the trustees acquired the use of the allotment for the term of two lives, those of Mary Finch, a widow of fifty-five, who (with Moses Pearce, an agricultural labourer) owned the property and Jessy (spelt elsewhere Jesse) Finch, another agricultural labourer of thirty-six who may have been her son. Remarkably the plot of ground was let provided that the intended 'chapel, meeting house or schoolroom shall stand upon iron arms and cast iron wheels and shall be movable on the death of the last two lives'. Nothing is known of this bizarre edifice, but in 1864 the trustees bought the former allotment from its then owner, George Moody, and in 1867 built a red-brick chapel which was to survive until 1991.

A further insight into the character of the communities in which life-holds lingered into the middle of the nineteenth century is provided not by documentary evidence but by an important work of literature. In 1887 Thomas Hardy's novel *The Woodlanders* was published. Set in a heavily forested and deeply secluded locality around the villages of Great and Little Hintock, the plot is set in the 1840s. One strand of the story turns upon a life-hold in the hands of Giles Winterbourne which lapses on the death of the last life, but which Winterbourne discovers (in an irony typical of the author) could have been renewed if he had been aware that such an option was available.

In 1913 Hermann Lea, a writer and photographer, published *Thomas Hardy's Wessex*, a touring guide to the actual locations upon which Hardy's fictional towns and villages were based and in which Hardy himself took a very active interest. In a chapter headed 'The Country of the Woodlanders', Lea described 'a region inhabited by simple minded people where old fashioned ideas and superstitions still linger'[5] – a description which, although patronising in tone, probably accurately reflected the character of the small hamlets and villages in the locality of the New Forest during the nineteenth century.

EVEN for agricultural labourers permanently employed on farms, wages (particularly in winter) were uncertain and dependent upon the weather. For the large number of labourers living in squatter cottages and relying upon casual work, it was essential to have various sources of income. One of the last surviving members of the Methodist congregation at Newtown, remembering her childhood in the 1920s, recalled that the hamlet was a 'poor village' where most of the householders worked on farms. Her own father had been a builder but, like the agricultural workers, was paid more in the summer than the winter, when he was liable to be laid off. Her mother kept a tin on the mantelpiece in which the extra summer shillings were saved as insurance for the lean days of winter, but less provident housewives spent the additional money as it came in – with the result that some children returned from school on bitterly cold afternoons to find that there was neither a fire in the grate nor food on the table.

Haymaking and harvesting provided the principal opportunities for farm labourers to earn additional wages, since both seasons called for extra hands and farmers paid a higher hourly rate than at other times of year. Agricultural labourers, whether employed on a permanent or casual basis, possessed a wide variety of skills and, being able to use a scythe and a riphook (sickle), could join mowing teams at haymaking and cut corn at harvest (which was less strenuous than mowing). Even after the widespread introduction of the mechanical haycutter and reaper binder towards the end of the century substantial numbers of men and women continued to be required in the hay and harvest fields. Women raked hay into piles in readiness for loading onto wagons, tied sheaves when corn was cut by hand and gathered them into stooks. Even where the reaper binder was used a strip had to be cleared manually before the machine could be brought into the field, whilst both hay and corn were carted away and made into ricks, an activity which called for some skill if the rick was to be securely built.

As the nineteenth century progressed the threshing machine, with its accompanying traction engine, elevator and van (to accommodate the crew), become universal, travelling from farm to farm during the winter months. Although the men who operated the machinery were employed on a permanent basis, some extra labour was required, and before mechanisation hand threshing with a flail could offer almost continuous winter employment. James Dibden, an aged inhabitant of Nomansland, told H.M. Livens in 1910 that he had been employed on piece rates to thresh two sacks of wheat, oats or beans a day, arduous work but undertaken under cover, for which he received 7s 6d a week.

If casual work offered some opportunities to labourers without permanent employment, two of the additional sources of income upon which they could rely are to be seen in the details of the two life leases of the chapel site at Newtown and in Alfred Gay's note on the death of Martha Hurst. The agreement of 1843 established the location of the 'garden ground' by referring to the adjacent properties. Its dimensions were 11 by 8 yards, and it was 'bounded to the east and south by a garden now in the possession of Moses Pearce, to the west by the highroad and to the north by an orchard owned by John Newell'. It is significant that the allotment let to the Primitive Methodist Trustees, the garden and the orchard all lay beside the highway, for broad roadside verges provided squatters with opportunities not only to build dwellings but also to enclose small areas of ground which they could cultivate and would, unless they were evicted, ultimately become their property. The importance of such gardens, allotments and orchards is apparent from the stipulation in the lease that the chapel on wheels 'shall be movable on the death of the last two lives', a condition clearly intended to make an asset available to the lessor's heirs if they were not supporters of the Methodist Society (congregation).

Gardens and allotments not only provided food for the household; they were also a potential source of income. In the middle of the nineteenth century the enumerators' schedules for most rural parishes included at least one resident who earned his living as a dealer, buying cottagers' surplus garden and dairy produce and hawking it in the nearest large town.[6] Dealers normally had a regular round, the burgeoning suburbs of mid-Victorian towns – of which Shirley in Southampton was an example – providing them with a ready market. Nor did a dealer trade in vegetables alone: fruit in season also formed part of his stock, and for this reason an orchard could contribute to the income of a household. The lease of 1843 implies that John Newell's orchard was not adjacent to his cottage, and it was by no means uncommon for fruit trees to be planted on small plots of ground well away from the owner's dwelling.

A traditional tale dating from the early 1880s and reflecting the value of even a single apple tree was remembered by Percy Hatch, who was verger of St Peter's Church, Bramshaw, for sixty years and its grave-digger for forty. The story claimed that when the Bramshaw Wesleyan Methodist Trustees rebuilt their chapel in 1883 they leased a strip of ground from the Warrens Estate to enlarge the site. The additional area encroached upon the garden of a neighbouring cottage, taking in an apple tree which had to be felled. The tenant of the cottage complained to Briscoe Eyre, the owner of Warrens and therefore much of the land and property in the village, that the tree had been worth £5 a year. Briscoe replied, 'Five pounds a year. I see that I have charged you too little rent. I shall have to take that into consideration in future' – a riposte which silenced the complainant immediately.

This has some basis in fact. The Wesleyans did lease a strip of land in 1883, but their agreement with the estate, which has survived, shows that it was only a yard wide and therefore too narrow to accommodate an apple tree. Nor does it seem likely that a single tree, no matter how reliable or prolific, would have borne a crop worth £5 a year when a farm labourer's wages were only 10s a week.[7] On the other hand the existence of this story indicates the importance of fruit in the cottager's economy.

Another reminiscence from the 1920s reveals the way in which the produce of an orchard was procured. In this instance a dealer from Canada Common in West Wellow, who regularly bought the crop from an orchard in Newtown, drove his horse and cart to the hamlet and took two of his children with him. The boy and the girl were sent into the trees, where their lighter weight and more nimble fingers enabled them to reach fruit which would have been inaccessible to an adult.

It was not, however, the fruit alone which made an orchard valuable. It could also provide grazing for a cow, which was a source of milk for the household and also an income, since the cream from any surplus could be churned into butter, a saleable commodity, while the skimmed milk was fed to the pig, the cottager's main source of meat. It seems likely that Martha Hurst's cow (and it is noticeable that Alfred Gay used the singular in his marginal note) was kept in this way. The inquest into her death (all sudden deaths were followed by an inquest even when they were obviously from natural causes) was the subject of a brief report in the *Salisbury Journal* for Saturday 11 September 1875.

The paper stated that the widow had died on the previous Saturday evening (4 September) and continued thus: 'It appeared that the deceased was milking a cow when she suddenly fell from the stool on which she was sitting and died in a few minutes. Mr Nunn, the surgeon, stated that the deceased had lately complained of palpitations of the heart and he had no doubt that her death was attributable to disease of the heart. The jury returned a verdict of died by visitation of God.' It was common in the nineteenth century to take the milking stool and pail to the cow rather than bringing the cow to a milking shed, and it seems likely that Martha Hurst had carried her bucket and stool to her cow, which must have been close to her cottage since she was evidently seen to collapse, and a witness at the inquest must have reached her in the few minutes which elapsed before she died.

PLAITFORD had its common, and it was often more valuable to have common rather than forest rights, since freeholders and leaseholders could usually run their animals on parish commons without a fee.[8] Moreover, when (as at Plaitford) the common was indistinguishable from and opened onto the Forest, stock could stray across the boundary at no expense to their owners – a situation which continued until 1964. H.M. Livens wrote that milk cows from Nomansland were turned out onto the Forest. Four houses in the hamlet had grazing rights, allowing their owners or occupiers to run animals at 1s 6d a head, whilst other inhabitants had to buy a licence and pay a marking fee and pasturing fee, which totalled 4s for each beast, for up to a maximum of ten. Mrs Macey, the shopkeeper and midwife, kept what Livens called a 'red cow' on the Forest, and employed a small boy named James Dibden to bring it in twice a day. Livens received his information from James Dibden himself, but recorded the old man's reminiscence in a self-consciously literary style which can scarcely have resembled the wording of the original. 'Starting at 6.00am it sometimes took all day to find the [cow] . . . The little cowherd would come home sometimes with a dry skin sometimes with a wet one. Pushing his way through the soaking fern [bracken] which was often higher than his head, he was liable to miss the object of his quest though she might be but a few yards from his track.' The wage that he received, 'which seems to have been considered agreeable to all three parties concerned, the boy, the cow and its owner . . . was one pint of skimmed milk a week'.

There is probably some exaggeration in this account, but it suggests that cows which fed on the sparse pasture of the New Forest gave relatively small amounts of milk; had yields been high, James Dibden would have expected a more generous reward. It also implies that whilst Livens wrote of the 'intense individualism' of the 'isolated smallholder and the forester', they suffered considerable privations, for if a boy was prepared to spend so much time and endure such discomfort for a pint of skimmed milk a week then he, his family and probably others like it must have relied upon a very meagre diet.

It is likely that surplus butter would have been bought by a dealer, but in the instance of a Landford woman it provided additional income in another way: she is remembered to have sold butter made on the farm adjacent to her cottage, in Romsey market, carrying it in two earthenware jars (known in the dialect of the New Forest as crutches) suspended from yokes across her shoulders. In hot weather it would melt, and was taken for much of the 6 mile walk over unmetalled roads as liquid.

Most villagers kept poultry, and eggs would have been another commodity that was offered to the dealer, but in many cottage homes subsistence relied upon more than casual labour on farms and the sale of excess produce from orchard, garden and dairy. Large families helped to support the household. Even after elementary schooling became compulsory, children were able to leave at ten. Many village girls immediately went into domestic service, whilst boys tended to find work more locally. In either instance a large part of their wages was sent home to support their family.

According to Livens, a large family was also an advantage in making and selling match faggots, the activity which, according to tradition, had cost the old woman shot for a deer her life. The manufacture of match faggots was almost exclusively undertaken by women and children. Stick wood was bought at a shilling a cart-load, broken into pieces by the children, placed in a hole in the ground, pressed down with a board, tied by the mother or one of the older children and trimmed with a hatchet. As a mother assisted by a family of eight or ten could produce a thousand faggots a day, a 'profitable business might be carried out', and 'A faggoter blessed with a large and healthy family, and good luck with his animals might by dint of incessant labour, gradually accumulate enough to buy his cottage or lay by something for his old age.' Yet by the time that Livens was writing, faggoting had declined drastically. He claimed that before the coming of the railway up to a dozen carts of kindling travelled from Nomansland to Salisbury, whereas in 1910 what he frivolously called the 'worshipful company of faggoters' had only two representatives in the hamlet, an aged man and woman.

Livens tended to accept the information he received uncritically, and although acknowledging some of the hardships of hamlet life he nonetheless tended to portray it in arcadian terms. The description of the faggoter who was able to accumulate a modest capital was in fact hedged about with qualifications. He required a large and healthy family at a time when infant mortality was high, and a poor diet would not have been conducive to health. He needed to be fortunate with his livestock and could only save from his income 'by dint of incessant labour'. The profit from match faggoting also came at a high cost. A woman with a family of eight or ten would have experienced years of child-bearing, the task of breaking enough sticks to make a thousand faggots would have been trying to children's hands and knees, whilst crouching or kneeling to tie the bundles would have been acutely uncomfortable over a long period. Employment of this kind would also have denied children schooling, as would James Dibden's work in searching for Mrs Macey's cow.

The decrease in faggoting indicated changing attitudes, but it was also symptomatic of another decline. In 1892 the now largely forgotten novelist Mrs Oliphant reviewed *Tess of the d'Urbervilles* and wrote disapprovingly that 'Tess was a skilled labourer, for whom it is very rare that nothing can be found to do'[9] – but for all that ended her life on the gallows, an adulteress condemned for the murder of her lover. Many of the labourers occupying squatter cottages and relying on casual work and subsistence agriculture possessed a wide variety of skills, yet their livelihood was precarious and depended upon the prosperity of agriculture. Through the middle of the nineteenth century farming flourished as the growing railway network provided a means of transporting food stuffs to the ever expanding towns (the dealer was a local example of the same trend), but during the last quarter of the century British farmers, who had endured a succession of bad harvests in the 1870s, began to experience competition from overseas. North American wheat, Australian wool and mutton and Argentinian beef were imported in ever-increasing quantities in the refrigerated holds of large steamships. Foreign produce which came to flood the market was both cheaper and of a higher quality than its British equivalent, and caused a slump in the country's agriculture. The number of inhabitants fell drastically in parish after parish as labourers were forced into the towns or to emigrate to the colonies. Plaitford, with its limited geographical area, was overpopulated and saw an early decline in the 1870s. Other villages were affected from the late 1880s and through to the turn of the twentieth century, a period in which Bramshaw's inhabitants fell from more than 1,000 to just over 700. It was the labourers, dependent upon casual employment and the sale of produce, who disappeared, their cob cottages collapsing as the roofs fell in and rain penetrated the walls, and their way of life and their place in the rural community being largely forgotten.

Chapter II
Master and Man

WHILST the majority of labourers inhabited mud-walled cottages built on scraps of waste land, the farmers who employed them were usually tenants of the gentry, and although a squatter settlement such as Nomansland might be independent of the influence of the upper classes and the Established Church, the traditional, although not inevitable, alliance of squire and parson held sway in the parishes around the northern borders of the New Forest as it did in most rural areas. The gentry and clergy, who were often related by blood or marriage, supported one another in maintaining their position at the head of their highly stratified communities, but whilst the presence of an estate ensured that its tenants and employees knew their place and whilst the attitude of the landed classes to the lower orders was at best paternalistic and at worst autocratic, there were advantages in renting property from, being on the staff of or living in proximity to a substantial landowner.

In 1862 John Wise described one of the routes that led to the Rufus Stone and passed 'through Minstead by a footpath which crosses Mr Compton's Park, dotted with cottages each with its garden full in summer and autumn of flowers – yellow Aaron – rods, candy tufts, colchicums and marigolds and tall sheaves of Michaelmas daisies'.[1] Henry Compton was a member of a long-standing family whose residence, Minstead Manor, was surrounded by, according to the late nineteenth-century editions of Kelly's Directory for Hampshire, a park of 400 acres, 'two hundred of which are planted with rhododendrons'. Wise's earlier description suggests that in the middle of the century the cottagers living in the vicinity of the house had both the means and the opportunity to cultivate flower beds, a luxury that was by implication rare in the dwellings of the labouring classes of the New Forest – which was in turn an indication of the severity of the forester's life. (Flora Thompson wrote in *Lark Rise* that every hamlet home had its narrow strip of flowers tended by the cottager's wife.)

The dwellings provided by the landowners were themselves more substantial than the mud-walled houses built by the labourers. When the Canterton Manor estate was sold late in the nineteenth century, the catalogue listed three cottages (among many others) identified only by their numbers on the accompanying plan, which contained respectively two rooms up and three down, three up and three down, and four rooms up and four down, with gardens, outhouses, woodhouses, piggeries and cowpens in the first two instances and a cowpen, piggery and cart house in the third. The size and use of the rooms was not indicated, but the properties were a marked contrast to the mud-walled dwellings which seldom had more than two rooms up and two down, and in some instances comprised nothing more than two or even one room on a single storey.

Nor did the gentry merely provide superior accommodation; they also created opportunities for employment, and with them local populations which had antecedents and places of birth that were more varied and therefore less inbred than those in hamlet communities. An estate, particularly where the mansion was close at hand, gave work not only to a frequently substantial domestic staff but also to coachmen and grooms (later to be augmented, then supplanted, by chauffeurs), gardeners (a photograph taken at Melchet Court in about 1913 showed the thirteen under-gardeners who worked on the estate[2]), carpenters and

Eleven gardeners and two decorators (wearing aprons) employed at Melchet Court, photographed in about 1913.

others engaged in the maintenance of the buildings (the photograph of the Melchet Court gardeners also included two decorators) and on the home farm, which in the vicinity of the New Forest was usually significantly larger than the equivalent properties let to tenants, agricultural workers, such as dairymen and carters who had specific skills and consequently commanded higher wages than the general labourers (although the estate farm would also employ more ordinary labourers than the tenant holdings).

Neither were the benefits of an estate confined to its tenantry and staff. When in residence the gentry would deal with village shopkeepers, whilst blacksmiths and other artisans would also benefit from the business which they provided. Carriage and saddle horses required shoeing, as well as those working on farms. An instance of the patronage given to local craftsmen occurred in 1922 when Briscoe Eyre of Warrens House died in Worthing. His widow insisted that the arrangements for his funeral should be entrusted to the Bramshaw carpenter, wheelwright and undertaker, Charles Young. Percy Hatch, the long-serving verger and sexton at St Peter's Church, Bramshaw, had been Charlie Young's apprentice at the time, and remembered having been the last to see the dead squire's face – for he had nailed down the lid of his coffin.

The advantages which the labouring and artisan classes derived from their association with the gentry and the aristocracy were nonetheless obtained within a rigid social order. In July 1884 Charles Bowles, a keeper from Plaitford, died at the age of forty-eight. The headstone marking his burial place records his name, age and the year of his death, and carries the words 'Looking unto Jesus' as well as a further inscription: 'Erected by Lord Ilchester in memory of a faithful and valued servant'. In the grounds of Brooklands House in the neighbouring parish of Landford a stone raised in the 1890s commemorates a pet dog, Oscar, with the Latin tag '*Semper Fidelis*', Ever Faithful. The phrasing of Charles Bowles's stone suggests that the relationship between master and servant was not wholly dissimilar to that between an owner and his or her favourite dog. The keeper's widow and children where wholly disregarded in the inscription, and it is not known if any provision was made on their behalf.

Nor were social distinctions confined to the relationship between the aristocracy and gentry and their employees. Three years before Charles Bowles died, one of the Earl of Ilchester's tenants in Plaitford had also erected a headstone over the grave of an employee in the churchyard there. Eliza Futcher was, in 1881, a seventy-four-year-old widow who occupied New Lodge, a relatively substantial and at that date modern house. She farmed 30 acres of land and evidently had greater social pretensions than the other small farmers in the village, for not only was she unique among her counterparts in employing two men but, with the exception of the rector, was alone among the residents of the parish in keeping a live-in domestic servant as well as a farm servant who would have performed both domestic and agricultural duties.[3] When in October 1881 James Hutchings, the farm servant, was (in the words of Alfred Gay's marginal note in the burial register) 'Killed by the fall of a tree in a gale of wind' at the age of sixty-nine, his employer provided him with a grave stone which commended his faithful service, briefly recorded the circumstances of his decease and piously added the text 'In the midst of life we are in death'.

Another example of the paternalistic nature of the relationship between a landlord and his tenantry is found in a tradition which survived to appear in print in 1998[4] and which in its published form recorded that at the end of the nineteenth century Lord Ilchester and his land agent would visit Plaitford each Michaelmas to collect rents from the farmers and cottagers and then provide them with a meal at the Shoe Inn. Michaelmas (29 September) was a quarter day when rents were traditionally paid, and it was the custom on many estates to provide a dinner for the tenants after the dues had been collected. (The rector and churchwardens at St Peter's, Plaitford, let a number of cottages, fields and allotments to villagers, and a surviving churchwarden's account book has an entry for Michaelmas Day 1904 and 1905 which reads 'Allowance to renters in lieu of beer 4/6d', a payment which continued, somewhat erratically, until 1923.) It is, however, inconceivable that either Lord Ilchester or his agent would have come to such a small and outlying part of the estate to receive the rents, and a local solicitor or estate agent would probably have fulfilled this function for them, yet the fact that they were described as having done so eighty-seven years after the Fox Strangways had sold their interest in Plaitford, Landford and Bramshaw is indicative of the reverence with which may of the lower orders regarded their masters.

The attitude of the tenants to their landlord is also evident in the tradition of Briscoe Eyre and the apple tree which, whilst being demonstrably apocryphal, nonetheless suggests that even a cottager could plausibly be assumed to have brought his grievances to the squire in person, a survival of a feudal relationship.

Briscoe Eyre was a liberal (according to the 1898 edition of *Burke's Landed Gentry* he was a member of the Reform Club), and in an address at the opening of Fritham Free Church on 31 August 1904 he told the congregation, in words put into reported speech by the *Romsey Advertiser*, that 'in the forest his strongest interest had been with the class of agricultural labourers who were rising to something better'. A quarter of a century earlier, in March 1880, he had drawn the attention of the vestry meetings in Bramshaw 'to the great injury to the pasturage and common rights by the inclosures proposed by Hans Stanley Esq. of Paultons',[5] going on to quote at some length other cases where a similar attempt to enclose forest commons had been successfully resisted. The clerks to the vestries dutifully copied the long submission into the respective minute books, but without any indication of the outcome of the protest.

Bramshaw had extensive commons which opened on the Forest, and commoning was widely practised here as it was in Nomansland and in all the Forest parishes (the cowpens included among the outbuildings belonging to the cottages at Canterton are evidence of this). Hans Sloane's proposed enclosures would have restricted the grazing available over a wide area and Briscoe,[6] who had become the first elected verderer in 1877, was evidently championing the interests of the 'class of labourers who were rising to something better', by combining their usual occupation with cowkeeping, although tradition remembered him to have been autocratic in his treatment of the lower orders.

One place in which the hierarchical and authoritarian nature of rural society was particularly obvious was in the parish church, which the squirearchy tended to regard as a private chapel. The seating of the congregation frequently reflected the status of the leading families, with the principal landowners either occupying their own self-contained pews or, where these did not exist, the foremost seats in the main body of the church. Where there were two or more landowning families they took the front seats, with one on the north and the other on the south side of the aisle, or sat immediately behind one another in the first, second and third pews according to their relative standing in the community, whilst their servants were similarly ranked behind them. In some instances the congregation at the morning service largely comprised the families and staff at the big houses, whilst the afternoon or evening attendance was made up of servants (who earlier had been preparing luncheon for their employers), tenants, cottagers and parishioners in general.

Percy Hatch, who had been a choirboy and organ blower at St Peter's, Bramshaw, remembered seeing Briscoe Eyre and his wife sitting at the front of their pew with their servants in rows behind them in order of seniority, with the kitchen and scullery maids in their outdoor uniforms at the back. As the sermon began the hall boy was sent to warn the coachman to bring the carriage to the church gate. At the end of the service Briscoe and Mary Eyre made their exit through the private door of their family pew (which Briscoe's grandfather had built over their vault in 1809) and were driven back to Warrens, with the servants following on foot.

The Eyres were first among the Bramshaw gentry, but other prominent residents automatically took the front seats in the main body of the church, an assumption of their status which is illustrated by a small wooden box attached to a low partition on the right of the foremost pew. The box, which has remained unopened and unregarded for decades, contains the Bible and prayer book used during the second half of the nineteenth century by Admiral Edmund Heathcote of Fritham Lodge, who was, like Briscoe Eyre, a member of a leading county family with widespread ramifications.

If the gentry were at the apex of rural society, the clergy, although superior to the vast majority of their parishioners in both education and income, had a less assured standing. In many instances the leading local landlord was patron of the living or exercised an influence which the parson could not ignore. Mark Cooper owed his appointment to the support of the Eyres,[7] and although his wife, Caroline Antonetta Asphasia Jacintha, was the sister-in-law and second cousin of George Edward Eyre of Warrens House (the father of Briscoe Eyre), he nonetheless wrote very respectfully of George Edward Eyre's stepmother in a note in the vestry minutes in which he referred to himself in the third person:

> The organ was presented to the church of Bramshaw through the Rev. M. Cooper, the incumbent by Mrs Eyre relict of the late George Eyre Esq. of Warrens in this parish and this lady very generously forwarded £45 that the organ & other expenses of putting it up might be discharged at her expense. Mrs Eyre visited Bramshaw in August 1846 and then very generously promised that she would present two additional barrels but (such is the uncertainty of Life) she departed from this world in the following January and her mortal remains were conveyed from her residence, 29 Eaton Place, London and deposited in the family vault in Bramshaw Church on Saturday, January 16th 1847 aetat 73.

Mark Cooper seems to have had an almost bureaucratic preoccupation with detail (most unusually he was the enumerator for part of Bramshaw in the census of 1841, a duty which normally fell to a less exalted member of the community), but besides his almost deferential tone and awareness of the status of the Eyre family, the paragraph from the vestry minutes contains another significant item of information. No record survives of the music played in Bramshaw Church before the introduction of the organ. There may have been a group of instrumentalists in the west gallery accompanying the metrical psalms which were still sung in the first half of the nineteenth century – the equivalent of the Mellstock Quire – or the singing may have been unaccompanied. (The parson diarist Francis Kilvert, who served as his father's curate in the north Wiltshire village of Langley Burrell from 1872 to 1876, recorded that the autocratic squire Robert Ashe, when asked to subscribe to the fund for the purchase of a harmonium, 'said that neither he nor any of his household should give a farthing for he disapproved of any music in church beside the human voice'.)[8] There is no suggestion that the introduction of an organ in St Peter's, Bramshaw, aroused any controversy – probably because of its source – but Mark Cooper's allusion to extra barrels which were denied to the church by the 'uncertainty of Life' indicates the nature of the instrument. Barrel organs were commonly found in Anglican churches in the middle of the nineteenth century, as no musical skill was required to turn the handle – but whilst they introduced hymns to the congregation, the number of tunes must have been very limited.

Forty years later, when St Peter's, Bramshaw, had a pipe organ (or at the very least a harmonium), Briscoe Eyre, who had inherited the Warrens Estate from his father in 1887, demonstrated a continuing influence over the parish church by insisting that the instrument should be moved from the south to the west gallery, because he objected to the organist looking down into his pew on the opposite side of the nave.

Yet if the parson was usually a little lower in the social hierarchy than the squire and had to defer to the demands of the principal landowner, his role was nonetheless in part to impress upon his congregation that the established order had divine sanction, a claim embodied in the long abandoned but still remembered verse from Mrs Alexander's children's hymn, *All things bright and beautiful*, which, having contrasted the rich man in his castle with the poor man at his gate, concluded with the lines 'God made them high and lowly | and ordered their estate.' It was to ensure that this distinction was maintained that landed proprietors insisted that their domestic staff should attend the parish church.

In 1851 the Home Office ordered that an ecclesiastical census should be taken, a questionnaire being issued to every church, chapel and religious meeting in the country. Among the enquiries made of each of the ministers or other church officers completing the form was one asking for the number of worshippers attending Sunday services. Mark Cooper characteristically added a lengthy footnote to his submission, which included the information that his morning and afternoon congregations numbered 210 and 220. 'The parish Church being very inconveniently situated at a distance of two, three or four miles from some parts of the parish very many only attended <u>once</u> a day and therefore of the afternoon attendance, a hundred or more are therefore present who were not present in the morning. This being considered, perhaps not less than 400 inhabitants attend in the course of the day from all parts of the parish.' The paragraph is clumsily written and the figures are suspect, the attendances have evidently been rounded up or estimated, and the arithmetic obviously wrong. If the morning congregation was 210 and over 100 of the 220 present in the afternoon had not been at the earlier service, then there would have been a total of approximately 300 individuals in St Peter's Church, Bramshaw, each Sunday and not 400 as Mark Cooper claimed. This was, even so, a large attendance (a further 150 inhabitants were recorded to have been present at services in the one Strict Baptist and two Methodist chapels in the village), and suggests that a significant number of villagers were being obliged by the estate to be present at services.

Percy Hatch remembered that numbers at the evening service immediately before the First World War were so great that members of the congregation were seated on the narrow stairs which led to the west gallery, but he also recalled the way in which the tenants and employees were coerced into attendance. Briscoe Eyre and his wife invariably went to London for the season, moving, with most of their domestic staff, into their town house, 18 Radcliffe Square. On their return Mary Eyre – whose father had been Vicar of All Saints', Margaret Street – would call on the Rev. John Whitworth Godden, the Vicar of Bramshaw, take the names of all the tenants who had failed to attend services whilst she had been away from the village, and then visit each one in turn to demand an explanation for their absence. No evidence exists to support this memory, but it is likely to have been a survival of a rumour current at the time – and reflected the way in which the gentry were perceived to have behaved towards the lower orders.

There was, however, one representative of what was then known as the Upper Ten Thousand who had an estate just beyond the north-eastern boundary of the New Forest and whose religious convictions meant that her attitude to the social order and denominational differences was highly unconventional. Louisa, Lady Ashburton, who owned Melchet Court in Sherfield English, a village 5 miles west of Romsey and immediately bordering upon Newtown and Lockerly, was descended from the Scottish nobility. Born in 1826, she was the second daughter of a minister in Sir Robert Peel's government. Noted in her youth for what the *Tatler* called in its obituary 'her dark and splendid beauty', a beauty which the *Romsey Advertiser* described as being of an 'oriental type', she became the second wife of the second Lord Ashburton in 1856 and was left a widow with one daughter in 1862. Her circle, unusually for a Victorian aristocrat, included writers, poets and artists, and she was a close friend of Thomas Carlyle, Robert Browning and Edwin Landseer. Then in 1873 – at least according to a local tradition, which has not been confirmed from any contemporary source – she came under a very different influence, attending a rally during Sankey and Moody's British Crusade and being converted to the cause of Evangelical Christianity. Fired with zeal, she spent the remaining thirty years of her life energetically promoting her faith. She established a mission in the London Docks, introduced a colporteur (someone who sold religious literature and engaged in evangelism) to her Hampshire estate, and built a mission hall in Landford Wood on the furthest extremity of her property, having by her own account been present at a meeting in the home of one of her tenants where the windows and doors had to be opened because of the heat. A service was held in the hall to coincide with her funeral in Scotland in February 1903, and Mr Dymond, the colporteur, who officiated, 'spoke of Lady Ashburton's love for the people of that neighbourhood and the earnest prayers he had heard her offer in her dining room at Melchet Court on their behalf' at what the *Romsey Advertiser* noted to have been one of the widely remembered evangelistic services in the house.[9]

A supporter of the temperance movement, Lady Ashburton became president of the Romsey branch of the Women's Total Abstinence Union and, again in the words of the *Advertiser*, 'took no heed of denominational differences but extended her bounty to all from the Salvation Army upwards'.

The Established Church and its adherents were generally hostile to dissent, although some members of the aristocracy and gentry were prepared to acknowledge the nonconformist denominations with the greatest middle-class support, in the belief that they exercised a restraining influence on the lower orders. Lady Ashburton's readiness to ignore denomination was exceptional, however. It is notable that she gave what was presumably financial assistance to the Salvation Army, since that organisation had yet to command the respect which it has since gained, a fact indicated by the *Advertiser*'s reference to 'all from the Salvation Army upwards'. (Indeed, the author knew an elderly resident of Southampton who, employed as a housemaid in the town during the opening decade of the twentieth century, went home to Poole for her annual visit to her family and attended the Salvation Army Citadel with her parents, who were members. After she had returned to work her employer learned of this and sacked her on the spot.)

Yet for all Lady Ashburton's willingness to ignore 'denominational differences' and to attend evangelistic meetings with her tenants, it is evident from her one recorded utterance[10] and from the tone of references to her in the local press, that she remained fully aware of the gulf between aristocracy and the mass of the people. She was reported to have a deep musical voice and to be 'tall, stately and of a commanding presence', and her command was evident when, following the death of her daughter, the Countess of Northampton, she had the existing parish church at Sherfield English demolished and a replacement erected as a memorial to her only child.

In common with most landowners, Lady Ashburton built an elementary school (in Sherfield English) in 1876. It was originally known as Melchet Court School, and her influence was evident in the appointment of the headmaster Francis Mowlem, who, besides his pedagogical duties, engaged in evangelism in the area.

In most instances landowners had a proprietary attitude to the village school. On 11 November 1874 Francis Kilvert wrote in his diary that 'a few days ago Mr Ashe came angrily in to Miss Bland the schoolmistress and ordered her to keep all the windows and the door of the schoolroom open except in very cold weather when one window might be shut. He said in a fierce determined way, "If you don't do as I tell you Miss Bland, instead of being your friend I shall be your enemy."'[11]

And if Robert Martin Ashe of Langley Burrell was extreme in his attitude, village schools were nonetheless subject to the often intimidating attention of the squire or his family. Elizabeth Merson wrote in *Once There Was The Village School* of visits to Bramshaw Boys' School by Mary Eyre, recording the experience of an unnamed teacher who recalled that as the squire's lady 'strode purposefully' into the classroom 'the boys leapt to attention, eyes fixed straight ahead whilst the master bowed and the assistant mistress curtseyed'.

Nor was the influence of the squirearchy confined to the school and the parish church. The patronage of the big house gave the principal landowner considerable influence among the tradesmen and others in the locality. Percy Hatch was still a pupil at Bramshaw Boys' School when he began Saturday work at William Domoney's baker's shop. William Domoney was not a tenant of Warrens but he served the estate with bread, a circumstance which gave rise to a reminiscence which must have been heard on his premises. One of the errand boys was returning from a delivery to Warrens House when Briscoe Eyre was approaching it. Briscoe was a woeful horseman, 'like a sack of spuds in the saddle', and as the boy passed him the bicycle basket clattered against the rhododendrons which grew on either side of the drive. Startled by the sound, Briscoe's mount shied, throwing him into a deep puddle. Regaining his feet, the squire walked with his legs splayed, 'for all the world as if he'd wet himself', a ludicrous spectacle which caused the boy too-evident amusement. Within the hour Briscoe appeared in the bakery, and demanded to see the proprietor. 'Domoney, if the boy you sent to Warrens this morning hasn't been dismissed by the end of the day, I shall give instructions that my custom is to be taken elsewhere.' No further explanation was given, but as soon as the youth came back from his round he was sacked, for if William Domoney had been defiant in the matter he would have foregone the trade of Warrens House and its tenants – whilst word would have been passed to Canterton Manor House with the same result, and ruinous consequences for the business. The authenticity of this story cannot be confirmed at so great a distance of time, and the account was probably made more vivid in its retelling, but it reflects the high-handed behaviour of the squire towards those who served him in the wider community as well as his attitude to his staff: whilst he was remembered to have gone in person to order the arbitrary dismissal of the errand boy, he would merely have given instructions to the cook or housekeeper to cancel the Warrens bakery account.

Another more scurrilous reminiscence suggested that it was not only landowners who were responsible for unequal treatment of the lower orders. The bailiff was an employee of the estate, but one who enjoyed a far higher standing than an ordinary workman. At the turn of the twentieth century the bailiff at Warrens was named Hall. On one occasion he was reputed to have been passing through an area of woodland, when he found his fifteen-year-old daughter *in flagrante delicto* with a farm boy. The youth was immediately sacked but as Percy Hatch (who was again the source of the story) remarked, the superior status of the girl made it likely that she was the greater transgressor.

For all its manifest inequalities and frequent injustices, the social order was accepted as unquestioningly by many of the lower orders as it was by their masters. As recently as the 1930s working people addressed the doctor and the clergyman as 'Sir', whilst the conventions governing the relationship between master (or mistress) and man were evident in the memories of a member of the outdoor staff at Lockerley Hall, who recalled them more than seventy years after they had been observed.

Henry Bungay, the son of George Bungay, a rick thatcher from Plaitford, was employed as garden boy at Landford House, but was dismissed from his post when his employer's lease expired. In 1906, at the age of seventeen, he found work as an undergardener at Lockerley Hall. Despite its name, Lockerley Hall was situated in East Tytherley, a village to the north-west of Romsey and close to the borders of Hampshire and Wiltshire. The owner of the estate, Frederick John Dalgety, had inherited the property from his father in 1894, resigning

Lockerley Hall from a postcard published by Dodridge and Gibbs of Romsey and postmarked at 9.30pm on 1 June 1905.

a commission in the 15th Hussars when he did so but still known in 1906 as Captain Dalgety. Captain Dalgety and his wife, the Honourable Pauline Caroline McLintock-Bunbury, the daughter of Lord Rathondell (an Irish peer whose surname recalled *The Importance of Being Earnest*), had married in 1897, when he was thirty-one and she was nineteen, and maintained a large household.

In 1901 they were served by a housekeeper, a butler, a cook and a French lady's maid, together with a footman, four housemaids, a kitchen maid, a scullery maid, a still room maid, four laundry maids, a nurse, a nursery maid (for their two sons aged one and two) and an odd man, all of whom lived in, a coachman, who was provided with a house, a second coachman, two stable helpers (as they were described), a head gardener, who also had his own house, and two under-gardeners, who were accommodated in the bothy, living quarters which had a counterpart in the gardens of every large country estate, together with a number of gardeners and others resident in the village. When Henry Bungay joined the staff in 1906 he received 7s 6d a week with bothy, milk and vegetables found and the services of an old woman from the village, who was brought in to prepare and cook meals. The establishment to which he had been appointed had, beside the usual walled kitchen garden, a pleasure ground adjacent to the mansion and an extensive range of glass-houses, all of which were under the supervision of James Budd, the head gardener, who in 1906 was sixty-eight years of age and approaching the close of his forty-seven years' service at Lockerley Hall.

Although it was common practice for the individual members of the staff to be employed in only one area of the gardens, and to jealously guard their knowledge and expertise, Henry Bungay worked in the orchid house, the nectarine house and the stove houses, which must have been extensive since they produced bananas, pineapples and tender ornamentals for decoration. Overtime was also available in the vinery when the bunches needed thinning, laborious work which entailed reaching up from steps to remove individual grapes with scissors made for the purpose, at a payment of 6d an hour.

One of the under-gardeners was always on duty to ensure that a constant temperature was maintained in the heated glass-houses, and when, in the limited leisure time available, the stable lads came to the bothy to play rings ("twas rings in them days – not darts'), the game would frequently be interrupted by a knock on the door, 'and there was old Jimmy Budd. "Who's on duty" he would say, "You, Bungay? It's two degrees too low in the nectarine house. Go and raddle them fires up boy. Raddle 'em up. Raddle 'em up."' Henry Bungay remembered the head gardener with evident regard, recalling that he spoke to his subordinates like a father and that he smoked cheroots, the smell of his small cigars warning that he was in the vicinity. When the cigar smoke was detected 'you'd look at the thermometer and if the temperature was too low you'd blow on it and push up the mercury and then Old Jimmy would come along and he'd say, "Cold in here for sixty-eight, Bungay. Cold in here." Well of course he knew what we were doing but he never said nothing. I expect he'd done it himself when he was young.'

'Old Jimmy' might have risen to an exalted position amongst the domestic staff and addressed the under-gardeners by their surnames, but he remained a working man, a fact emphasised by the census of 1901 which showed that he occupied the head gardener's house with his wife and unmarried daughter Rosa, who worked on her own account from home (was self employed) as a dressmaker. His relationship with his staff was probably influenced by his background, whereas the under-gardener's standing with the gentry was of a wholly different character.

If a gardener met a gentleman he had to touch his cap but say nothing. If he encountered a lady he was to make the same gesture but to accompany it with the greeting 'good morning (or afternoon) ma'am', but in neither instance was he to add anything further unless invited to do so. Usually he would be completely ignored. Henry Bungay remembered this discourtesy without resentment, rather implying that he accepted his place in the social order by recalling that he visited the pleasure grounds to see their keeper Tom Gambling, but insisting that he did so only if Captain and Mrs Dalgety were absent from the property. Tom Gambling was 'a funny little, hunch-backed old man', who nonetheless laid out beautiful carpet bedding, displays made up of thousands of annuals planted in elaborate geometrical patterns and maintained from a plank raised above the border, their coloured foliage trimmed with sheep shears. Invariably when Henry Bungay came into the pleasure grounds he would be met with the question, 'Has thee kicked the heels of thee's boots, boy?' because hobnails collected gravel from the path, which dropped onto the lawn and damaged the blades of the mower. On occasion the maids brought the gardeners cups of coffee, but it was again emphasised that this only occurred in the family's absence.

Yet whilst the under-gardeners knew – and accepted – their place, they were able to appreciate the preposterous aspect of one ritual performed annually by the wife of their employer. Pineapples were one of the most prized products of the Edwardian glasshouse. At Lockerley Hall, when Jimmy Budd sent word to the mansion that the first pineapple had ripened, usually near to Christmas, a procession came down to the stove house with the butler at its head, carrying a silver tray which had a knife on it. He was followed by Mrs Dalgety and her house guests. When they reached the ripe pineapple Mrs Dalgety took the knife and cut it, after which it was placed on the tray and borne back by the butler with the gentry following behind. The undergardeners made every effort to watch this spectacle, which caused them considerable amusement, although they had to ensure that they did so without being seen by any of the participants.

Henry Bungay left Lockerley Hall in 1908, retaining the references which Jimmy Budd had given him until his death at the age of ninety-one in 1979. From Lockerley Hall, which he remembered as the best place he ever had, he moved to Paulton's Park at Ower to be employed by the Sloan Stanley family. He was not happy there. Plants were offered for sale, a practice which he clearly regarded as inappropriate in a gentleman's establishment ('they never sold a plant at Lockerley Hall'). When he left in 1911 he emigrated to Canada, where he remained until the 1920s – returning as a married man to the village where he was born, and where he spent the rest of his long life.

Henry Bungay's must have been among the last references that Jimmy Budd wrote. The *Romsey Advertiser* reporting the funeral of the former head gardener in its edition of 27 January 1911, noted that he had suffered 'a sudden attack about three years earlier'. After the attack, which was attributed to 'pressure on the brain', he had continued to occupy his 'onerous position' for a further twelve months until he was forced to retire to Kingston, taking with him a silver loving cup presented by Captain Dalgety in recognition of nearly half a century of service. When his body was brought back to Tytherley for burial the funeral was attended by, amongst others, 'the staff of gardeners from Lockerley Hall'.

ALTHOUGH many of the lower orders were content to know their place, there was, in some sections of rural society, a sullen resentment of the upper classes for which the principal evidence is anecdotal. Percy Hatch recalled that his paternal grandfather, Henry, had served as verger and sexton at St Peter's, Bramshaw, during the final quarter of the nineteenth century but had quarrelled with the vicar of the day, the Rev. Samuel Waring Mangan, who held the living from 1882 to 1889. Among his other duties the sexton had to mow the churchyard, and Henry Hatch had been accustomed to keep the hay which he made there to feed to his own animals. Percy Hatch remembered that the vicar (whom he untypically referred to by surname alone) had claimed the hay as part of his emolument, and that the ensuing quarrel between sexton and parson had been so acrimonious that Henry Hatch had resigned his position and the salary it provided (which would have been a significant supplement to his income), rather than accede to the clergyman's demands.

Another more colourful anecdote in which a parishioner defied the parson came from the period in which Alfred Gay had voluntary responsibility for Nomansland. Remonstrating with a young woman of the hamlet who was notorious for her wantonness, he was told, in words which he was most unlikely to have heard in the rectory drawing room, that if she wished to bestow her favours freely she would do so, 'and there won't be you or any parson in England that'll stop me'.

Nomansland was a community where an Anglican clergyman was unlikely to receive a favourable hearing, its name a byword for rowdy behaviour and its only place of worship a Primitive Methodist chapel. Primitive Methodists were generally less sympathetic to the Established Church than their Wesleyan counterparts. It was Primitive Methodism which gave rise to a widely remembered and enduring story that, by implication at least, indicated an antipathy to the landowning classes. Richard Jefferies wrote of the cottage preacher in 1879, and, referring to his earnest and immovable conviction, added: 'Men of this kind won Cromwell's victories; but today they are mainly conspicuous for upright steadiness and irreproachable character mingled with some surly independence.'[12] One labourer's display of independence provoked an extremely harsh reaction from his employer. William Moody was a farm worker on the Embley Estate in East Wellow, where every employee was expected to attend the parish church. When he became a Primitive Methodist local preacher he was at once dismissed, evicted from his tied cottage and left homeless on the roadside with his wife and six sons. A memorial tablet was erected in Newtown Primitive Methodist Church after his death, and one of the church officers recalled in the 1980s being required to repeat the inscription from memory when making boyhood visits to an aunt in London. William Moody's great-granddaughter remembered in 1991 that she had heard the story of the eviction from her grandfather, Charles Moody, who had been a child at the time,[13] whilst an account of the incident was collected from a former member of Longdown Methodist Church in the New Forest as recently as 1992.

Yet despite these memories, an examination of contemporary sources suggests that some details are open to question. In Primitive Methodism an intending local preacher passed through two stages before being accredited. He began as an exhorter and then went 'on trial'. Once the trial period was successfully completed accreditation followed. A Salisbury Primitive Methodist Circuit Plan for the Quarter from February to April 1844, which listed the preachers appointed to take services in the Salisbury Primitive Methodist Circuit and the Ringwood and Fordingbridge Mission, included Newtown amongst the widely scattered churches and an exhorter, 'Moody, Wellow' in the list of preachers. Since only the surname and place of residence was given, it is impossible to state conclusively that this was William Moody, but as there is no evidence of any other local preacher with that name in the circuit it is highly probable that he was the individual concerned. The census of 1851 shows William and Mary Moody to have been living at Dunwood Hill, East Wellow, with their six sons and a daughter (who was forgotten in the story).[13] The three eldest boys, aged between nineteen and nine, were farm labourers like their father, but by 1861 they and their parents were no longer in Wellow, and when trustees were appointed for the brick-built chapel in Newtown in 1867 William Moody, a general dealer of Shirley in Southampton, was among their number. As William Moody preached four times between February and April 1844, yet was still employed as an agricultural labourer in Wellow in 1851, it seems improbable that he was dismissed for his involvement in Methodism or his failure to attend Anglican services; the circumstances of his departure from the Embley Estate are unexplained.

The real significance of this tale does not rest upon its factual basis, but in the gross injustice which was perceived to have been done to a poor labourer by a powerful and wealthy member of the landowning classes, whose second daughter, Florence Nightingale, was at about the time of William Moody's dismissal and eviction being fêted as a heroine of the Crimean War. Some members of the lower orders clearly failed to regard their social superiors with reverent esteem.

A LTHOUGH the aristocracy and gentry were to retain a dominant position in rural society throughout the Victorian and Edwardian eras and beyond, their position was undermined by steadily increasing death duties and the drastic changes in society which were brought about by the First World War. The effect of the war is suggested by two anecdotes repeated by Percy Hatch. In one the verger and sexton recounted that Albert Biddlecombe, a tenant farmer on the Warrens Estate, successfully defied Briscoe Eyre by refusing to reduce the unprecedentedly high wages he was paying his men, even though his rates were causing disaffection among the squire's less well-remunerated hands. Scarcity of labour, with large numbers of farm workers serving under arms, was changing the relationship between landlord and tenant and master and man.

The other anecdote also involves Albert Biddlecombe, who, late in the war, encountered Mrs Jefferys of Canterton Manor mounted astride rather than side saddle, a posture which would have been considered very daring before 1914, since it involved wearing breeches. 'Why, Mrs Jeffreys,' the farmer is reputed to have said, 'fancy seeing you riding in that fashion.' He received the reply, 'Well, Mr Biddlecombe, it's easier for a woman, do you see? She hasn't a man's encumbrances.' An answer which caused both surprise and amusement, leading Albert Biddlecombe to remark, 'Imagine her knowing about that what with her being a lady and all.' The exchange and the comment it provoked both reflected a society in transition.

Chapter III
The Labourer at Home

THE second chapter of *The New Forest, Its Traditions, Inhabitants and Customs* is entitled 'The Forester' and has, as its penultimate subheading, 'Nature's Loafers'. This description is applied to what the text calls 'the ordinary inhabitant and labourer – so to speak of him for courtesy's sake – of the Forest'. Labourer was a courtesy title because, according to Rose de Crespigny and Horace Hutchinson, a forester would 'labour a day, perhaps a week, even at great strain, a month, but a year no'. Engaging in regular work was not 'according to his traditions . . . not among his inherited qualities'. Instead the natives of the Forest, who were slow witted and slow moving but endowed with a degree of low cunning, were content to find the necessities of life in their surroundings, and as well as providing extra labour at haymaking and harvest gained an income from casual work peculiar to their locality. De Crespigny and Hutchinson listed as sources of seasonal employment: fern cutting (bracken being used as litter for livestock), leaf gathering (to make leaf mould for the gardens of large houses), holly cutting (at Christmas) and beating for shoots, all of which were supplemented by commoning, most inhabitants of the Forest (like those at Nomansland) keeping some animals which they ran on the commons and heaths. Thus 'the Forester is like the Olympian gods, living easily but there is no doubt that in neither case does the "easy life" lead to a very high standard of moral excellence' but rather to 'lounging through the woodland and across the marshes in company with the spirit of Pan and his attendant fairies and dryads'.

The allusion to the easy life of the Forester and the fanciful references (typical of the period) to the spirit of Pan and his accompanying fairies and wood nymphs indicates how little the co-authors knew of the harsh and precarious circumstances of the labouring classes in rural communities. The exact nature of the collaboration between Rose de Crespigny and Horace Hutchinson is not recorded, but it is likely that the former provided the material for their book whilst the latter (who is primarily remembered as an authority on golf but was also a prolific author, having written fifty-two titles on a variety of subjects by the time of his death in 1932) composed the text. Percy Hatch remembered Mrs de Crespigny and her husband Philip (who according to local tradition was the descendant of an émigré family) to have lived in straitened gentility in Bramshaw, and recalled that Philip de Crespigny invariably attended St Peter's Church in hunting pink.

What Rose de Crespigny and Horace Hutchinson failed to recognise was that, far from revealing an innate indolence, the way of life of the Forester and equally of many of the inhabitants of rural communities elsewhere was the result of necessity. From the eighteenth century onwards the population of the country had been increasing, not only in the industrial north and Midlands but also in the largely rural south. As a result there were more labourers in villages than permanent positions for them to occupy, with the majority forced to live from hand to mouth. Furthermore, by 1899, when *The New Forest, Its Traditions, Inhabitants and Customs* was published, the exodus to the towns and colonies was well under way as the depression in agriculture became more severe.

Indeed, declining opportunities to live by casual means forced the Forester and others who remained on the land to accept regular employment where they could find it. Percy Hatch remembered that his father Albert had, in the years preceding the First World War, been working at Brook, a hamlet within the boundaries of Bramshaw and no more than a mile from his home. For the sake of an extra shilling a week he took a job in Romsey, and with it a 14 mile round journey, on foot, to and from the town. In the same way employees of the Schultze Gunpowder Company's Factory at Eyeworth in the north of the New Forest walked considerable distances to work a twelve hour shift in what were, in some instances, very hazardous conditions. One long-standing Schultze Company employee, George Matthews, who himself walked from Woodfalls to Eyeworth, was later to recall that men involved in the initial stages of gunpowder manufacture, and therefore dealing with a solution of 75 per cent nitric and 25 per cent sulphuric acid, were issued with pieces of chalk which they put into their mouths to neutralise the fumes that otherwise corroded the enamel of their teeth. The Schultze Company nevertheless paid 18s a week to unskilled men, 5s more than the usual wage for a farm worker, and did so for fifty-two weeks a year without interruptions for the weather or the seasons, with the result that there was a ready supply of labour for their factory which was at its most prosperous as the depression in rural areas grew more acute.

For those who continued to find employment in agriculture, working hours, particularly at the busiest seasons when extra hands were required, were very long, whilst agricultural labour was not without hazards. Marian Harding, the daughter of a tenant farmer in Plaitford, who was born in 1896 and lived to be 107, remembered seeing her mother take off her father's boots after he had come in from haymaking, because he was too weary to unlace them for himself. She also recalled that her grandfather, who rented the largest farm in Plaitford, let his men plant potatoes in the headlands on Good Friday (the headlands were a strip of ground left fallow to allow the plough to turn at the end of every furrow). This was a practice which ensured that weeds did not infest this otherwise uncultivated area and seed into the main part of the field, but is also an indication of how little leisure was available to farm workers. Good Friday was one of the few holidays in the agricultural calendar, yet it was given up to plant a family's staple crop. Indeed, the tradition that potatoes should be set on Good Friday (which is a movable feast and can vary by more than a month from year to year) must have arisen because it provided time for this activity. In the same way Christmas Day, which according to Flora Thompson in *Lark Rise* was kept with relatively little ceremony in farm workers' houses, was sometimes chosen as a date for weddings or on occasion funerals, the congregation being able to attend without losing a day's wages.

The severity of the agricultural labourer's life was also illustrated by a fatal accident which occurred in Landford in June 1912. George or (as he was known for reasons which have now been forgotten) Captain Bungay, the rick thatcher from Plaitford, must, because of the nature of his work, have moved from farm to farm, whilst his employment would have inevitably been seasonal. The Churchwarden's Account Book for St Peter's, Plaitford, indicates that he was also deriving income from other sources: three entries dated 1906, 1909 and 1911 show him to have received payments for thatching church cottages, whilst he not only rented his own dwelling from St Peter's Church but also what was described as 'an old cottage, uninhabitable and orchard'. The orchard was evidently the reason for the outlay of 35s paid annually to the rector and churchwardens, since it must have been exceeded by the return on the sale of the fruit, an inference made all the more probable because the derelict cottage and fruit trees were retained by his widow Sophie after his death.

It was, however, the evidence given to the inquest into the rick thatcher's fatal accident which is indicative of the harshness of the labourer's circumstances. Percy Hatch, whose mother was a native of Plaitford and still had immediate family in the village in 1912, remarked that George Bungay 'had too much beer and fell off a rick'. Marian Harding, who had known the thatcher in her childhood, remembered him to have been a quiet and gentle man when sober but entirely the opposite when the worse for drink, which was his more usual condition. Percy Hatch had been a seven-year-old pupil at Bramshaw Girls' and Infants' School at the time of the fatality, but he had evidently heard and remembered in old age the gossip circulating in Plaitford in the wake of the accident. On the other hand the report of the inquest carried by the *Romsey Advertiser* makes no reference to the influence of alcohol, as it would have done if George Bungay was drunk at the time of his death. Instead it prints, at some length, the evidence of Dr E.O. Scallon of Romsey, suggesting another – significant – reason for the fatal accident.

Robert Blake, who had been 'pitching up hay onto the rick where the deceased was working', heard him fall, 'at once jumped from the load', which must have been on a four-wheeled wagon, 'and went to his assistance'. Dr Scallon stated that he had been summoned to attend the injured man, but arrived to find that the rick thatcher had died in the cart taking him back to Plaitford. By conducting a post mortem, the doctor established the cause of death to have been a haemorrhage resulting from 'a complicated fracture of the breast bone which was in an oblique position from left to right',[1] but also concluded that whilst the body was well nourished the heart was enlarged and there was pleurisy in both lungs.

George Sturt (who took the name of his home village, Bourne, near Farnham, as his pseudonym) wrote in *The Memoirs of a Surrey Labourer*, which was published in 1909, 'Because they can so little afford to be ill, it is habitual among the very poor to neglect an illness long after other people would be seriously alarmed by it.' Drunkenness was undoubtedly both a cause of and a response to poverty, and it is indicative of hardship that George Bungay was continuing to work whilst suffering from a serious and painful complaint. Dr Scallon informed the jury that 'there was no evidence of the deceased having had a seizure or an attack of syncope [a fainting fit]', but the effects of pleurisy are likely to have been a factor in his fatal fall. His being on a rick when he was in such a condition shows how necessary it was for labourers to avoid losing wages through illness.

The dwellings of many labourers in rural areas were equally indicative of the fact that they were not 'living easily'. In 1891 concern about the standard of working-class housing led to an additional column being included in the census forms. Enumerators were required to record the number of households in their district living in four rooms or fewer. Overcrowding was most prevalent in towns, and in Salisbury some of the worst conditions were in small courts which led off the main thoroughfares and survived as relics of the medieval city. Among them was Derby Court, which opened onto Milford Street. In 1901, when enumerators were again instructed to record the number of households occupying fewer than five rooms, there were six families resident in Derby Court, of whom two were accommodated in four rooms, one had three rooms and three lived in two rooms apiece. In one instance the two rooms were situated above a greengrocer's shop and were the home of Alfred Humby (who would appear to have been the shop man), his wife, fourteen-year-old son (a porter in a drapery establishment) and three daughters, aged seven, five and one. He was also, on the day that the census was taken, entertaining a visitor, Henry Humby, a forty-two-year-old horse dealer and presumably a relative, who must have spent the night on the premises to be included in the entry.

At the same time Salisbury retained something of a rural character. No. 3 Derby Court had among the five occupants of its three rooms Thomas Durrant and his second son George, who were agricultural labourers, whilst 82 Milford Street, a four-roomed dwelling a few doors from the entrance to the court, was occupied by, among others, a father and son both named John Hayter and both hay trussers.

If overcrowding was a problem in the poorest streets in Salisbury, many of the villages along the northern border of the New Forest also had

Cottages at Nomansland from another hand-coloured postcard by F.G.O. Stuart. The construction of mud-walled cottages in successive layers is evident from the gable end of the dwelling nearest the camera. The apex of the wall is partly filled with a hurdle, whilst a gap above allows items of washing to be hung out to dry.

a significant number of households occupying properties with no more than two rooms up and two down. In 1891 Nomansland was included in the enumerators' schedules for Downton and had a predictably high number of residents living in houses with fewer than five rooms. Twenty houses in the hamlet were stated to have four rooms, two households were accommodated in three rooms and one occupied a two-roomed dwelling, whilst there were, according to the census return, only eight properties with five or more rooms, including the Lamb Inn and the grocer's shop.

A similar proportion of cottages with fewer than five rooms was listed in parts of the adjacent parish of Redlynch, which also lay within the Downton enumeration district. In Lover, the lower end of the village, thirteen out of the eighteen dwellings were stated to have four rooms, whilst in Kiln Road (which runs through the centre of the parish and was once the site of a brickyard) eleven cottages from a total of fifteen were recorded to have only four rooms, whilst one had three.

Some evidence suggests that even these figures conceal the real character of the poorer dwellings. Richard Jefferies in an essay entitled 'The Labourer's Daily Life', which first appeared in 1874, wrote of many of the cottages built by the labourers themselves: 'The ground plan is extremely simple. It consists of two rooms, oblong and generally of the same size – one to live in and one to sleep in, for the great majority of squatters' hovels have no upstairs rooms. At one end there is a small shed for odds and ends.'[2]

If the 1891 and 1901 enumerators' schedules for Nomansland and Redlynch list a high proportion of four-roomed dwellings, it is the returns for Plaitford which suggest that at least some of the cottages were closer to Jefferies' description than the census implies. In 1901 there were still a substantial number of dwellings on Plaitford Common where the 'miserable houses' had been situated fifty-three years before, yet very few of these were listed as having fewer than five rooms. One four-roomed cottage was occupied by George Bungay and his family. Although long demolished, it is remembered to have been built on a single storey with mud walls and three very small rooms, together with a lean-to which served as a kitchen. The roof was thatched, whilst it was recalled that during the Bungays' occupancy it had earth floors. It seems probable that the four and five rooms included lean-to sheds and outhouses, and that the living accommodation was more restricted than the enumeration suggests.

Even where there was an upper floor, the construction was often very crude. In some instances the bedrooms were approached by a ladder rather than a staircase.

The interior of the poorer cottages was described in 'The Labourer's Daily Life':

> The chimney is placed at the end of the room set apart for day use. There is no ceiling, nothing between the floor and the thatch and the rafters, except perhaps for one end where there is a kind of loft . . . The furniture of this room is of the simplest description. A few chairs, a deal table, three or four shelves and a cupboard with a box or two in the corner constitute the whole. The domestic utensils are equally few and strictly utilitarian. A great pot, a kettle, a saucepan, a few plates, dishes and knives, half a dozen spoons and that is about all. But on the mantelpiece there is nearly sure to be a few ornaments in crockery bought from an itinerant trader. The walls are whitewashed. The bedroom is plainly and rudely furnished.

In the first of two letters written to *The Times* in 1872, Jefferies described a two-roomed cottage which accommodated a family of eight, the labourer who built the dwelling, his wife, grown-up daughters and younger children, and another squatter cottage occupied by twelve people, whose ceilings were so low that a tall man could stand 'with his head right through the opening for the staircase and see along the upper floor under the beds'.[3] In this description Jefferies, who himself stood well over 6 feet, seems to imply that in the cottage in question something approximating to a ladder led to the upper storey.

Yet the enumerators' schedules show that it was unusual for parents and children over the age of eleven or twelve to be living under the same roof. Where older children were still at home they were usually boys, employment for girls being largely in domestic service which entailed living-in, away from their parents' cottage. As a result it was often the case that a mother, father and no more than four or five younger members of the family were resident in the same dwelling at any one time.

There were exceptions, even so, and most parishes had one or two households who lived in the crowded conditions which Jefferies described. In 1861 John Hurst and his wife Martha (who was to drop down dead whilst milking her cow fourteen years later) were living on Plaitford Common with their two daughters aged twenty-two and one, five sons who were between fifteen and five, and their two-year-old granddaughter, a total of ten people occupying what was likely to have been a two-up, two-down cottage with perhaps an additional lean-to and outhouses. Four decades later George Bungay and his wife were living in their single-storey cottage with two of their daughters, Ellen aged twenty and Florence who was eighteen, and their two youngest sons, Henry who was thirteen and Hubert who, at eight, was still a pupil at Plaitford School. Ellen Bungay was a housemaid, her sister was recorded to have been a kitchen maid whilst Henry was garden boy at Landford House in the next village. The two young women were representative of a class of domestic servants found in squatter cottages and living out. Housemaids and kitchen maids began their day at six and were sometimes required to work into the early hours of the following morning. The nearest large properties, Melchet Court at Sherfield English, Embley Park at Wellow, Warrens in Bramshaw and Landford House all lay in adjacent parishes and at some distance from Plaitford Common. There were very few servants employed in Plaitford itself, and it is unclear whether Ellen and Florence Bungay were working in their immediate locality, had places of employment further afield to which they made their way on foot each day, only had casual work augmenting the domestic staff in big houses when major social events called for extra helpers, or were, in the standard phrase of the enumerators' schedules (which was not used in their case), 'out of place'. Henry Bungay, as gardener boy, would have started work no later than seven o'clock in the morning, and must have walked 2 miles to and from Landford House daily.

Whatever the ages of the occupants, the crowded conditions in dwellings with fewer than five rooms meant they had very little privacy. Flora Thompson in *Lark Rise*, wrote that families in two-up, two-down cottages attempted to retain some degree of seemliness by putting all the boys in one room whilst the girls and their parents slept in the other, a screen or curtain separating the mother and father's bed from that of their daughters. Where an elder son was living with his parents and several younger sisters, a bed was made for him in one of the downstairs rooms, but in either instance it was 'at best a poor, makeshift arrangement, irritating, cramped and inconvenient'.

In *Tess of the d'Urbervilles* Thomas Hardy suggests that there was less careful segregation in the sleeping arrangements of the sexes. In his description of Tess's baptism of her dying baby, Sorrow, he depicted her rising at one o'clock in the morning and going 'to a second and a third bed under the wall, where she awoke her younger sisters and brothers, all of whom occupied the same room', to witness, kneeling and with their hands together, her christening of the infant before its approaching death.

Richard Jefferies, in a comparison essay to 'The Labourer's Daily Life' which he entitled 'Field Faring Women',[4] ascribed an unwholesome influence to the conditions in cottage homes: 'The overcrowding in cottages leads to what may be called an indifference to decency. It is not that in families, decency is wantonly and of a set purpose disregarded, but stern necessity leads to a coarseness and indelicacy which hardens the mind and deadens the natural modesty of even the best girls.'

Evidence of what to the Victorian middle classes would have been grossly indelicate is to be found in the use of the privy. Flora Thompson gave an example of the attitude of the middle classes to the matter when she wrote, in *Lark Rise,* of the mortification caused to a Victorian child who had been taught to approach the earth closet unobserved when an old woman hung the text 'Thou Lord alone seest me' in her privy. Flora Thompson's mother had been a nurse in a well-to-do household, and had evidently acquired the values of her employees and passed them on to her eldest daughter.

Other evidence suggests that cottagers had an altogether earthier attitude to domestic sanitation. Two- and three-seater privies were by no means uncommon, sometimes with a smaller seat for the children, and oral tradition suggests that they were used by more than one person at a time. In an instance from Redlynch a couple who had made a late marriage were remembered to have walked hand in hand down the garden to use their two-seater privy together.

Privies had to be emptied, and in some areas this was undertaken by one or two men with a horse and cart who cleared the earth closet for a small payment and ultimately deposited the contents on the fields. In others the cottagers themselves emptied the privy and buried the soil in the compost heap, or disposed of it by similar means. Richard Jefferies, describing the two-roomed cottage with its eight occupants in his first letter to *The Times* in 1872, wrote that the dwelling had no garden and 'the refuse and sewage was flung into the road or filtered down a ditch into the brook which supplied part of the village with water'. Such an instance must have been extreme, although Jefferies complained that it was among the squatters that 'fever and kindred infectious diseases break out'. An attack of cholera in the downland village of Bowerchalke is recorded to have taken place in 1883, and whilst the source of the epidemic is not identified it must have been as a result of the sort of contamination which Jefferies described.[5]

Drinking water was itself a scarce commodity in most rural households, and in the majority of dwellings it had to be carried for some distance and husbanded with great care (the rainwater butt provided for other uses, such as washing). Marian Harding remembered that the drinking water for the farm in Plaitford in which she spent much of her childhood was brought in buckets carried on a pair of yokes over two fields and a stile. Communal wells sometimes provided a locality with drinking water, whilst a cottage with its own well possessed an amenity which would be used by the residents in the surrounding dwellings. In *The Memoirs of a Surrey Labourer*, which describes the final years at the turn of the twentieth century of Fred Bettesworth, the labourer of the title, George Sturt recorded Bettesworth's complaint that the well serving his cottage was drained by his neighbour, a laundress who drew off the water in pursuit of her occupation.

A well with a pump was a particular luxury, most water being raised by windlass and bucket or merely by bucket and rope. Well buckets were especially made for the purpose. With a small circumference at the base and the mouth and a large one in the middle, they were intended to draw the greatest amount of water with the least amount being spilled. They were nonetheless heavy, and according to Marian Harding accounted for many accidental drownings. Having wound up the windlass, the victim (and it was usually the women who went to the well) reached over to catch the rope and haul in the bucket, only to have it jerk back, causing her to overbalance and topple headfirst into the water, which, being below ground, was intensely cold. Heavy clothes that dragged a victim down meant she had very little prospect of surviving.

One particularly revealing instance of a death by drowning occurred in Nomansland in 1866. The *Salisbury Journal* for Saturday 14 April, reporting the inquest on Anne Moody, an eleven year old from the hamlet, described how she had gone to a neighbour to borrow a jug and fetch water, only to be found down the well half an hour later and brought up dead. The account indicates that the residents of Nomansland relied upon a communal well, whilst the fact that the child had to borrow a jug from a neighbour recalls Jefferies' description of the sparse furnishings in the squatter cottages. Moreover, the fact that Anne Moody had gone for a mere jugful of drinking water shows what a scarce commodity it was.

Hot water was even more scarce. Henry Bungay, remembering his boyhood on Plaitford Common, remarked that it was necessary to find a few sticks and light a fire even to boil a 'kittle' (the pronunciation being the same as the spelling of the word in early Stuart probate inventories, a necessity which meant that many cottagers washed in cold water, whilst shaving was a weekly occurrence.[6] Baths were infrequent and taken by the fire, with successive members of the family following one another in the same water, the first finding it warm and clean, the last having to use it when it was dirty and tepid. Usually it is children who are remembered to have taken a bath in this way. The arrangements in households where grown-up children of both sexes were living seem never to have been described, although in the cramped conditions of two up, two down cottages there can have been little opportunity for privacy or modesty. Yet whilst such practices would have been viewed as grossly indelicate by the middle classes, the cottager, as one witness to the communal use of the privy remarked, merely took them for granted.

Substantial amounts of warm water could only be obtained by heating a copper or in a wash-house where one existed. Farms usually had their own wash-house, and one might be shared by a group of cottages, but where this was the case time and substantial quantities of fuel were required to bring the copper to the boil, a significant factor in making Monday the traditional washing day in both urban and rural households.

Fuel was not plentiful. Coal was expensive, having to be transported over considerable distances. Richard Jefferies wrote of labourers who could not afford to burn coal on weekdays but would buy 28 pounds for 6d on a Saturday night to cook their Sunday dinner.[7] In the Forest some properties had the right of estover, or assigns which entitled them to a specified number of cords of wood, whilst the right of turbary, to cut turves for fuel, was, according to Rose de Crespigny and Horace Hutchinson, 'very much prized by the poorer classes', the two authors noting that in 1899 'the Forest people are allowed to pick up fallen and dry sticks for fuel and to break down such dead branches as they can get hold of "by hook or by crook"'.[8] The right to cut turf was also available to those with rights of common beyond the Forest boundary, whilst many cottagers would have collected wood from copses and hedgerows even if they did not have any specific entitlement to do so.

According to Richard Jefferies, labourers and their families were inured to cold. In *Hodge and His Masters*, which was published in book form in 1880 but had appeared as a series of newspaper articles in the previous decade, he wrote that 'a servant fresh from an outlying hamlet, where her parents probably could procure but little fuel beyond what was necessary for cooking, at first cares not an atom whether there be fire in the kitchen or not. Such girls are as hardy as the men of their native place. After a time, hot rooms and a profusion of meat and good living generally saps and undermines their natural strength. Then they shiver like town bred people.'

Jefferies, in his description of the poor labourer's cottage, noted that the room in which the family lived was often divided by a screen, not for the sake of privacy but because the wind drove the rain under the door, making the area immediately beyond both cold and wet. Smoke blew back from the chimney and filled the part of the room sheltered by the screen but here the labourer, his wife and children would sit on winter evenings crowded around the meagre fire and lit only by its glow, the need for strict domestic economy precluding the possibility of purchasing candles.

Memory suggests that by the opening decades of the twentieth century the need for such stringencies had passed. Percy Hatch knew an old Bramshaw woman, Ursula Babey, who came to the door of her cottage carrying a candle if a caller arrived after dark. Should the visitor be invited in the candle was snuffed out and conversation continued by firelight. This was evidently sufficiently unusual to be worthy of comment, and was attributed to the fact that Ursula Babey was very poor.

A recollection which suggests that in some strata of rural society domestic life was more comfortable in the first decade of the twentieth century than it had been among the labourers forty years before came from the author's great-aunt Ellen (Nellie) Ings, who remembered that the village of Redlynch presented a lace pillow to Queen Mary at the time of the Coronation in 1911. Mrs Robinson of Redlynch House, who had revived lace-making in the Downton area at the turn of the century, chose Nellie and her elder sister Bessie to make the band of lace which was to be placed around the middle of the pillow (it was evidently more reminiscent of a hassock than a cushion). Nellie recalled sitting at the table under the light of the oil lamp whilst she and her sister worked with their bobbins, their mother was engaged in needlework and their father read to them from that week's edition of the *Salisbury Times*.

The family, represented in the village for several generations, were Wesleyan Methodists, artisans, kept a small grocer's shop, owned two mud-walled cottages which they let out for rent and enjoyed a higher standard of living than the ordinary labourers. Reading aloud had long been a common practice: George V was reputed to read aloud to Queen Mary, and it had been the custom among the Wordsworths and in Jane Austen's circle a century earlier. The Liberal *Salisbury Times* was the preferred local newspaper amongst nonconformists and covered their activities. The *Salisbury Journal* had a bias towards the Church of England and the Conservative Party, and ignored them. National newspapers did not circulate widely in rural communities until later in the century.

Something of the radical spirit of nonconformity was perhaps evident in the sequel to the making of the Coronation lace. After it had been completed the band was sent to Mrs Robinson, who failed to acknowledge the effort involved in its manufacture. Bessie was prepared to accept the situation but Nellie, who was only sixteen (and would live to be ninety-eight), went to the big house and protested so vigorously that Mrs Robinson came out in person to present her with 7s 6d – a substantial part of a housemaid's weekly wage.

Kelly's County Directory for Wiltshire for the year 1898 listed James Ings as a master grocer in Redlynch, although it was his wife,

Sarah, who was effectively the proprietoress of the shop. Florence Mary, the elder sister of the lace-makers, who had left home at the age of eighteen in 1900, remembered accompanying her mother in a donkey cart as she went to Downton to purchase stock. This stock was varied and oddly miscellaneous, including bolts of calico and flannel for underwear, butter which was sold with the impression of a wooden stamp on its surface, bread which was bought in, sweets, lard cakes that were made on the premises, and joints of pork and bacon together with pig offal which were particularly saleable commodities, the demand for meat leading to the keeping of pigs in sties at the top of the garden. James Ings and his brother William regularly killed a pig for the shop, but since both were in employment this only occurred in the evening. Nellie, who had by then come home from school, held the lantern for her father and uncle as they undertook the noisy and bloody procedure, and recalled it phlegmatically over eighty years later.

The ready sale of pork and bacon suggests that whilst the cottager's pig was traditionally a ubiquitous animal, it was either kept less widely than has been assumed or failed to provide sufficient meat through the year. Marian Harding recalled the butcher's cart coming out from Romsey in the early twentieth century with meat hung from racks. By the time it reached Plaitford it was at the end of its round, the best cuts had long gone and those that remained were begrimed with the dust of the road. Her mother never patronised the vehicle, a ready supply of meat being provided by the rabbits which her father shot in his fields.

A tradition relating to the cottager's pig survives at Nomansland, where one of the streams running through the Bramshaw Woods Inclosure about half a mile from the hamlet is still known locally as Chitterling Gutter, a name acquired because the women brought (in scenes which must have been reminiscent of Jude's first encounter with Arabella Donn) the offal from the pig, to wash in its water.

Whatever the source of their meat, Richard Jefferies claimed that the culinary skills of the cottagers' wives were very limited and that the labourers' diet was correspondingly bad: 'The labourer, from so long living upon coarse, ill cooked food, acquires an artificial taste. Some men eat their bacon raw; others will drink large quantities of vinegar, and well they may need it to correct by its acidity the effects of strong unwholesome cabbage.'[10]

Cabbage was a staple part of the cottagers' diet together with bread, which according to Jefferies was usually of good quality but rarely baked at home, the baker's shop having by the 1870s superseded the domestic bread oven, an assertion supported by the enumerators' schedules, which show one or more bakeries in most villages. Potatoes were also eaten in quantity. Half-cooked and uneaten food was thrown into the road, the housewives who maintained a degree of cleanliness indoors thinking 'nothing disgusting' out of doors, with the result that in the vicinity of a cottage there was a smell of 'soaking saturated cabbage for yards and yards round about'.[11]

Fruit had for the most part to be sold, but one item which was considered to be a particular delicacy was variously described as pot liquor, kettle broth or kettle soup. The kettle in question was the large pot to which Jefferies referred in his description of the squatters' kitchen utensils. This was suspended over an open fire with the meat and vegetables boiled in separate muslin bags immersed within it. The liquor, broth or soup was the water in which they had been boiled, infused with their juices.

In the first of his two letters to *The Times*, Richard Jefferies stated: 'Pot liquor is a favourite soup. I have known cottagers apply at farmers' kitchens not only for the pot liquor in which the meat has been sodden, but the water in which potatoes have been boiled – potato liquor – and sup it with avidity. And this is not in times of dearth or scarcity, but rather as a relish.'[12] Thomas Hardy took kettle broth on the day before he died, whilst H.M. Livens recorded in *Nomansland, A Village History* that one dweller in the hamlet, John Moody, who was known for his prodigious appetite, was remembered to have visited a neighbour and sat down to 'a huge bowl of "kettle soup" as wide as James Dibden's broad brimmed hat'. Kettle soup also featured in another, probably apocryphal, anecdote which Livens included in his pamphlet. A 'benevolent lady' asked a hamlet child if her mother had taken castor oil and received the reply, 'Please ma'am, mother tried it first in one thing and then another but she couldn't take it no how, so at last she mixed it with the kettle soup but she couldn't take it even then.' Whatever the truth of this story, and it suggests middle-class amusement at the supposed simplicity of the lower orders, it does suggest that kettle soup was a normal part of the cottagers' diet.

Not all household necessities were produced by the labourers or purchased in the shops in the village or hamlet, and visits to the nearest town were sometimes essential. Henry Bungay remembered that his mother Sophie walked the 5 miles from Plaitford Common to Romsey every Friday in order to do her household shopping. At the end of the school day he and his younger brother, Hubert, walked towards the town to meet her, usually reaching Sounding Arch on the Embley Estate, a distance of about 3 miles, before they did so. Once Sophie and the two boys had encountered one another, Henry and Hubert took the shopping bags and they all walked home together.

The presence of calico and flannel in the stock of a small village shop is a reminder that some items of clothing had to be made at home. By the time that Richard Jefferies was writing farm workers had largely abandoned the traditional smock frock[13] in favour of slops, ready-made clothes and corduroys, although they continued to wear gaiters and nailed boots which could weigh 7 pounds. 'Cheap outfitters in the towns' and 'pack drapers' who employed 'several men carrying packs who work through the villages on foot'[14] were a source of garments. When items of clothing had to be cut out and stitched in the home, or when an elder daughter in service sent a parcel of hand-me-down clothes she had received from her employer and these needed alteration, a housewife who was not adept with her needle had to turn to the seamstress whom the census returns show to have been present in nearly every village. Jefferies noted that even so it was the farmers' wives who supplied the needlewomen with most of their work.

Marian Harding remembered a birthday present which she received from an aunt living in London. She had to leave home for Plaitford School before the postman arrived, but on her return she found the anticipated parcel awaiting her. Opening it, she discovered that it contained a pinafore, a garment worn by small girls until immediately after the First World War but one unlike any owned by her fellow pupils, since it was trimmed with lace at the arms and around the neck, and embroidered. The delight the present gave was still treasured almost a century later, and was an indication that even in the household of a small farmer necessity rather than luxury prevailed.

L ABOURERS had no luxuries and few recreations. In some villages fairs were organised by benefit clubs or branches of friendly societies, although these could be occasions of excessive drinking and rowdy behaviour. In 1862 John Wise wrote that 'Wrestling and cudgel playing have been continued till the last few years close to the northern boundaries of the Forest. The old Hocktide games were till a late period kept up in the northern parts.'[15] The exact nature of the Hocktide games is not specified, but Hock day was the second Tuesday after Easter and the season around it was traditionally a period of hearty if somewhat coarse merriment. The northern New Forest was more remote and isolated than the south, and this may have accounted for the survival of traditions abandoned elsewhere.

Team games had become far more organised by the turn of the twentieth century, often with the support of the parochial clergy. Football and cricket matches between village sides were reported at some length in the local newspapers, de Crespigny and Hutchinson noting the existence of five cricket pitches within the Forest boundaries, whilst there were others in surrounding parishes, some, as at Hamptworth, being estate grounds.

One activity survived from an earlier period. This was squoyling, hunting squirrels with squoyles, short sticks weighed with lead (according to Wise there was also a lighter, wholly wooden, equivalent called a snog). De Crespigny and Hutchinson claimed that squoyling or, as they called it, squogging (from squog, a dialect word meaning squirrel) developed the forester's skill in throwing a cricket ball or a stone. New Year's Day was a favoured date for squoyling, and the squoyles taken on that day were made into pies or baked in a coating of clay, in the way that gypsies cooked hedgehogs. Louis Hatch, who farmed on the Hamptworth estate as his father had before him and who was born in 1896, the same year as Marian Harding to whom he was distantly connected, recalled, in a memoir first published in 1987,[16] that as a boy he had heard the shouts of the squoylers from Nomansland as they ranged through the Bramshaw Woods. His father, Moses, was a native of the hamlet and as a young man had participated in the squoyling; he still retained his squoyle, a modified whip handle. Lou Hatch did not join the Nomansland party as they did not welcome outsiders; indeed, the settlement had a reputation for insularity, aggressiveness and disorderly behaviour which continued for decades afterwards. Its residents seem to have embodied John Wise's observation that with the Forester 'heartiness and roughness still go hand in hand', although the comment which accompanied it, referring to 'heaviness of intellect', seems again to reflect the upper classes' prejudice with regard to the lower orders.

Chapter IV
Birth and Marriage

ON Sunday 31 March 1901, the day of the census, Sophie Bungay was absent from the three-roomed cottage on Plaitford Common which she occupied with her husband, two grown-up daughters and two youngest sons. Such absences often occur in enumerators' schedules and are usually unaccountable, but in Sophie Bungay's case an explanation may lie in the fact that she was the village midwife and might have been called to a confinement. She had no formal training but was nonetheless (according to her seventh child, Henry) far from unskilled, for she attended over 350 births without losing a mother or a baby. It is impossible to establish the accuracy of this figure, but if correct it lends weight to Flora Thompson's claim that village nurses were competent practitioners who had received some instruction from the local doctor and, being able to recognise complications, could summon help as soon as it was needed.

Sophie Bungay's niece also remembered her aunt's involvement in more than 350 successful lyings-in, but added that when government regulations did away with unqualified midwives the registered nurse who was appointed in Plaitford lost both the mother and the child at the first confinement she attended, with the result that any Plaitford woman who was approaching her time asked that Mrs Bungay should be present during her labour, even though the former lyer-in could take no part in delivering the baby. Unfortunately this reminiscence cannot be supported by contemporary evidence. Legislation passed in 1902 prohibited any unqualified nurse from describing herself as a midwife, but it was not until 1905 that a system of certification was established and only in 1910 that uncertified nurses were prevented from attending a birth. An examination of the burial registers for St Peter's Church, Plaitford, shows that no adult was interred in the graveyard between 1909 and 1912, and that whilst two infants were buried in March and April 1910, one was seven and the other fourteen months old, so both were likely to have been delivered by Sophie Bungay. On the other hand, the survival of such a tradition suggests both resentment of a stranger imposed by government regulations and loyalty to a cottage midwife who, although born in the neighbouring parish, was one of the village's own people.

Even so, Richard Jefferies wrote in 1874 that a cottage was not a fit place for a confinement. In a two-up, two-down dwelling the mother and the midwife had to occupy one bedroom, whilst the father and sometimes seven or eight children were forced to sleep in the other or make what arrangements they could on the ground floor. Furthermore, the newly confined mother returned to her domestic tasks after only three or four days, with the consequence that she would 'linger in a sickly state for months', although deaths in childbirth were rare.[1]

According to Jefferies it was the labourers who had the largest families. (In a sketch named 'John Smith's Shanty' he has the wife of an old labourer of doubtful character say to a well-to-do spinster, who besides distributing tracts and blankets reproves her for having her fifteenth son, 'Lor', Miss, that's all the pleasure me an' my old man's got,' an utterance which occurs in a work of fiction but has an authentic ring.) Moreover, the 1861 census returns suggest that Martha Hurst provided an example of a lying-in under the circumstances that Jefferies describes. The enumerators' schedules and the burial registers for Plaitford show that between 1838, when she was twenty-one, and 1860, when she was forty-three, Martha Hurst was confined eleven times and bore twelve children (among them twins in 1848), and that she gave birth to her latest child, Mary, when there were eight other occupants of the four-roomed cottage in which she was living.

Despite Jefferies' observation, large families in rural areas were not the exclusive preserve of the labouring classes. An instance of fecundity in a higher stratum of society is found in the Rev. Alan Broderick, the Vicar of Bramshaw from 1861, and his wife Ellen, who were photographed at the time of their golden wedding, surrounded by their sixteen children – three of whom had been baptised in St Peter's, Bramshaw. According to Alan and Ellen Broderick's granddaughter, who visited the church in the late 1980s, others were to follow after they left the Forest parish. She recalled that her father, the second of the sixteen children, had obtained a commission in the army and been posted to India. Such postings entailed a long absence from England, and when he finally returned home it was to find his mother awaiting him on the steps of the parsonage with three small children standing in a line beside her. They were the youngest of his brothers and sisters who had been born since his departure, and he was formally introduced to each one in turn.

Such formality would hardly have been found in a cottage home, and whilst the survival of all of Alan and Ellen Broderick's sixteen children may in part have been attributable to good fortune and a strong constitution, it must also have owed something to the superior living conditions in the parsonage. Infant mortality was high among the labouring classes in both urban and rural communities. John and Martha Hurst lost their second daughter, Susannah, within twelve hours of her birth in 1840, whilst their twins, Ellen and Edward, were born in 1848 and died when they were three days old. Indeed, the burial registers for St Peter's, Plaitford, record 298 interments between 1837 and 1901, of which seventy-two were of children aged five years or less. On the other hand, if the registers are examined over shorter periods a significant difference between the earlier and later decades of Victoria's reign emerges. Between 1837, the year of the Queen's accession, and 1851, when the Great Exhibition was staged, there were 100 burials in Plaitford churchyard, of which thirty-one (almost one in three) were of children aged five years or under. From 1852 to 1869 there were ninety interments, among which were the burials of twenty-six children of five years or less. By contrast, the period from 1870 to 1886 saw only ten children aged under six interred in the graveyard out of a total of seventy-one burials. The proportion remained the same between 1887 and 1901, when six out of forty-one interments were of infants, but it dropped again in the first decades of the twentieth century, children of five and under accounting for only four burials out of thirty-eight during the years from 1902 to 1918 (and these included two in successive months in 1910 and an accidental drowning).

Whilst no final conclusions can be drawn from the evidence of one small parish, Plaitford was probably representative of many similar communities, and there are indications from its locality that attitudes to the death of children changed between the 1860s and 1900s. At the close of the third quarter of the nineteenth century Richard Jefferies had written that whilst the labouring classes felt a natural affection for their children, the severity of rural life hardened them to deaths among their offspring. He described an exchange between a farmer and one his employees. '"Well John", the farmer says to his man, "your wife has been confined hasn't she? How's the young one?" "Aw sir, a' be main weak and picked and likely to go back – Thank God," replies the labourer with intense satisfaction especially if he has two or three children already.'[2] Jefferies explained that picked meant 'thin, sharp featured, wasted, emaciated', and that 'to go back' was a euphemism for dying, the child going back to the place whence it had come.[3]

In 1875, a year after the article containing this conversation was published in *Fraser's Magazine*, the *Salisbury Journal* reported an inquest under the heading 'Hamptworth, Fatal accident to a child'. The inquest was into the death of William Curtis, the son of a farmer, Walter Curtis, 'who was accidentally kicked or trodden by one of his father's horses, whereby he sustained such severe injuries that he died on Monday morning'. The coroner's jury returned a verdict of accidental death, and the newspaper summarised the proceedings in only two sentences. The inquest into Anne Moody's death after falling down the well at Nomansland was reported at slightly greater length, but forty years later, on 3 May 1907, the *Romsey Advertiser*, under the headline 'Sad drowning fatality at Plaitford', described the death of a five-year-old girl, Tinny Lovell, and did so in terms which indicate a very different response to the loss of a child – and perhaps to a corresponding decrease in infant mortality. Tinny Lovell was the daughter of Henry Lovell, a farm labourer employed by George Curtis, Marian Harding's uncle, and had been christened Ellen Sarah. According to Marian Harding, she owed her nickname to her father, who had an impediment in his speech. Coming downstairs after seeing his youngest child for the first time, he was reputed to have said, 'Isn't she tinny?' The mispronunciation of tiny became attached to the little girl in an example of the rough humour of rural communities.

According to the *Romsey Advertiser*, which devoted 10 column inches to the inquest, the funeral and the wreaths and crosses laid on the grave, the red-haired child went out to play with her elder sister on the afternoon of Saturday 26 April 1907. The older girl soon returned to her mother crying and very wet, and saying that Ellen Sarah had fallen into the stream which ran past their cottage. The mother (who unlike her husband was not named in the newspaper report) at once ran to the bank but, seeing nothing, continued to Powell's Farm, a distance of at least a quarter of a mile, returning with George Curtis who, 'at a spot pointed out by the elder girl, found the little child in the water'. Marian Harding remembered that her uncle had drawn out the body with two dung graplins, long-handled forks with the tines turned over, which were used to rake manure from the back of a cart. The *Romsey Advertiser* added an account of evidence given at the inquest: 'The sister told the mother that the deceased fell into the stream – which was swollen by recent rains – and she held her hand as long as she could but becoming exhausted had to release her hold. She too fell in the water but managed to get out by climbing up the bank.'[4] The jury, hearing Dr Scallon's evidence that Ellen Sarah had suffered 'asphyxiation caused by drowning', returned a verdict of accidental death.

The account of the funeral which took place two days after the inquest, on Wednesday 30 April, recorded that the pupils of Plaitford School 'had received a half day's holiday' to attend the burial at St Peter's Church where they joined the large congregation of relatives and friends who heard the headmaster's wife play 'a very suitable voluntary before the service', the Dead March from *Saul* after it and 'There's a friend for little children' during the funeral itself, whilst John Holmes, the headmaster, led his pupils 'in singing the hymn "Within the churchyard side by side" by the grave'.

The *Advertiser* opened its account of the death of Tinny Lovell by saying that the drowning had created 'a very painful sensation in the village', and there seems to have been a profusion of wreaths and crosses, many from classmates at the school, although in evident recognition of the social order the first wreath whose tribute was quoted by the paper was the one sent by the rector, the Rev. Richard Roberts (the little girl had been a member of St Peter's Church Sunday School). Those from the schoolchildren followed, many addressed to 'dear little Tinny' and quoting lines from the hymns or from the New Testament. They included a typical example from the future Marian Harding: 'With much love for our little schoolmate from Marie Curtis we have met her on earth may we meet her in heaven' – a sentence which can hardly have been chosen by a ten-year-old girl and must have been selected by her parents. Almost a century later Marian Harding remembered her brother running into the farmhouse kitchen to announce that Tinny Lovell had drowned. The wreaths from the family were listed last, followed by the names of the four young women who carried the coffin and that of the undertaker, Oliver Kendal of Landford, another of Marian Harding's uncles.

Yet it is not the details of the death nor those of the funeral and floral tributes which make the *Romsey Advertiser's* account significant. The final sentence noted that 'the whole district deeply sympathises with Mr and Mrs Lovell in their great sorrow'. The local press no longer reported the loss of a child – albeit in particularly distressing circumstances – in the almost perfunctory manner seen in the 1860s and 1870s, whilst the numerous wreaths and the tributes attached are a clear indication that such bereavements had ceased to be viewed with an almost callous sense of relief but as a cause of communal grief arising from the relative rarity of deaths in infancy.

IF infant mortality was high in rural communities in the middle decades of the nineteenth century, so too was the incidence of illegitimate births. W.E. Tate, in his pioneering work *The Parish Chest*, wrote that any student of village records would inevitably find that many referred to illegitimacy, and the same can be said of contemporary works of literature whether they were novels or texts describing the life of the fields. Characters such as Hetty Sorrel in *Adam Bede* (which is set in the late eighteenth century but was published in 1859), Fanny Robin in *Far From the Madding Crowd*, which appeared in 1874, and Tess from 1891 all bear illegitimate children (in each case with tragic consequences), whilst W.H. Hudson wrote of the inhabitants of the Sussex Downs in 1899 that 'they are not very thrifty and not very pure. In some villages illegitimate children are as plentiful as blackberries.'[5] Flora Thompson in *Lark Rise* claimed that whilst there were no hamlet children born out of wedlock in the 1880s, the number attending school with a different surname to their younger brothers and sisters showed that such births had been common in the previous decade. (Under the law as it then stood a child was legitimate only if its parents were married at least one month before its birth; if the marriage took place afterwards it retained its mother's surname.) Flora Thompson also wrote of a conversation between Laura, the main protagonist in *Lark Rise*, and her mother in which the latter recalled the marriage of a hamlet girl, Patty, the last at which the hat was passed round to pay for the cradle. It was, however, Richard Jefferies who wrote on cottage morality at the greatest length, and whose observations reflect most fully the evidence of other contemporary sources.

W.E. Tate argued that illegitimate births were rare before the middle of the eighteenth century but became common after the widespread enclosure of the open fields, because land ceased to be available for the building of squatters' cottages. On the other hand, in the villages along the northern boundary of the New Forest where farms were small, open fields were unknown and squatting continued into the early decades of the nineteenth century, illegitimate births were of frequent occurrence, so here at least alternative explanations have to be sought.

W.H. Hudson suggested that the lax morality encountered on the Sussex Downs in the 1890s might have been the result of 'too much beer', whilst Jefferies, who acknowledged that it was often difficult for a young man to rent a cottage, nonetheless claimed that the village girl who grew up in a dwelling without privacy and who therefore lacked modesty, was often barely literate and experienced the coarse humour and crude behaviour of the hayfields where men and women worked in close proximity, was particularly liable to have children out of wedlock: 'Young, full of animal spirits, giddy and ignorant, she thinks no harm of a romp and finally falls.' Jefferies also noted that 'The number of poor girls from fifteen to twenty-five in agricultural parishes who have illegitimate offspring is very large.'[6] It is impossible to establish the exact number of children born in these circumstances who were to be found in any one parish, but the baptismal registers give some indication, as do the enumerators' schedules. Thus the registers for the parish of Minstead show that between 1841 and 1849 twenty-six illegitimate children were brought to baptism, whilst between 1851 and 1858 a further nineteen were christened. At least one single woman had a child baptised in each of the years from 1837 to 1858, with the two exceptions of 1840 and 1850, whilst in 1844 eight children born out of wedlock were christened, although this was from a total of seventy-two baptisms recorded during the year.

Parish registers do not necessarily provide such a revealing indication of the extent of illegitimate births. Only eleven illegitimate children were baptised in St Margaret's Church, Wellow (where Florence Nightingale would later be buried), between 1839 and 1859, although the village had a larger population than that of Minstead, and it is hardly likely that the young men and women of the parish would have been more chaste than their counterparts across the Forest boundary. At the same time the number of christenings at Wellow was substantially fewer than in Minstead (in 1844 only twenty-two children were baptised, of whom one was born to a single woman), although the reasons for the discrepancy can only be a matter of speculation.

The enumerators' schedules give some additional evidence. The census of 1861 included, among the members of John and Martha Hurst's numerous family, a two-year-old granddaughter Sarah. It was not uncommon for grandparents to take in one or more of the offspring of married sons and daughters in order to relieve the burden of maintaining a burgeoning family, but Sarah Hurst was born in Plaitford into the only household to have that surname, whilst John and Martha Hurst's older children had all been girls. It is likely, therefore, that Sarah was the daughter of Elizabeth, the eldest of these, who was twenty-two, single and seven years senior to the next of her six brothers and sisters who were also living under their parents' roof.[7] She does not appear in the census return for Plaitford in 1851 when she was twelve and probably already a domestic servant, perhaps belonging to the category of village girls who, according to Richard Jefferies, went into farm service and encountered young labourers who also slept in the house and were 'immoral almost without exception'. Such girls flirted, 'romped' and ultimately fell, losing their situations and either having to return to their families as (in somewhat different circumstances) did Tess, or be confined in the workhouse lying-in ward in the manner of Fanny Robin.

Although the Victorian era is often regarded as one of exaggerated prudishness, the frequency of illegitimate births among the labouring classes in villages and hamlets supports Jefferies' claim, made in 1874, that 'general looseness and indifference prevail[ed] as to morality' in that stratum of society. The fact that so many single women brought their children to be baptised indicates that they saw no stigma in their circumstances, especially as the great majority of christenings took place during the regular morning and evening services. The officiating clergy seem to have accepted the situation without demur. Indeed in many instances illegitimate children were entered in the baptismal register with their father's rather than their mother's surname. An example of this occurred in Plaitford in 1838, when written across the columns for the child's and the parents' names and the father's occupation was 'Elizabeth Hurst, daughter of Martha Jones, single woman'. Comparable entries occur elsewhere in the Plaitford registers, as well as in those of Bramshaw and West Wellow, the only suggestion of disapproval occurring in Bramshaw in 1843 and 1844.

Mark Cooper, a Low Churchman, recorded in 1841 the baptism of 'John, the illegitimate son of Caroline Russell and John Boham', an entry succeeded by an additional note written two years later: 'See page 19 No. 146'. This reads: 'Edward Henry, the second illegitimate child of John Boham by Caroline Russell his domestic servant of the same place' – with a note appended a year later, in 1844, 'See page 25 No. 198'. This is the record of the baptism of 'Mary Anne, the <u>third</u> illegitimate child of John Boham, Fursley, Weeks Farm, by his domestic servant Caroline Russell. See page 19 No. 146 of the register.' Two reasons for Mark Cooper's indignation are evident in these entries: the regularity with which John Boham and Caroline Russell brought illegitimate children for baptism, and the difference in their status, which made it unlikely that they would marry. (Flora Thompson wrote in *Lark Rise* that hamlet society in the 1880s was indulgent in its view of young women who had married after the birth of their first child.) There may, however, have been another factor giving rise to the parson's sense of outrage. The Vestry Minutes for the Wiltshire part of Bramshaw show John Boham to have been the Overseer of the Poor. Overseers had, under the 1834 Poor Law Act, to assess and collect the poor rate; from 1601 until 1834 they had administered the Poor Law at a local level. The office was an unpopular one, and a significant part of the rate was used for the maintenance of single women with children. John Boham's conduct would have been at variance with his parochial responsibilities, since he was setting a conspicuously bad example to the young men and women of the village – which might ultimately have led to an increased charge on its householders.

In 1844 a Poor Law Amendment Act allowed the mother of an illegitimate child to apply to the Petty Sessions for an order requiring its father to provide for its upkeep. Richard Jefferies saw the frequency with which such orders were claimed and granted as an indication of the lax morality in rural communities. Young women who obtained contributions in this way, augmented by some parish relief, were no worse off than before giving birth, whilst a cottager's daughter who had borne the child of a farmer's son would find herself in a more favourable position, since she could receive a regular income from either a private settlement or by order of the justices. At the same time she would suffer little or no reproach.

'The girl who has had an illegitimate child is thought very little worse off by her friends and her own class, especially if her seducer is a man who can afford to pay for it – that is the great point. If she is fool enough to yield to a man who is badly off, she may be jeered at as a fool but rarely reprimanded as a sinner, not even by her own mother. Such things are not looked upon by the rural poor as sins, but as accidents of their condition'.[8] Yet even as Jefferies wrote this paragraph in 1874 attitudes were changing. At the end of the decade, in *Hodge and his Masters,* he noted that the numbers of illegitimate children had diminished, a trend also indicated by Flora Thompson in *Lark Rise* when she commented on the absence of illegitimate births in the hamlet in the 1880s. This impression is reinforced locally by a decline in the number of single women bringing children for baptism. Thus, and as an example, in the registers for St Peter's Church, Bramshaw, the only entries recording the christening of illegitimate children at the latter end of the nineteenth century were accompanied by the note 'born under canvas' – gypsies having, in many cases, no regular marriages.

Jefferies suggested that the trend had occurred because village girls valued themselves more highly, taking airs, dressing 'so far as their means will go as flashily as servants in cities' and standing on their own dignity. Apart from its effect in reforming morals he saw this as foolishness, yet he also hints at two reasons for the change of attitude which did not arise from idle vanity. On several occasions in the articles which he wrote in 1874 he attributed the cottagers' lax morality to a lack of self-respect arising from ignorance. Through the nineteenth century elementary education had become increasingly widespread. The National Society had established schools in many villages by 1850, and in most parishes along the northern edge of the New Forest the enumerators' schedules for 1851 and 1861 show that a large number of children were scholars, although few remained at school after the age of eight (and can therefore have only received a rudimentary education). With the introduction of a universal system of elementary schooling after 1870, parishes such as Wellow on the Forest boundary and Awbridge just beyond that saw the erection of board schools where previously there had been no adequate provision. The number of children listed on census returns as scholars even before 1870 indicates that the labouring classes were placing an increasing value on schooling, and by the final decades of the nineteenth century girls whose mothers and grandmothers had been illiterate could read and write and had mastered simple arithmetic, gaining at the same time a greater sense of self-esteem.

As opportunities for elementary schooling increased so too did employment in domestic service; and this in turn influenced the conduct of young women in rural communities. Richard Jefferies observed in *Hodge and his Masters* that 'an illegitimate child of her own may fetter the cottage girl. Thus she goes out in the day time to work at the farmhouse and returns home to sleep.' Service in a farmhouse was less well paid and less desirable than employment in a more fashionable establishment. Village girls might begin as maids of all work to a farmer's wife, but they usually aspired to more remunerative situations in well-to-do households. Such ambitions must have encouraged them to refrain from the loose behaviour seen in earlier generations.

Another influence on cottage morality is to be found in the extension of middle-class mores to the lower orders, the casual attitude to morality seen in the middle decades of the century giving way to a sense of respectability. This respectability was embodied, after her emergence from her early widowhood, by Queen Victoria. The village celebrations held to mark the Golden and Diamond Jubilees in 1887 and 1897 show the esteem in which she was held; and the daughter of a carpenter in Sherfield English was given the name Lillian Jubilee Littlecott, as she was born in 1887.

After the Queen's death in January 1901 the *Salisbury Journal* printed a number of eulogies delivered by the city clergy and other prominent residents. These invariably referred to her piety, high-mindedness and virtue, together with her influence on her subjects. Typical among them was the extract from the address given at St Edmund's Church by the rector, the Rev. J.D. Morrice, who claimed that 'it was not too much to say that to make her kingdom the kingdom of God was the aim of the Queen', and that she had elevated the monarchy 'by goodness, by keeping from the court what was evil, by showing sympathy with schemes likely to raise the public morality but most by the blamelessness of her private life'. The Chairman of the Board of Guardians for the Alderbury Union (who were responsible for the administration of poor relief in the locality) was similarly reported to have said, in remarks which preceded the main business of the weekly meeting, 'Her Majesty's reign had been a beautiful one . . . Her trust was in God . . . God had been the secret of her good life, the purity of her court and the great influence she had exerted throughout every country in Europe and throughout the world. (Hear Hear).'⁹

No record survives of the preaching of the country clergy, although it was probably in the same vein, whilst the *Salisbury Journal* and the *Salisbury Times*, whose leading articles conveyed similar sentiments, were read over a wide area of south Wiltshire and clearly reflected the attitudes which were increasingly influencing even cottage homes.

The effects of domestic service and the growth of respectability were illustrated in the family of woodman James Gange and his wife Susannah, who had settled in Earldoms, a hamlet situated between the villages of Landford and Whiteparish on the south-eastern boundary of Wiltshire, at the end of the eighteenth century. One of their granddaughters, Sarah Batten, who in 1851 was a servant in London, gave birth to an illegitimate daughter in 1859 (two of her aunts had done the same a generation earlier), but by 1861 had returned to domestic service in Christchurch leaving her child, Alice, in Earldoms to be brought up by her mother. Sarah Batten, who remained single, continued in service until at least 1891, but whilst it is not known whether her employers were aware of her offspring, Alice herself, who was to become the wife of a policeman in Cowes on the Isle of Wight, believed her mother to have been married, an impression which suggests that even as Richard Jefferies was writing in 'Field Faring Women' of the looseness of rural morality, the laxity which he described was giving way to the acute sense of propriety which is usually associated with the Victorian era.

A particularly striking witness to the growth of respectability in the late nineteenth century is to be found in the churchyard at Bramshaw where an inscription on one of the headstones reads, 'In loving memory of John Pile Giddings who died 12 March 1891 aged 95 years also of Mary Ann beloved wife of the above, called home 8 July 1918 aged 85 years. Peace, Perfect Peace.' The wording, with its closing quotation from a popular hymn, is conventional but misleading. In 1866 Alan Broderick baptised three of the children of a single woman, Mary Ann Parsons of Nomansland, including them in the register with their father's surname. The christening of Walter Pile, Mary Anne and Clara Giddings was followed in 1869 by that of their younger brother John. In 1871 the enumerators' schedules for Nomansland listed John Pile Giddings, a farmer of 3 acres who was aged sixty-five (ten years younger than his age according to his gravestone), as the head of a household which comprised his six children (the four baptised at Bramshaw among them) and his housekeeper Mary Ann Parsons. The headstone implies that John Giddings and Mary Ann Parsons married after 1871;

the enumerators' schedules show that they cannot have done so, for entered beside Mary Ann's name in the column headed 'relation to head of family' is the word 'niece'.

Morality was at its most lax in isolated hamlets. The majority of single women bringing children to be baptised at St Peter's, Bramshaw, were from Nomansland, and two illegitimate children from the settlement were christened at Plaitford in the 1890s after such baptisms had become rare elsewhere.[10] Oral tradition occasionally hints at incestuous relationships, although documentary evidence of their occurrence is seldom encountered. John Pile Giddings was born in Urchfont near Devizes and Mary Ann Parsons in Salisbury, but the family connection between them must have been known to Alan Broderick, to the enumerator in 1871, to the schoolteacher (four of their children were listed as scholars) and probably to the community at large. It was, even so, evidently overlooked. By 1918 when John Pile Giddings had been dead for twenty years, the inscription added to his headstone after Mary Ann Parsons was buried with him drew a veil of respectability over the actual but evidently forgotten nature of their domestic arrangements, and reflected the extent to which propriety had come to prevail even in a notoriously disorderly hamlet such as Nomansland.

Despite writing at length on the looseness of cottage morality, Richard Jefferies regarded agricultural labourers as a marrying class, but noted that their marriages were 'sober dull tame clumsy and colourless'. (They were, however, sober only in their drab hues since cottage weddings were followed by an afternoon and evening of drunkenness.) The wedding party walked to church, but 'the procession is so dull – so utterly ungenial – a stranger might pass it without guessing that a wedding is toward. Except for a few rude jests, except that there is an attempt to walk arm in arm . . . except the Sunday dress utterly devoid of taste, what is there to distinguish this day from the rest?' Jefferies himself offered, at least by implication, one reason for the lack of what he called poetry on these occasions. Cottage brides were rarely married more than three months before their first confinement, their condition being all too obvious on their wedding day (indeed, he claimed that some parsons' wives, anxious to improve the morals of their husbands' parishioners, offered a good piece of furniture to any young woman whose first child was not born until at least nine months after her wedding – although Flora Thompson's allusion to the last marriage at which a collection was made for the cradle suggests a change in attitudes). There must have been some exaggeration in Jefferies' claims, and the life to which a village bride was going can hardly have encouraged conviviality at her wedding. Two or three decades of childbearing were likely to have followed the marriage service, with the necessity of bringing up a large family on an inadequate income and in a cramped, comfortless and often insanitary cottage whilst, if Jefferies was correct, hardship quickly robbed rural marriages of affection. Labourers escaped their crowded dwellings to frequent the ale house. Here they steadily drank themselves into a state of intoxication – although not of rowdiness, returning to occasionally dispense blows which their spouses usually accepted with resignation. *John Smith's Shanty*, which claimed to have been taken from life, concludes with John Smith, the labourer who gives his name to the title, coming home in liquor, knocking down his wife Martha when she asks for a shilling to feed their children, being brought before the bench on a charge of assault and (having failed to mount an adequate defence) being sentenced to a fortnight's hard labour, during which Martha and the younger children are forced to go to the workhouse, where the eldest daughter Polly has already been confined with an illegitimate child.

Although the name John Smith indicates that the character is in some senses representative of a whole class of labourers, the narrative and especially the account of the court proceedings suggest that Jefferies was drawing on a case which he had reported as a journalist on the *North Wiltshire Herald* and the *Wiltshire and Gloucestershire Standard* in the later 1860s and early 1870s, and that a prosecution of the kind which he describes was sufficiently unusual to attract the attention of the local press. In *Lark Rise* Flora Thompson acknowledged that the men of the hamlet spent their evenings in the Waggon and Horses, but claimed that beer was too expensive at tuppence a pint to admit of any drunkenness (although she does lead her readers to infer that Laura, who in the book represents her younger self, saw her father, a stone-mason, lapse into habitual inebriation).

Jefferies remarked in *Hodge and His Masters* that village girls who entered domestic service encountered footmen, grooms and artisans who had more refinement than the farm labourers among whom they had grown up, and who could look forward to better prospects. As a result they sought to marry into that class of society rather than returning to their home villages to find husbands, thus causing a decline in purely rural marriages.

There are indications of the effects of domestic service on the population of the communities on the north-eastern border of the New Forest. In Whiteparish, a substantial village just within Wiltshire and immediately between the southern edge of the chalk downs and the boundary of the Forest, the 1881 census shows that there were thirty unmarried labourers aged between seventeen and thirty in the parish, whilst there were only two single women of comparable age still living in labouring families and two servant maids employed in farmhouses. The registers for Plaitford record that twenty-seven marriages were solemnised in the parish church between 1837 and 1850, and that in thirteen of these the bridegroom was a labourer (the bride was never shown to have any occupation), whilst among the others were two wheelwrights, two woodmen, a copse man and a miller, two shoemakers, a yeoman, a farmer, a hostler, a policeman and a warehouseman. Between 1870 and 1883, another thirteen year period and one in which Jefferies was writing the essays later collected in *The Toilers of the Field* and in *Hodge and His Masters*, and at a time when the number of domestic servants was increasing, there were twenty-five weddings in St Peter's Church, Plaitford, but in only five of these was the bridegroom a labourer, the occupations of the other twenty being more varied and less directly connected with agriculture than had been the case thirty years before. Indeed, the number of labourers marrying at the church was exceeded by that of building workers, with four carpenters and two bricklayers (there had been none between 1837 and 1859), and almost equalled by outdoor staff from domestic establishments (two gardeners and a coachman). Amongst the remainder only a farmer and a shepherd were exclusively engaged in agriculture, whilst two blacksmiths and a wheelwright would principally have been involved in working with farm horses or vehicles. Of the remainder a carrier and a dealer may have traded, at least in part, in farm and garden produce, a wool sorter from Notton near Lacock was employed in cloth manufacture, which still continued in parts of Wiltshire, and a grocer (from Derby), a gas fitter (resident in Plaitford) and a sailor (whose place of abode was 'off Cowes') had no association with the land or those who worked on it.

Percy Hatch, remembering his early years as verger and sexton at St Peter's, Bramshaw (he was appointed in 1932), recalled some weddings which were not wholly dissimilar to those described by Richard Jefferies in the early 1870s. The wedding party walked to the church with the bridegroom dressed in his Sunday suit and the bride wearing her best frock, whilst the service was followed by a tea at the bride's parents' house, after which the newly married couple went to the cottage which they were to occupy without any kind of honeymoon. Yet even if instances of these drab wedding procedures persisted well into the twentieth century in the villages on the borders of the New Forest, other marriages in the locality were celebrated with rather more ceremony and by the turn of the century were being reported in the local press. One such was described in the *Romsey Advertiser* on 8 April 1907. The bride, Miss Hilda Mabel Vinall, was the daughter of a bricklayer who lived in Landford, whilst the bridegroom, George Legge, was a resident of

Redhill where the bride evidently worked. Hilda Vinall did not come to St Peter's, Plaitford, in her best frock but in a cream wedding dress and veil with trimmings of orange blossom, whilst her sisters, Alice and Winnie, who were the bridesmaids, were also dressed in cream with blue waistbands, black chiffon hats and bouquets of daffodils. Such details were clearly intended to interest women readers, as was the information that the bride's going away dress and matching hat were of dark heliotrope, but they indicate that what the *Advertiser* called a 'very pretty wedding' was essentially different from the prosaic marriages which Jefferies had described and Percy Hatch subsequently observed, and probably reflected a degree of refinement which the bride had acquired in urban employment. References to the gold locket and chain that George Legge gave to his new wife and the silver hatpins which he presented to the bridesmaids create the same impression, as does a reference to the wedding breakfast and 'the large number of useful and handsome presents' given to the newly married couple. There were, even so, aspects of the occasion which recalled colourless village weddings. The wedding breakfast was provided in the bride's parents' house, where, after the departure of the bride and bridegroom, 'their friends remained and spent a very happy evening together' – although without any suggestion of insobriety. 'Mr and Mrs Legge left the old home for the new one', travelling to Redhill to do so but clearly without a honeymoon: such a luxury was denied to working people by the absence of paid holidays, which were not introduced for another three decades.

One detail at the close of the newspaper report described how 'Mr Kendal and staff performed their duty of respect in the old-fashioned way to the satisfaction of all, in the anvil salutes before and after the wedding'. Oliver Kendal, the Landford wheelwright, was at the time a neighbour of the Vinall family, and in less than a month would be the undertaker at Tinny Lovell's funeral (whilst one of the bridesmaids, Winnie Vinall, was to be among the four young women who carried the coffin).[12] Although primarily engaged in the manufacture and repair of four-wheeled wagons and other agricultural vehicles, he also provided the iron tyres for their wheel rims (Marian Harding remembered that a blacksmith came into the wheelwright's shop whenever these were required) and in consequence had an anvil. Traditionally smiths fired their anvils on the feast of their patron saint, Clement (28 November) by filling three holes in the upper surface (these were intended to hold cutting tools) with gunpowder, which was then ignited with a fuse. The ensuing explosion was very loud and could reputedly lift the anvil off the ground. The first of Oliver Kendal's salutes was presumably given as the bride left for the church and the second on her return with her husband.

According to the closing sentence of the *Advertiser*'s report, Mr and Mrs Legg went 'with the best wishes of all the locality for a happy and prosperous life'. One intending bride who came to St Peter's Church, Plaitford, in 1894 was not to enjoy a happy or a prosperous life with her prospective husband. Margaret Annie Elkins was the twenty-five-year-old daughter of Timothy Elkins (a farm labourer who occupied what was almost certainly a two-up, two-down cottage on Plaitford Common). She was to have married a widower, Sidney Ford, but as Alfred Gay tersely noted in the wedding register, 'This marriage was not proceeded with in consequence of the non-appearance of the expected bridegroom.' No further details are provided, so Sidney Ford's circumstances are unknown, whilst the feelings of the bride (whose situation bears some resemblance to that described in the music hall song 'There was I waiting at the church') can only be imagined.

Chapter V
Deaths

A HEADSTONE in Bramshaw churchyard commemorates three members of the same family: John Wells, who died in 1858 at the age of thirty-two, his mother Sarah, who followed him three years later aged seventy-two, and his father James. Thirty years elapsed between the death of Sarah Wells and her husband, for he lived to be 103. Centenarians were relatively rare in Victorian England, although Heywood Summer wrote of his encounter with a gardener whom he called Old Tame.[1] Old Tame had been resident in Bramshaw as a young man (the surname occurs on headstones in the graveyard there) but spent his final years in Boldrewood in the heart of the Forest, where he died in 1900, also at the age of 103. James Wells and Old Tame were exceptional, but longevity was by no means unknown in the parishes on the north-eastern boundary of the New Forest in the nineteenth and early twentieth centuries. In Plaitford between 1837 and 1851 thirteen individuals buried in the churchyard were aged seventy to seventy-nine, a further twelve were aged eighty to eighty-five, and three were respectively ninety-one, ninety-two and ninety-four. In the neighbouring village of Sherfield English during the same period the number of burials was sixty-one, forty fewer than in Plaitford, and of these ten were of parishioners or former parishioners aged seventy or over, including three who were ninety, ninety-one and ninety-four.

In the closing years of Victoria's reign, from 1886 to 1901, twelve individuals interred at Plaitford were aged from seventy to eighty, together with a further eight whose ages were between eighty and eighty-six. In Sherfield English during the same period there were eighty-three interments, of which thirty-one were of men and women aged between seventy-one and ninety-six. By the close of the century half the burials in Plaitford were of parishioners who were over seventy, whilst in Sherfield English one in three fell into the same age range.

As with the number of deaths in infancy, evidence collected in two small parishes over little more than two widely separated decades cannot be regarded as a general indication of longevity, although it is probably representative of many similar communities. Mortality was highest amongst children under five in the middle decades of the nineteenth century, but deaths occurred at every stage of life and a significant proportion of interments in the early Victorian period were of individuals aged fifteen to forty. In Plaitford in the first fourteen years of Victoria's reign almost a fifth of parishioners buried in the churchyard were aged between sixteen and thirty-seven, whilst in Sherfield English fifteen out of the sixty-one burials, nearly a quarter of the total, were of those aged seventeen to thirty-seven. One of the reasons for such a high rate of mortality amongst the residents who should have been the healthiest and most vigorous in their villages is suggested by the cause of death in the case of John Wells – consumption. Tuberculosis was particularly prevalent amongst the young, and must have carried off many who died in early adulthood. After his final illness John Wells left a remarkable relic. In 1851 he was living with his parents and younger brother Isaac, and must have shown some promise for, whilst his father was a gardener and his brother a coachman, he was described as a schoolmaster's assistant, although he can have had little prospect, at twenty-five, of qualifying as a teacher. Despite being entirely untutored, he produced a Lord's Prayer, elaborately drawn in pen and ink, and illustrated with a praying Christ and small, circular pictures of Cain murdering Abel, sowing and reaping and a young man standing in front of a large country house. The first of these drawings seem to have been derived from seventeenth-century originals and the last from one of the late eighteenth century. In the left-hand margin, faint and incomplete, are the first three commandments.[2]

Frequent mortality in Victorian society and the fact that most people died at home meant that children encountered death at a very early age. The half-holiday which allowed the pupils at Plaitford School to attend Tinny Lovell's funeral provides an instance of this, as does the way in which they sang a hymn beside her grave. (Another occasion when a hymn was sung in these circumstances occurred in a far more exulted stratum of local society in 1878. After the Dowager Countess Nelson, the widow of the second and the mother of the third Earl, had been interred in the family vault at Standlynch near Downton, the mourners were reported to have stood at the graveside – although whether this was in the vault itself or at its door is unclear – and sung the (to modern ears) morbid and now largely forgotten hymn, 'A few more years shall roll.)[3]

The author's great-aunt, Florence Mary Ings, who was born in Redlynch in 1882, provided an instance of a child being made actively aware of a death, for she had amongst her earliest memories the recollection of being lifted up to look into her great-aunt's open coffin. The great-aunt, Mary Beauchamp (née Ings), was survived by her husband James, who had been coachman at Redlynch House (where Downton lacemaking was afterwards revived) and, somewhat to the family's disapproval, took a gypsy from Hale, a neighbouring parish within the Forest Perambulation, as his housekeeper.[4] When Uncle Jim Beauchamp was dying, Florence was sent to enquire about him. Her knock was answered by the housekeeper, a tall, dark, gaunt woman, and her question was met with the answer, 'He's dead and I've just laid him out. Do you want to come and see him?' Having been led upstairs, she found Uncle Jim propped up in bed with a bandage tied around his head to hold his lower jaw in place – in the manner of Morley's ghost. Nor was this the only occasion when the young Florence Ings was sent to enquire about a relation during a final illness. Her Uncle William had a daughter, Gertrude, who was categorised as an 'imbecile from childhood' in the final column of the enumerators' schedules of 1891. She was so severely handicapped that she could not sit upright, and her parents had a special cradle made by Eastman's, the carpenters at Downton, to support her. Gertrude did not survive into adulthood, and when she was near the end Florence was sent to her uncle's house to find him holding her cousin in his arms. 'We shan't have her for very long now' was his answer to her enquiry, and Gertrude died during the night.

Marian Harding, too, remembered an early experience of death. In March 1910 her younger sister Blanche died at the age of fourteen months. Her mother called in Sophie Bungay (who was the village layer-out as well as midwife) but was too distraught to be of any assistance. Mrs Bungay turned to Marian and said, 'You'll help me my dear, won't you?' and the thirteen year old held the scissors and performed various small tasks as her sister was prepared for her coffin.

Marian Harding also recalled being sent, with other pupils at Plaitford School, to collect spring flowers to line the grave of Caroline Roberts, the rector's wife who died in May 1904. The practice of lining a grave was widespread, although it is unclear to what depth it was dressed with blooms. The last recorded instance of the custom in the locality was again in Plaitford in 1926, when the wife of Marian Harding's cousin was buried after dying in childbirth, leaving six sons. The *Romsey Advertiser*, reporting her funeral, wrote that the grave was lined with evergreens and flowers picked by the children of Plaitford School.

The inscriptions carved on headstones reflected conventional piety for the most part, with lines and even verses from hymns, biblical texts or appropriate sentences being usual, and gravestones in different churchyards sometimes having the same epitaph. An undistinguished quatrain which is found on more than one headstone reads, 'Day by day we do but miss him | Words would fail our loss to tell | But in time we hope to meet him | Ever more with Christ to dwell' – the pronoun varying according to the sex of the deceased. Monumental masons evidently had standard patterns for stones and phrasings for epitaphs, although the wording occasionally indicates that the occupant of a grave must have endured prolonged suffering. In an example in St Andrew's churchyard in Landford, 'Whom the Lord loveth he chasteneth' is inscribed on a stone, whilst at Plaitford the headstone placed over the grave of Mary Hutchings, the wife of one farm labourer, John Hutchings, and the mother of several others, who died in 1879 at the age of fifty-four, carries a quotation from Psalm 119: 'I know, O Lord that thy judgements are right and that Thou in faithfulness hast afflicted me.'

Medical assistance was expensive, and unless they belonged to a friendly society was largely beyond the reach of cottagers. Even where it was available it was often of a very limited effect, whilst diagnosis could be unreliable. When, in 1855, Edward Macey met his end falling down the stairs in the house that he had built for himself in Nomansland, the *Salisbury Journal* in giving a brief account of the inquest that followed the accident left no doubt that the deceased had been fatally injured after missing his footing on the top of the staircase, but noted that the verdict was death by apoplexy.[6]

The outcome of another inquest in Downton nine years later also called into question the accuracy of the surgeon's diagnosis. At about seven o'clock on the morning of 15 April 1864 an eighty-five-year-old man, William Arney, 'was observed by a neighbour lying outside his back door quite dead'. The jury was informed that he had become increasingly feeble, and when Mr Caesar, the surgeon, stated 'that the cause of the old man's death was natural decay, a verdict was returned accordingly'. Yet there had also been evidence that two days before his demise William Arney had 'complained of pains in his chest and spat up a good deal of blood', symptoms which suggested that he succumbed to more than old age and decrepitude.[7]

The course of a long final illness was followed in a series of entries in the minutes of the Quarterly Meeting of the Romsey Primitive Methodist Circuit. Between March 1909 and March 1911 the meeting sent a succession of letters at three-monthly intervals to one of the local preachers, Brother (as Primitive Methodists always addressed each other) Samuel Collins, a builder from Awbridge. A proposal to forward a further 'letter of sympathy to Bro. S. Collins on his long months of affliction and physical weakness' was made at the meeting on 8 March

1911, but it is doubtful if the letter was ever sent or even written, for Samuel Collins died three days later. Instead, the Rev. T.C. Rigg, the superintendent minister, included a note in the minute book, 'to place on record our very high and loving appreciation of the beautiful life and abundant labours of the late Samuel Collins of Awbridge'. The entry continued by listing the work which he had undertaken and concluded, 'We shall treasure his memory as one of those good men it has been our privilege to know and labour with. He died a triumphant death implicitly trusting in the Lord Jesus Christ . . . He fell asleep in Jesus March 11th [1911] aged 79 years.' The *Romsey Advertiser*, reporting the death, added that Samuel Collins had been bedridden for two years.

Other deaths were recorded in a very different manner. The active interest which the Victorian local press took in inquest proceedings meant that cases of suicide and misadventure were frequently reported, whilst the marginal notes which some clergy wrote in their burial registers drew attention to the interment of parishioners who died in such circumstances. Alfred Gay marked the burial of two suicides in Plaitford in 1875 and 1878 in this way. In the latter case the inquest which followed the death of Alfred Elkins, a young man of nineteen whose sister would be left standing at the altar sixteen years later, was overlooked by the *Salisbury Journal*, and the only surviving details are in the register: 'Suicide by hang'g at Broxmore [Park, Whiteparish] temp. insanity.' In the former case the Salisbury paper carried an account of the inquest. The jury heard that the deceased, Edwin Tutt, a blacksmith who was aged forty-eight, was living with his father and other members of his family, having returned from Leatherhead two months previously 'for the benefit of his health'; he had, however, 'been in a low and desponding state for the last fortnight'. The report then gave an account of his suicide. 'On Tuesday morning [14 September 1875] about eight o'clock, his sister called him in his bedroom and about two minutes afterwards he was seen coming down the stairs with blood flowing from his throat. Mr Nunn, the surgeon [who only days before had given evidence at the inquest into the death of Martha Hurst], in examining the body, found the windpipe completely severed as well as the principal arteries. The jury returned a verdict that the deceased had killed himself in a fit of temporary insanity.'[8] This report was evidence of both the interest felt by the local press in the lurid details of such occurrences, and of the difference between the living conditions of artisans and those of squatters. The Tutt family had been blacksmiths in Plaitford for decades, and their house was clearly sufficiently large to allow the returning Edwin (who was shown on the census of 1861 to have been a widower) to have his own bedroom.

Twelve years earlier, on 17 July 1866, the *Salisbury Journal* printed an account of a suicide which occurred in the parish of Redlynch. According to the newspaper the deceased, William Scovell, a widower of sixty-three, was to be married to a widow on the morning of his death. Despite his age and the fact that he and his bride were both marrying for the second time, he was to have been brought to St Mary's Church by coach. When the coachman arrived at his lodgings, however, he did not answer the door. His landlord was called to break into his rooms, where he was found hanging from the bedstead by his braces.

Until 1823, when the practice was abolished, anyone who took their own life was buried at a crossroads or other unconsecrated site, and even after they were permitted to be interred in the churchyard it was traditionally in what Thomas Hardy described as 'that shabby corner of God's allotment where He lets the nettles grow and where unbaptized infants, notorious drunkards, suicides and others of the conjecturally damned are laid'.[8] The graves of Edwin Tutt and Alfred Elkins are unmarked, and it is not known if such an area existed in the graveyard at Plaitford, but the Bramshaw burial registers show that in 1897 and 1901 the vicar, the Rev. John Whitworth Godden, interred two unbaptised and unnamed children. The second interment is reminiscent of the experiences of Tess, since the entry in the register records that the child was a five-day-old 'female infant' born to Emily Dibden, a single woman of Nomansland. Whereas the fictional Sorrow was 'buried by lantern light at the cost of a shilling and a pint of beer to the sexton', the daughter of Emily Dibden had 'a few prayers' read over her by the Vicar.

Death or serious injury were also liable to occur in the course of a labourer's daily work, as George Bungay's fatal fall from a rick illustrated, although the attitude of both employers and the authorities to such incidents was suggested by the reporting of an accident involving an eleven-year-old boy which took place in Landford at the latter end of 1864. The steam-driven agricultural machinery which was used with increasing frequency during the second half of the nineteenth century represented a particular hazard, the moving parts being without guards. At about two o'clock on the afternoon of Tuesday 15 November 1864 a threshing engine was at work in the yard of Landford Farm, when a ploughboy, Edward Charles Reynolds, came out of the barn carrying a broom, slipped and fell against the spindle of the machine, which trapped his leg and drew it round. The machine was stopped as quickly as possible and the boy was taken to Salisbury Infirmary (probably by horse and cart over uneven roads). According to the *Salisbury Journal* the house surgeon, Mr W.G. Lush, giving evidence at the inquest which was subsequently held at the hospital, 'stated that when the deceased was brought into that institution, he was suffering from a comminuted fracture of the leg and thigh [i.e. one in which the bones were shattered]. He was sensible but in a too prostrate condition to undergo any operation. He never rallied and died the following day.'[9] Yet whilst the report called Edward Reynolds a poor boy, the newspaper not only noted the verdict of the jury – accidental death – but emphasised the way it had exonerated all parties, and especially commended Henry Gwyer, the farmer, who was Countess Nelson's principal tenant in Landford. The *Journal* wrote that it was 'quite evident that no blame was attached to anyone and they [the jury] also expressed satisfaction at the conduct of Mr Gwyer who caused the poor boy to be immediately taken to the infirmary and afterwards brought from Landford every person who could give any information on the subject'. Accidents of this kind were by no means uncommon, but the inquest evidently accepted them as unavoidable – whilst the way in which the jury commended Henry Gwyer's promptitude in sending the injured boy to hospital and his readiness to release his employees to give evidence about the incident suggests that many farmers in similar circumstances would not have allowed such an accident and its consequences to interfere with the work of their farms.

Henry Girdlestone, the rector of Landford, preaching 'on the death of a poor parishioner' in 1863, told his congregation that he wished his own funeral to be of the utmost simplicity, and that he was leaving £10 in his will to inaugurate a burial fund which he hoped would be maintained by contributions from the principal residents of the parish, be administered by the incumbent and churchwardens and provide a means by which the richer villagers would assist with the burial expenses of the poor.[10] Whether such a fund came into being is not known, but Henry Girdlestone's bequest suggests that the cost of providing funerals was over-extending bereaved cottage families, whilst his insistence that he would have a plain funeral seems to suggest that elaborate interments among the leading families were encouraging the labourers to have more expensive mourning than they could afford.

Accounts of funerals given in the local press, which usually date from the late nineteenth century onwards, generally confined themselves to the voluntaries and hymns and to the wreaths and the tributes which accompanied them, together in many instances with a description of the coffin and the inscription on the name plate. Some authors, however, indicate that most village funerals were conducted without the ostentatious display of mourning usually associated with Victorian burials. In the majority of parishes interments would have been too infrequent to provide an undertaker with a living, and a general builder or carpenter and wheelwright usually assumed the role.

Walter Hood, wheelwright, joiner and undertaker in West Wellow, was remembered as having kept his workshop doors open. If they were shut and hammering was heard it was because he was making a coffin, and this in turn was often the first indication of a death in the village.

Richard Jefferies, writing in 1879, gave an account of the uses of a four-wheeled wagon, and included a paragraph describing the way in which the vehicle played a part in every stage of a labourer's life. He concluded: 'many a plain coffin has the old wagon carried to the distant churchyard on the side of the hill. It is a cold spot – as life was cold and hard; yet in spring the daisies come and the thrush will sing on the bough,'[11] but whilst Jefferies wrote of coffins being carried to the graveyard in a wagon, memory recalls that they were as likely to have been wheeled to the burial ground on the parish bier with the mourners following on foot. The bier was a trolley kept for the purpose and made available to any bereaved villager. In Whiteparish it stood in the north aisle of All Saints' Church until relatively recently, although it had long since ceased to be used.

Newspaper reports suggest that in many instances the coffin was carried by friends, neighbours or relations of the deceased – as was the case with the four young women from Plaitford who were the bearers at Tinney Lovell's funeral (and indeed when the Honourable Henry Nelson, a son of the Dowager Countess and younger brother of the third Earl, was fatally injured in a riding accident in 1863, his coffin was carried into the family vault by six labourers from the estate).

For centuries the only monuments to the dead were either the churchyard crosses, which served as a general memorial and almost entirely disappeared after the Reformation, or the effigies and tablets within the church which commemorated the leading families of the parish. The local representatives of the landed classes were frequently buried in their own vaults beneath the building. Percy Hatch, the verger and sexton at St Peter's Church, Bramshaw, remembered being amongst the last to enter the vault occupied by the Eyres of Warrens House before it was sealed in the 1930s. The coffins of the adults were laid on shelves projecting from the walls, whilst that of a child was on a wrought-iron stand in the middle of the floor. The account of Countess Nelson's funeral, printed in the *Salisbury Journal*, described how her coffin was placed between those of two of her sons who had predeceased her and near to that of her husband, indicating that they, by contrast, were all laid on the floor. Percy Hatch remembered, to his surprise, that the Eyre vaults were 'dry as a cork', although by an irony the font was subsequently relocated above it (the Eyres having converted to Roman Catholicism and ceasing to attend the parish church). The water used in baptism services audibly splashed the coffins as it drained away through the floor.

The first headstones to have survived in most graveyards date from the late seventeenth or early eighteenth centuries, and because they were cut from the heavy material which was difficult to transport they were small. The earliest example in Plaitford churchyard, which commemorates Jane, the widow of Richard Gauntlett who died in 1710, is 28 inches high by 21 inches wide and, as with many early stones, has a skull carved above the inscription as a *memento mori*. Headstones became larger and more numerous during the eighteenth and early nineteenth centuries, but it was not until after development of the railway system allowed heavy freight to be carried widely that they were erected in significant numbers. Monumental masons established businesses, even in smaller towns, and by the opening of the twentieth century Graces of Romsey were inserting a weekly advertisement in the local paper.

The growing number of gravestones called for churchyards to be extended. Mark Cooper included a characteristic note when he recorded one interment: 'The first burial in the new ground which was Meddy Eades, Bramshaw, October 20th, 97 years. New churchyard consecrated by the Bp. of Salisbury on October 19th 1848, where N.G. in margin in New Ground.' Many subsequent entries have the initials N.G. written

St Peter's Church, Plaitford, from a postcard by Sam Taylor of Andover. The grave of Tinney Lovell is on the left of the picture with the headstone, surmounted by a wheelcross, which was donated by the Sunday School.

beside them, one of the earliest recording the burial of John Boham, the erring farmer and overseer of the poor who died at the age of forty-one in May 1849.

Yet whilst headstones became more widespread during the nineteenth century they were far from universal, many graves being unmarked. It was, in the majority of instances, farmers, artisans and others from a slightly more affluent stratum of rural society who had stones. Very few labourers or their families were commemorated in this way (John and Mary Hutchings were exceptions) and the same was true of children. In Plaitford only two children have headstones: Tinny Lovell, whose monument was provided by the teachers and pupils of the Sunday School, and Jessie Elizabeth Curtis, the six-year-old daughter of George Curtis, who retrieved Tinny Lovell's body from the stream where she had drowned. A surviving story claims that George Curtis's wife, Eva, took two of her children to Fordingbridge to have their tonsils removed and brought one back living and the other dead. This is unsubstantiated, but it is perhaps significant that the Romsey section of the *Andover Advertiser* should in November 1898 have included a short paragraph noting the erection of a 'very handsome memorial' to Jessie Curtis, describing the stone and kerb and concluding that 'the work was very satisfactorily carried out by Mr J. Grace, Station Road, Romsey', who may have been the source of the information. That grieving parents should have erected a monument to their six-year-old daughter which was so substantial that it attracted the attention of the local newspaper suggests that the circumstances of her death might have been exceptional.

If a relatively small proportion of graves had stones or, more infrequently, cast-iron wheel crosses, others were marked by less durable memorials. A survey of St Mary's churchyard in Redlynch made in the late nineteenth century showed a number of monuments which no longer survive. These lost markers must have been grave-boards. Grave-boards were a cheaper alternative to stones and were usually supported by vertical posts, with the board itself running the length of the grave. A rare example remains in the south-west corner of the burial ground at Redlynch, although the inscription has gone and the board is very dilapidated. Most grave-boards eventually rotted away, but they often outlasted the memory of the individual they commemorated and could easily be removed. The undertakers in Redlynch at the turn of the twentieth century were named Plaskett, and it is remembered that they used a grave-board with the inscription still legible to repair their hen house.

Most cottagers were interred beneath anonymous mounds. At the close of *Hodge and his Masters* Richard Jefferies wrote: 'Hodge died and the very grave digger grumbled as he delved through the earth, hard-bound in the iron frost for it jarred his hand and might break his spade. The low mound will soon be level and the place of his burial shall not be known.' Some families commemorated several deceased members by having their names inscribed on the same stone. John, Sarah and James Wells provide an example of this, whilst a headstone on the south-east side of St Peter's Church, Plaitford, records the deaths of John Hurst, his widow Martha, 'who departed this life suddenly', their second son George, who died six months before his mother at the age of twenty-five – both deaths presumably inspiring the choice of text, 'Watch for ye know not the day nor the hour wherein the Son of Man cometh' – and their granddaughter Sarah, who died in 1880 at the age of twenty-two. It seems improbable that four individuals should have been buried in the same grave, particularly as at least one death was unexpected and all occurred within a decade of each other. Some of the interments must have taken place elsewhere in the churchyard in unmarked graves.

The graveyard in Bramshaw is on two levels, separated by a 10 foot high bank, and was extended more than once after 1848. In the upper churchyard, according to Percy Hatch, nothing remained in the sandy soil after seven years, even coffin handles disappearing within that time, whereas the heavy clay of the lower churchyard retained a coffin for decades. The verger and sexton recalled being asked to dig the grave of an elderly parishioner who wished to be buried with her younger sister. The sister had died in her mid-teens, fifty years before, but when the grave was reopened her coffin proved to be as sound as on the day it was lowered into the ground, even the name plate being perfectly legible.

Before the widespread erection of gravestones, burial grounds were used over and over again until the older parts of many village churchyards were higher than the adjacent paths or roads. Evidence that this practice continued after headstones became more numerous is to be seen in the juxtaposition of stones from widely differing periods, together with the removal of grave boards, although this in turn meant that human bones unearthed when a grave was dug were treated with less reverence than might have been expected in an era which was so morbidly preoccupied with death and with mourning. A painting by the minor artist Henry Alexander Bowler called *The Doubt, Can These Dry Bones Live?*, which was exhibited in 1856, indicates that this was the case. It shows a young woman leaning pensively over a headstone in a country churchyard and looking at a newly refilled grave, a skull, a femur and part of a rib cage protruding randomly from the disturbed earth. The artist intended the study to be a comment on the religious uncertainties of the period (it preceded the publication of

On the Origin of Species by three years), but the way in which he showed bones amongst the backfilling for a grave, albeit in a picture laden with symbolism, suggests that such a detail must have been plausible to a mid-nineteenth-century audience.

Another instance of irreverence shown not merely to human remains but to a whole area of a graveyard also comes from Bramshaw. St Peter's Church stands on a natural hillock overlooking what, until 1871, had been a branch of the Sarum to Eling Turnpike. Percy Hatch claimed that his predecessor as verger at the church had seen human bones dug out of the opposite bank, the construction of the turnpike in the middle of the eighteenth century having cut through the mound and obliterated part of the burial ground. Such a tradition seems improbable, although the fact that it survived into the twentieth century is perhaps significant – whilst the hillock falls almost vertically from the churchyard to the road below, suggesting that a cutting was made to accommodate the progress of the highway.

Every resident had the right to be buried in their parish churchyard, but until 1880 the funeral service had to be conducted by an Anglican clergyman and had to be in accordance with the rites of the Church of England. To avoid this, some dissenting congregations had a burial ground attached to their meeting houses: this was most frequently true of the Strict and Particular Baptists who embraced an especially severe form of Calvinism. Strictly excluding non-members from what they called 'the ordinance of the Holy Communion', they believed that they were particular beneficiaries of the sacrifice of Christ and that they had been chosen from before the beginning of time to be admitted to heaven, the rest of humanity being equally destined for perdition. Some Strict and Particular Baptists were buried in parish churchyards as the Thirty-Nine Articles of Religion, the doctrinal basis of the Church of England, are Calvinist in their teaching, but an exclusivity which made them sit beside dying members of the congregation and question them to establish that they were in fact amongst the elect also led them to have their own burial grounds, The Strict and Particular Baptist Church at Fritham, the Rehoboth Chapel at Downton, the Ebenezer Chapel at Lockerly Hole and Sperrywell Baptist at Mottisfont all have a graveyard. The Romsey Primitive Methodist Circuit also had its own burial ground surrounding what, until 1932, was known as West Wellow Primitive Methodist Church. The doctrines of Methodism are the reverse of those of the Strict and Particular Baptists, for they embody the conviction that salvation is available to all who believe, but the Primitive Methodists, who drew their support principally from the labouring classes, felt themselves to have been subjected to persecution both by the Anglicans

– many of whose clergy were intensely hostile to dissent – and by their often more socially elevated counterparts, the Wesleyans.

An emphatic assertion of nonconformity was made in the funeral of Elizabeth Emily Collins, the eldest daughter of Samuel Collins, the Primitive Methodist preacher of Awbridge. Emily Collins, as she was known, was thirty-nine at the time of her death in February 1898, and as a result of the Burial Law Reform Act of 1880 would have been entitled to interment in St John's Churchyard, Lockerly, by a Primitive Methodist minister using a form of service appropriate to the connexion.[11] Instead the *Andover Advertiser* reported that she was interred in 'the family burial place at the Ebenezer Chapel in Lockerly Hole'. Whether the Collins family regarded the graveyard at Canada Common as too far from Awbridge for convenience, or whether a burial plot at Lockerly had been acquired before the Primitive Methodist Circuit had its own burial ground is not known, but whatever the case the decision to be buried there suggests a determination to remain nonconformist even in death. Samuel Collins's building business must have brought a measure of prosperity, for the report in the *Andover Advertiser* suggested that his eldest daughter's funeral was conducted with some ceremony. The service, which took place on the afternoon of Sunday 28 February 1898, attracted a congregation of more than 400, whilst the hearse and four mourning coaches 'slowly wended their way to the Ebenezer Chapel' where the funeral was 'very impressively conducted by the Deacon, Mr N.T. Southwell . . . The remains of the deceased lady were borne to the graveyard by her old companions, and were enclosed in a handsome polished coffin with brass fittings, on the lid being a brass plate bearing the inscription – Elizabeth Emily Collins died February 22nd 1898 aged 39 years.' One of the wreaths carried the verse:

> Sleeping in Jesus, how sweet is her slumber,
> No features by anguish appearing distressed;
> Already her spirit has joined to the number,
> Of those who in Christ are eternally blest.

Thirteen years later Samuel Collins's triumphant death was followed by a funeral service conducted by the Rev. T.C. Rigg, the Romsey Primitive Methodist Circuit minister (who wrote the fulsome obituary in the Quarterly Minutes). This appears to have taken place entirely in the Ebenezer graveyard at Lockerly. The coffin was carried by six prominent members of the congregation at Newtown Primitive Methodist church and about two hundred mourners were present. A memorial service at Newtown on the following Sunday also attracted a large attendance. Today nothing remains of the Newtown Church, and only the weathered gravestones in the burial ground mark the site of the Lockerly Ebenezer Chapel.

Chapter VI
Outdoor Relief, Charity and Self Help

THE Poor Law Amendment Act of 1834 is notorious in popular memory for having forced paupers into the workhouse, where married couples and parents and children were separated and made to endure extremely harsh conditions. In reality the operation of the New Poor Law was often less rigid and less severe than tradition has assumed.

The Old Poor Law, introduced in 1601, gave responsibility for the indigent to the parish and distinguished between impotent and able-bodied paupers. The impotent were incapable of earning their living through age or infirmity, and were supported by the rate levied from every householder, whilst the able-bodied were assumed to be idle and were therefore put to work. The Poor Law of 1601 had been subject to successive (though often minor) amendments and modified by local practices – the Speenhamland and Roundsman systems were examples of these[1] – but whilst it continued to be effective in the industrial Midlands and north, it had been overwhelmed in the southern counties by a rapid increase in rural poverty, the result of a rising population combined with the depression in agriculture which followed the ending of the Napoleonic Wars.

The 1834 Act was based upon the premise that if outdoor relief – paid to the poor in their own homes – was drastically reduced, and if the only options open to the great majority of paupers were either to enter the workhouse (where conditions were to be worse than those of the poorest labourers) or find their own means of support, then they would choose the latter course and the burden on the ratepayers would ease correspondingly. In order to achieve this end, the Poor Law Amendment Act required parishes to combine into Unions (which varied in size and sometimes crossed county boundaries), each Union having to build its own workhouse.

The Unions were placed under the immediate supervision of a Board of Guardians[2] elected by the landowners (who, depending upon the extent of their properties, could have up to six votes) and the ratepayers (with one vote each). The guardians met regularly to deal with the business of the Union, and as the nineteenth century progressed their proceedings attracted the attention of the local press. Richard Jefferies, who became familiar with their activities as a journalist, noted in the final chapter of *Hodge and His Masters*: 'Tenant farmers sit as guardians of the poor for their respective parishes, the clergyman and the squire by virtue of their office as magistrates and the tradesmen as guardians of the market towns.'

The meetings took place in the boardroom of the workhouse, which Jefferies seems to suggest, by implication at least, offered a standard of comfort which was sharply contrasted with that experienced by the inmates. 'The boardroom ... is a large and apparently comfortable apartment. The fire is piled with glowing coals, the red light from which gleams on the polished fender. A vast table occupies the centre and around it are arranged the seats for each of the guardians.' By the time that *Hodge and His Masters* was published in 1880 the New Poor Law had been in effect for well over four decades, and Jefferies wrote of the 'stout elderly farmers' who sat around the boardroom table and were regularly re-elected because no one else wished to compete for the thankless responsibility of addressing every aspect of the Union's business in the minutest detail for one full day a fortnight.

A brief item in the *Romsey Advertiser* of 18 March 1907 suggested that by the early twentieth century the office of guardian was more eagerly sought after and commanded more public attention. The paragraph recorded an accident to a Bramshaw farmer, Edward Dibdin, who had been thrown from his cart whilst driving through Wellow and injured in the face and arm. The paper concluded by stating that 'Mr Dibdin was one of the contestants for a seat on the Romsey Board of Guardians'. Teddy Dibdin, whom Percy Hatch remembered to have seen cycling into a headwind with his very full beard parting over his waistcoat buttons, was resident within the New Forest Union but saw sufficient advantage in being on the Romsey Board to offer himself as a candidate for a seat, a view evidently shared by others as there was clearly an election. Moreover, the fact that a local newspaper should have identified him by his candidacy is indicative of the public interest in the position.

From the outset the principal priority of the guardians was to provide for the poor at the least possible expense, and the *Salisbury Journal*, clearly aware of this fact, took note of the effects of the Poor Law Amendment Act in other parts of Southern England. In October 1836, the paper informed its readers, 'The Provisions of the Poor Law Act have been introduced into the Isle of Wight ... It is gratifying to learn that the savings effected to the ratepayers in the month of July when the new system was adopted, as compared with July 1835, amounted to 500L [£] whilst in the following month of August, the diminution of expenses was more than sufficient to pay all the salaried officers of the Union.'

A year later the *Journal* looked even further afield for evidence of the effectiveness of the legislation, printing an extract from the 'Statement of the Board of Guardians of the East Kent Union' who met in Deal: 'We have practical, the best of all proofs, of the return to more independent habits and practices of forthright thought; that value is given to character; that the labouring classes are really and truly benefited by the alteration rather than oppressed as some would have it believed, by this absolutely necessary change, obtaining more independent employment for themselves as proved by the actually diminished, indeed as respects this Union, totally extinct item of outdoor relief to be able bodied.'

Yet whilst the guardians of the East Kent Union were congratulating themselves on their success in extinguishing outdoor relief to the able-bodied poor and in promoting industry among the labourers, the demand for economy meant that many paupers continued to receive some assistance in their own homes. This commonly occurred when aged parents were living with and being partially supported by their children, although there were other instances where the payment of a dole from the Union entailed substantially less expense than removing a pauper to the workhouse.

The enumerators' schedules for most parishes include residents who were listed as paupers and were evidently living in these circumstances. The parish of West Wellow in the Romsey Union, provided in 1851 typical examples of those receiving outdoor relief. The census for that year showed George and Mary Snellgrove, who were aged sixty-four and sixty-five, to have been paupers living in their own cottage with two of their sons, George, a widower, and William, who had never married, together with a grandson, John, all of whom were agricultural labourers and evidently contributing to their parents and grandparents' means of subsistence. Another entry showed Hannah Russell, a thirty-eight-year-old widow and a pauper washwoman, who was almost certainly living in a squatter cottage with three of her children, James and Harriet, who were respectively seventeen and twelve and both agricultural labourers, and a second son, eight-year-old William. The combined income of the mother and the two elder children, supported by some outdoor relief, was evidently sufficient not only to allow the household to subsist but also, in an indication of the value already being put on schooling, for William to be a scholar, thirty years before school attendance became compulsory and at a time when it would have required a small weekly payment.

Although George and Mary Snellgrove and Hannah Russell were typical recipients of outdoor relief, other less obvious candidates also appear in the 1851 census returns. An eighty-two-year-old widow, Elizabeth Penny, who was amongst Hannah Russell's neighbours, was listed as a pauper although she was the sole occupant of her cottage, whilst in the parish of Sherfield English, which was also in the Romsey Union, outdoor relief was being paid to a twenty-five-year-old widow, Sarah Bell, who had lost her husband within the preceding year, since she had a three-year-old daughter and a three-month-old son. Considerations of humanity may have played in keeping such paupers in their own homes, although they must have possessed some means of support to prevent them being taken into the workhouse.

Richard Jefferies suggested that because so many of the guardians were farmers, the individual inmates of the workhouse and claimants for poor relief would, in agricultural Unions, be known personally to one or more members of the Board, and as a result would be treated more favourably than the Poor Law Amendment Act had envisaged. Describing the decline of Hodge, his representative labourer, into decrepitude and helplessness, Jefferies wrote: 'His case came before the Board of Guardians. Those who knew all about him wished to give him substantial relief in his own cottage, and to appoint some aged woman as nurse – a thing that is occasionally done and most humanely. But there were technical difficulties in the way, the cottage was either his own or partly his own, and relief could not be given to anyone possessed of "property". Just then, too, there was a great movement to curtail outdoor relief; official circulars came round warning Boards to curtail it and much fuss was made.' With the result that the old labourer was taken, against his will to the workhouse.

Jefferies noted that Unions kept such comprehensive records that they could find details of any claim made since the implementation of the 1834 Act, but very few of the 'account books, ledgers, red bound relief books, stowed away, pile upon pile in the house archive' have survived, and *Hodge and his Masters* provides evidence that assistance to the able-bodied continued, albeit on a temporary basis, in the late 1870s. Describing the procedure for the fortnightly meeting of the Board of Guardians, Jefferies wrote of those who applied in person for financial support: 'A group of intending applicants has been waiting in the porch for admission for some time. Women come for their daughters; daughters for their mothers; some want assistance during an approaching confinement, others ask for a small loan to be repaid by instalments, with which to tide over their difficulties. One cottage woman is occasionally deputed by several of her neighbours as their representative. The labourer or his wife stands before the Board and makes a statement supplemented by explanation from the relieving officer of the district.'

It is not clear whether the reference to a directive from the Local Government Board which forced Hodge into the workhouse had any parallel in fact, but by the close of the 1870s when *Hodge and his Masters* was written the first effects of the depression caused by bad harvests and the mass importation of foreign foodstuffs were being felt, and claims of the kind which Jefferies described must have been made with increasing frequency. Certainly sources from the late nineteenth century show an ambivalence towards outdoor relief. Thus in October 1898 the *Hampshire Advertiser*, reporting a meeting of the Board of Guardians of the New Forest Union, wrote that 'The cases of outdoor relief before the Board were very light and the relieving officer was congratulated thereon.' By contrast, in the preceding January, the advertisements that were printed on the front page of the *Andover Advertiser* included a panel in which the accounts of the Mayor's Out-Door Paupers Christmas Dinner Fund for 1897 were reproduced, with a note giving the names of the managing committee, cordially thanking the ladies and gentlemen who assisted in the collection and concluding by stating that 'The committee distributed, on Christmas Eve, 123 bread and 123 meat tickets.'

A decade later the Liberal Government of 1906–16 introduced a series of measures which prepared the way for the eventual establishment of the Welfare State. Among these was the old age pension which, whilst it was only 5s a week and paid to persons over seventy who were of good character, marked a change in attitude to provision of the aged. This was developed further with the passing of the National Insurance Act in 1911, whilst in 1913 the name workhouse was abolished in favour of poor law institution, and outdoor relief was largely restricted to the aged and infirm.

Employees of the Poor Law Union did not enjoy a high standing but one, the relieving officer, who was mentioned by Richard Jefferies in the final chapter of *Hodge and his Masters* and was commended by the New Forest Union in 1898, could exert a considerable influence over the circumstances of paupers. Relieving officers were responsible for assessing applicants for assistance from the Union, for establishing whether they should be allotted outdoor relief or if they should be admitted to the workhouse, and for distributing any dole to the poor in their own homes. According to Jefferies, the fortnightly meeting of the Board of Guardians spent a considerable amount of time examining the relieving officers' account books and hearing their reports: 'Each has his records to present and his accounts to be practically audited, a process naturally interspersed with enquiries respecting cottagers known to the guardians present.'

Yet whilst Jefferies indicated that the guardians viewed the recipients of outdoor relief with sympathy and interest, the provision made for them was often very meagre and could take the form of food and clothing. In *A Shepherd's Life* W.H. Hudson wrote of an old man he met in a downland churchyard in the first decade of the twentieth century who was paid 3s a week by the Union, whilst James Chalk, the relieving officer in Downton in the Alderbury Union, was known locally as 'Starvo', a nickname reflecting the popular perception of the amount of relief which he provided.

The relieving officers themselves required some education, which placed them above the cottagers but did not give them the same status as the guardians. Isaac Fielder, a relieving officer for the New Forest Union, was probably representative. The fifth of six children born to Mary and Joseph Fielder, he was baptised in St Peter's Church, Bramshaw, in 1805. Nothing is known of his early life, and it is not until 1835 that any further record of him can be found. In that year the Easter Vestries for the Wiltshire and Hampshire parts of Bramshaw recorded 'That a person be appointed i.e. Isaac Fielder, to keep the accounts of both sides of the parish with a reasonable salary', a resolution which suggests that he already had a reputation as an efficient book-keeper. He was described as a relieving officer at the time of his marriage in 1839, whilst the minutes of the Board of Guardians for the New Forest Union show that in 1848 he was being paid £65 per annum, well over twice the wages of an agricultural labourer. Isaac Fielder continued in his post until about 1870, when he developed an unspecified illness which left him suffering from paralysis. Craven's Directory for Hampshire continued to list him as 'Relieving Officer and Registrar of Births and Deaths' in its 1871 edition, although the census taken in the same year described him as a 'Superannuated Relieving Officer', whilst the minutes of the Board of Guardians showed him, in October 1871, to have been receiving a pension of £10 a quarter.

More unusually, Isaac Fielder was an active dissenter, being appointed as a trustee of the newly erected Bramshaw Wesleyan Methodist Church in 1839 (when he was again described as a relieving officer), but subsequently transferring his allegiances to the Strict and Particular Baptists. He was appointed a Strict Baptist preacher in 1849 and the (unpaid) lay pastor of the Rehoboth Chapel in Downton in 1858, perhaps following two of his brothers, George and Ezekiel, who had become Strict Baptists before him. All three of his brothers were shoemakers, and he may have gained his position with the Poor Law

Union by virtue of a better schooling (although George had a sufficient level of literacy to have acted as the enumerator for the hamlet of Fritham in 1841). Yet despite living in the imposingly named Barford House in Bramshaw and being listed as a farmer as well as a relieving officer and registrar in Craven's Directory of 1871, he probably supplemented his income by keeping cattle on a few acres of land attached to his house or on an adjacent common.

No record survives of the manner in which Isaac Fielder fulfilled his official duties, but his local antecedents and long period of service must have meant that he was thoroughly acquainted with the people of his district (which comprised the Wiltshire and Hampshire parts of Bramshaw, Minstead and Lyndhurst), and must have known the circumstances of the labourers and others who became destitute within it.

George Fry, another relieving officer, who served in the larger and better remunerated Southern District of the Union, completed fifty years' service in December 1900, and to mark the occasion gave the Board of Guardians 'some interesting facts in connection with the discharge of his duties', although the clerk failed, tantalisingly, to elaborate further.

Although the 1834 Act gave responsibility for the poor to the Union and the Board of Guardians, there is some evidence that in the decades immediately following its introduction parishes continued to play a part in addressing the problem of poverty. Until 1890 Poor Law Unions and other bodies dealing with paupers were permitted to raise loans in order to pay the passage of those wishing to emigrate to the colonies. (A *Punch* cartoon which appeared in 1848 under the title 'Emigration a Remedy' depicted on its left-hand side a family homeless and despairing in an English city, and on the right the same family living in comfortable colonial prosperity.)

On 8 October 1846 the vestry in the Wiltshire part of Bramshaw paid the final instalment of a loan of £50 which had been advanced by George Edward Eyre of Warrens House 'to defray the expenses of the emigration of Joseph Price'. No minute survives to provide further details of Joseph Price's departure from the village, but in 1847 authority was given to the churchwardens and overseers to borrow £40 'for defraying the expenses of the emigration of poor persons having settlements in this parish and being willing to emigrate'. A year later the minute book recorded that the vestry was to borrow or raise money out of the poor rate for the purpose of enabling parishioners to emigrate. The loan was apparently because several villagers had applied for the cost of a passage to Canada. The applications made by William Thompson, a widower (who was to be accompanied by his two young sons), Charles Macey and

Samuel Blake, a single man who had been a stoker on a steamship, were all accepted, whilst the minutes provided a sequel to the emigration of Joseph Price:

> Joseph Price senior, who states that he has a son, Joseph Price junior and his wife and family living in Westminster in Upper Canada, is desirous of going, they having written to him to say that they can take charge of him to end his days with them and to come with his grandson Charles Margery . . . Joseph Price also makes application for his passage out to Canada to be paid by the parishioners of Bramshaw which the vestry approve of, considering Joseph Price to be a hale man and quite equal to the voyage. He was in his youth a seaman and would be a good experienced companion for the younger men who wish to emigrate to Canada from this parish. The vestry therefore willingly accede to his application and request the sanction of the Poor Law Commissioners.

Nor was it only prospective emigrants who requested grants from the vestry. In 1849 the minutes recorded that 'Widow Curl applied on behalf of her daughter who is anxious to be apprenticed to a Mantua maker[3] that she may earn her own living, she being disabled from going into service and requested aid for effecting the same. Agreed that the request be taken into consideration after the Easter Vestry.' Widow Curl was evidently asking the parish to pay the premium on her daughter's apprenticeship, although there is no indication of the final outcome of her application.

In the same way the results of the Vestry's deliberations in the case of William Beavis, 'now a lunatic and mad, chargeable to the parish', are unrecorded, and indeed after 1853 the minute book makes no further reference to the poor, a possible indication that by that date the Board of Guardians had become wholly responsible for dealing with cases of want. An entry made on 10 March 1852 seems to confirm this impression: 'According to the public notice given in the usual manner, the books of the overseers and way warden [who was responsible for maintaining all the roads in the parish with the exception of the turnpike] were produced for examination but after one hours sitting the Deputy overseer removed the books in consequence of non-attendance of the parishioners.' If the Vestry had had greater control over the use and distribution of the rate which they collected, there would presumably have been more interest in their accounts.

H.M. Livens claimed that the poor rate was first levied in Nomansland in about 1850 (the hamlet was incorporated into the Alderbury Union in 1869 but there is evidence that its paupers were being admitted to the New Forest Union Workhouse before that date). The overseers first approached the oldest inhabitant, George King, but he refused to pay, with the result that his clock was distrained. His brother William, who was landlord of the Lamb Inn, learning of the action, paid the outstanding rate and recovered the timepiece, the incident proving salutary in that it prevented further resistance to the levy among the inhabitants of the settlement.

The overseers continued to assess and collect the poor rate, which was demanded from every householder regardless of income, until the office was abolished in 1925. The Churchwardens' Account Book from St Peter's Church, Plaitford, records that in 1906 and 1907 the wardens paid the poor rate on property which was owned by St Peter's to Alfred Bowles, one of the farmers in the parish, who was serving as overseer at the time. (Marian Harding remembered Alfie Bowles's wife to have kept a parrot which called out, 'There's someone at the door, Sarah' whenever a visitor arrived.) In 1912 the rate due from the church was received by Frank Curtis, Marian Harding's father, who was by then overseer and, like Alfred Bowles, a farmer in the village; his brother George occupied a seat on the Board of Guardians for the Romsey Union.

Yet if the principal provision for the poor was made by the Union with some limited contribution from the parishes, initiatives were nonetheless taken by the local charities or private individuals. The Mayor of Andover's Out-Door Pauper's Christmas Dinner Fund was an example of this, whilst Coal Clubs, which often enjoyed the support of local clergy and gentry, were established in some villages to provide a supply of fuel for the poor. H.M. Livens wrote of an apparent attempt to deal with the able-bodied poor in Nomansland, describing a plot known as the Parish Piece where the unemployed were put to work, bringing an area of hitherto waste ground into cultivation and, in the process, avoiding the necessity of entering the workhouse. Men occupied in this way were described as being 'on the stem', although Livens could offer no explanation for the phrase which, he claimed, was current seventy to a hundred years before he was writing (i.e. between 1810 and 1840)[4]. The reference is vague, and makes no attempt to suggest who was responsible for administering the Parish Piece or providing subsistence for those without work, but *Nomansland, A Village History* also referred to two instances in which the Hamptworth Estate, which adjoined the hamlet, rented allotments to its inhabitants. Seven plots had been provided in this way in the 1850s but they had reverted to 'birch coppice' by 1910, whilst a field known as The Allotments was still being cultivated in the first decade of the twentieth century, Livens remarking that 'An idea of the value sets upon such a piece of garden land by those who cultivate it, may be gathered from the amount of attention it receives. There are at the present time about a dozen occupiers who raise no inconsiderable part of their livelihood from their respective strips.' Livens's observation, and the fact that allotments had long been a significant source of income to labourers in rural communities (as indicated by the Newtown Chapel lease of 1843), suggest that the estate was ready to make land available in this way in order to allow the occupiers to provide for themselves and not have to seek relief from the Union.

The parish of Plaitford saw what was probably an effort to relieve the distress caused by the depression which affected agriculture from the 1870s onwards. The large number of inhabitants occupying squatter cottages and relying upon casual work meant that the village was particularly susceptible to the effects of the depression, and its population fell by about a quarter between 1871 and 1881.[5] Tradition claims that Alfred Gay purchased houses and land which he converted into allotments and endowed to St Peter's Church, and although there is no evidence to support this memory the churchwardens' accounts for 1904 show that St Peter's was receiving rent for four houses (including George Bungay's mud-walled cottage), land and allotments, which comprised twenty-seven plots, although these were, in fact, occupied by only seven tenants and had never been 'let to multiple holdings by one tenant'. If Alfred Gay provided the twenty-seven plots, it was almost certainly in the knowledge that they could (as Livens later noted) make a significant contribution to the income of cottagers who would otherwise have been forced to leave the land. The fact that they were in the hands of only seven tenants (who included the landlord of the Shoe Inn and other artisans and tradesmen) and had never been sublet to individual plot-holders, suggests that in this case the rector's intentions had not been fulfilled.[6]

Yet whatever relief might have been given to the poor, many cottagers sought to provide for themselves in old age or sickness. H.M. Livens's description of the match fagotter who 'by dint of incessant labour' and good fortune could lay something by for his later years is an example of this, whilst Richard Jefferies noted the value of £10 or £20 in savings to an aged labourer who was still able to undertake some work. Describing Hodge in his old age, Jefferies wrote: 'Three score years and ten did not set the limit of his working days; he still could and would hoe – a bowed back is no impediment but rather an advantage at that occupation. He could use a prong in hay making; he could reap a little and do good service tying the cut corn. There were many little jobs on the farm that required experience, combined with the plodding patience of age and these he could do better than a stronger man.' An aged labourer undertaking such tasks could subsist on his wages for much of the year, especially if he received assistance from his children whilst a guinea or two from his £10 or £20 store would tide him over the depths of the winter when no work was available.

Census returns do not indicate exactly how the aged labourers included in their columns supported themselves, but the enumerators' schedules for most parishes list occasional cottagers who were continuing to work over the age of seventy. The 1881 census for Plaitford, taken in the year after the publication of *Hodge and his Masters*, showed Charles Mussell to have been employed as an agricultural labourer at the age of seventy-four. (Alfred Gay, recording Charles Mussell's burial in 1883, added a note in the margin of the register, 'Dropped down dead in Wellow from apoplexy'.) Another seventy-four-year-old, Charles Roud, was employed as a farm servant (although the burial register showed him to have been eighty-three when he died in 1888, a discrepancy of a kind often found at a time when many cottagers were uncertain of their exact age), whilst an artisan Michael Hood was also working, apparently without assistance, as a wheelwright when he was seventy-six. A decade earlier John Martin (or Martyn according to the census of 1861) had been listed as an agricultural labourer even though his age was given as eighty-three. He was living with, and presumably partly supported by, his son Joseph, an army pensioner, whilst Thomas Bungay, who was seventy-six, was also an agricultural labourer, as was his sixty-seven-year-old brother James, who was living under the same roof, and William Dibdin who was seventy-two. Nor was Plaitford untypical. In the neighbouring parish of Landford in 1881 an agricultural labourer, a garden labourer, a (female) broom dealer, a small farmer occupying 28 acres, his wife who was a laundress and a grocer were all aged between seventy-two and seventy-nine.

Not all the residents in rural communities who survived into old age continued to work, however, and some aged inhabitants were listed with their former occupation or with the word 'annuitant' or the phrase 'living on own means' written in the column for rank, profession or occupation. The farmers, tradesmen and other more affluent residents would have been in a position to purchase an annuity or to support themselves from their capital, but some villagers described in this way were less obviously able to maintain their independence in old age, and can only have done so with the support of a friendly society.

Friendly societies had become widespread in rural areas in the nineteenth century, and their importance is emphasised by the extent to which the local press reported their activities (although it is likely that the households which took papers such as the *Salisbury Times* were

Quavey Road, Redlynch, depicted on a postcard franked in the village on 13 December 1907. The author's great-grandmother's shop is half-way along the road on the left. The identities of the children and the lady cyclist are unknown.

also those which could afford the subscriptions, the poorer labourers being unable to do so). The societies fulfilled three functions, providing sickness insurance, pensions in old age and a death grant to meet funeral expenses (while some insured items such as tradesmen's tools or made provision for unemployment). They varied from national bodies such as the Ancient Order of Foresters, The Manchester Unity of Oddfellows or the Rechabites (who were supported by nonconformists and demanded that their members should be total abstainers: they derived their name from an Old Testament family who lived as nomads and took no wine) to county and even village societies. Members usually paid an entrance fee on joining and, having undergone a medical examination or submitted a medical history, underwent a probationary period – often a year – in which no benefits would be paid. Subscriptions were calculated on the basis of the amount of benefit which each member was likely to be claiming at certain specified ages, together with a surcharge to cover the expenses entailed in managing each account. The larger societies had branches in towns and villages, and employed local agents to collect subscriptions and seek new members.

In the early nineteenth century the friendly societies had aroused suspicion because their activities were accompanied by quasi-masonic rituals, whilst their social gatherings were often occasions of drunken rowdiness. An alteration in their standing was evident in a report of the twenty-third anniversary of the Redlynch branch of the Modern

Society of Foresters printed in the *Salisbury Journal* in May 1869. The newspaper's account described how the members had assembled at the Kings Head at ten in the morning and, led by a brass band, had made their way in procession to St Mary's Church where they heard the vicar, the Rev. Theodore Redhead, preach 'an excellent sermon' on the text 'For bodily exercise profiteth little but godliness is profitable unto all things, having promise of the life that now is, and of what is to come'.[7] The members then returned to the 'lodge' which met in the public house, to eat 'a most excellent dinner' served by the landlord 'Bro[ther] Chalke' who was himself a member. The parson took the chair, and 'after the cloth had been removed' and 'the statement of the society' read to great satisfaction he gave 'a most edifying address', the report concluding that 'The day was spent in a very pleasant manner by the members, harmony and goodwill being maintained towards one another. The day continued with a dance.' Although they met in lodges, courts or, in the case of the Rechabites, tents (as their namesakes were nomadic), and gave their members the title brother, and whilst, like the Redlynch branch of the Modern Order of Foresters, they often assembled in a public house, friendly societies were gaining in respectability, a fact evident from this *Journal* report. The harmony and goodwill which marked the day's proceedings emphasised, by implication, their sobriety.

When in 1877 Harry Churchill, the headmaster of the National School in Landford, resigned after suffering what was probably a mental breakdown, the rector, Francis Girdlestone, presented him with a purse of £50 subscribed by the managers, parents and Landford branch of the Wiltshire Friendly Society. In reply the retiring headmaster, whose high moral character had been commended by the rector, stated 'that he thanked all members of the Wilts Friendly Society most sincerely for their kind expressions'.[8] Despite the support of the clergy and, increasingly, the patronage of the gentry, friendly societies were essentially working men's organisations, and Harry Churchill had probably assisted with their accounts.

The standing of the societies in the early twentieth century is evident from a newspaper report which appeared in the *Romsey Advertiser* in September 1904. The report described the annual parade of the Wellow branch of the Hampshire Friendly Society and the Oddfellows' lodge in the village. On this occasion the societies did not attend a public house but marched directly to the (Anglican) Mission Room, with their banners and the Berthon and Volunteer Band (from the Berthon Boatyard in Romsey) leading the way. The service at the Mission Room seems to have emphasised one of the principal purposes of the societies by including the hymns 'Thine arm O Lord in the days of old | was strong to heal and save' and 'Thou to whom the sick and dying | Ever came nor came in vain', whose third verse read:

Still the weary, sick and dying
Need a brother's, sister's care
On Thy higher help relying
May we now their burdens share
Bringing all our offerings meet
Supplicants to Thy mercy seat.

The same emphasis was evident in the vicar, the Rev. G.C. Elton's choice of text: 'We that are strong bear the infirmities of the weak'.[9] Although the tone of the service may have been influenced by the decision to send the collection to Salisbury Infirmary, it is also evident that the two societies saw their main responsibility as the provision of sickness insurance for their members. After the act of worship the parade reassembled to march onto the common, where the band played the National Anthem – processions evidently providing a spectacle for the parish at large.

Friendly societies offered amusements in a more direct way through the fetes which many branches organised annually.[10] In June 1906 the *Romsey Advertiser* reported on the fete or festival, as such occasions were often known, held by the Bramshaw branch of the Hampshire Friendly Society. It was similar, in several respects, to the anniversary meeting of the Modern Order of Foresters in Redlynch thirty-seven years earlier. The Schultze Company brass band led the members in procession from the boys' school to the church and then, after a service, led them back to the school, where the men were provided with a luncheon at which the vicar presided. The newspaper's principal interest was in the long succession of toasts and speeches which followed the meal and included a vote of thanks to the *Romsey Advertiser* and its 'Romsey representative for the careful and full reports of all the Bramshaw meetings, reports ... which had been appreciated' and concluded with a toast to 'the ladies proposed by MR. HENRY KING in felicitous terms. This time honoured toast has been proposed for many years past by the same member of the Society and Mr King again did justice to it, alluding to the importance of the women in the life of the man.' The fete which followed was dismissed in a sentence that referred to 'all sorts of attractions including Bartlett's roundabouts' (the Bartlett family were well known as showmen in the locality from the middle of the nineteenth century until the beginning of the Second World War), whilst the day concluded with a dance at which the Schultze Company Band provided the accompaniment, and which

A (probably Friendly Society) fete on Lockerley Green, 1906.

attracted a large attendance. The branch of this friendly society was evidently contributing a significant event to the village's social calendar.

At the same time the vote of thanks to the *Romsey Advertiser* and its reporter were an oblique reference to a dispute between the branch and the agent, William Henbest, who had failed to supply a full list of members paying for the services of Dr White of Lyndhurst, whose practice included Bramshaw, and Doctor Whitely of Downton, who attended patients in Nomansland. As a result two members who had called the doctor on the assumption that their account would be paid by the society had received bills, and others who had not required medical attention but had assumed that it would be available on the strength of their subscriptions had found that their names had not been forwarded to the appropriate doctor. The details were, however, less significant than the amount of coverage which the Romsey paper gave to what it called 'a lively meeting'. The report extended into three columns, and the allocation of so much space to an event that only immediately affected one of the numerous villages in which the *Advertiser* circulated is an indication of the importance attached to friendly societies and of the interest which such an incident was expected to arouse in the wider locality.

The strength of feeling which the agent's lapse caused among the members of the Bramshaw branch was less evident from the lengthy discussion of the matter itself (which had occupied the committee for three hours and the AGM for two) than in the debate on the festival which took place afterwards. This included a claim that the money taken on the gate in 1905 and handed to the agent had exceeded the amount shown in his accounts. The *Romsey Advertiser*, reporting the meeting as if it were the proceedings in Parliament, described what followed: 'THE AGENT: I shan't have anything to do with any other festival. I shall leave it to the committee. MR. MEECH: I think the committee can do it quite as well. Some commotion was caused here by an altercation between the agent and Mr Meech, and at one moment a fight looked imminent but owing to the persuasion of the Vicar and Mr Cooper both men resumed their seats.' Although the vicar was in the chair and despite the election of Briscoe Eyre, the squire, as branch president, the way in which the agent and Jim Meech – who was a baker from the hamlet of Fritham – had almost come to blows was another indication that the friendly societies were essentially working men's organisations.

The solidarity between the members, again a reflection of social class, was demonstrated at Lockerly in May 1903, the *Romsey Advertiser* reporting that a special meeting of Court Lockerley 7847 Ancient Order of Foresters had been held in the King's Arms, and had unanimously agreed to postpone the Whit Monday fete because of the death of one of the members, Brother F. Maidment. The report noted: 'This is the first experience of a death since the Court was established in 1890. A vote of condolence to the widow was passed and members of the Court offered their services as bearers. It was also resolved to obtain a wreath as a mark of brotherly sympathy.' The fact that Fred Maidment's death was the first which had occurred in the Lockerly branch during its thirteen years' existence was suggestive of a decline in mortality in the later nineteenth century, but the death had not been from natural causes and, according to the paper, 'had startled the village and other places in the district'.

Frederick Charles Maidment, a miller's carter of excellent character and abstemious habits, was an affectionate husband and father, with two sons aged four and nine months, who occupied his time when his working day was over in his garden, in assisting with the household tasks and in looking after his two boys. On the evening of Monday 18 May 1903 he had put his eldest son to bed, cradled the baby, Wilfred, in his arms and sat with his wife Edith until nearly ten o'clock, when she went upstairs ahead of him. He then took down his razor which he kept on the mantelpiece, collected a benzoline lamp, carried his younger son, who had remained downstairs, into what was described as the wash-house and wc, placed the lamp on the seat of the closet and cut the child's throat with such violence that he not only severed the main arteries and windpipe but also the spinal column. Covering the dead infant's face with a red handkerchief, he then walked through a patch of nettles and proceeded 300 yards to Holbury Mill, where he drowned himself in the stream.[12] The *Romsey Advertiser* reported the murder, suicide, inquest and double funeral in considerable detail, and in doing so showed how closely the members of friendly societies identified with one another. In its account of the burial the newspaper described the scene on Lockerly Green where Frederick Maidment's cottage was situated, and after pointedly referring to the sheep grazing there, amongst whom were 'ewes with lambs by their side that bleated with the cry so peculiar to them', the paper continued:

> Presently from out of the middle of the three cottages . . . came two coffins, a long one containing the body of a man and a small one which held the body of a child. The first was borne on the shoulders of some stalwart Foresters, Maidment having been a member of Court Lockerly, and the second was carried underhand by other brothers of the Order. Behind came the widow and mother of the dead baby, leaning on the arm of a relative, then other relatives and friends, fellow workmen and a long line of Foresters, who attended as a last mark of respect. As the procession came slowly over the green the picture was a striking one. The sun flashed from the polished fittings of the man's coffin as it came over the slope and the figures behind looking additionally sombre by contrast. Through the narrow lane with its hedgerows, the footsteps keeping time, and the tramping sound having a very weird effect as no other sound could be heard.[13] In the fields on the right, the horses and ploughs stood still as the bodies passed and this cessation of labour was the more effective because so spontaneous.

Lockerley Green from a slightly faded photograph, c. 1900. Sheep and lambs graze as they are described to have done in the account of the funeral procession of Frederick and Wilfred Maidment.

Then, after an 'extremely solemn' funeral and committal and surrounded by sobbing women and by men, many of whom 'were unable to hide what they were too plainly feeling', Mr Edney of East Dean (the neighbouring village) 'read the lines appointed to be read at the burial of a Forester'.

The common experience of hardship in rural communities created a strong sense of unity amongst the inhabitants. Friendly societies which sought to relieve the burdens of sickness and age gave their members the opportunity both to provide some security for themselves and, as they paid their contributions whether they claimed benefits or not, of assisting other significantly styled 'brothers' who were facing difficulties which might have otherwise forced them to resort to the Poor Law Union and the workhouse.

Shocking and tragic though the deaths of Frederick and Wilfred Maidment may have been, the response of Court Lockerly in sending a wreath 'in brotherly sympathy', in carrying the coffins and in marching in file and in step behind the funeral procession, showed the artisans' and labourers' fellow feeling for each other in the face of the adversity which was common to them all, a feeling which expressed their identity as members of what Flora Thompson called 'The Besieged Generation'.[14]

Chapter VII
The Workhouse – The Paupers' Daily Routine

Although the Poor Law Amendment Act of 1834 had ensured that every parish was incorporated into a Union and that any pauper could be admitted to a workhouse, its provisions had been anticipated by earlier legislation. From the end of the seventeenth century some parishes had sought private Acts of Parliament in order to build poorhouses, but in 1723 Knatchbull's General Workhouse Act had empowered them to do so without requiring further parliamentary approval, and had given smaller parishes the opportunity to combine into Unions for the purpose. Yet despite the existence of enabling legislation, special acts continued to be passed, and in Salisbury in 1770 the three city parishes, St Edmund's, St Martin's and St Thomas's, formed a Union by this means and established a workhouse in Crane Street.[1]

In 1782 Thomas Gilbert's Act had promoted the formation of Unions in order to provide poorhouses which were to be occupied exclusively by the aged and infirm; the able-bodied were to be put to work and orphan children to be boarded out with what were described as 'respectable persons'. Gilbert's legislation also required independent inspectors to be appointed. These provisions did not meet with a favourable response, and very few Gilbert's Unions were formed (it required the agreement of two-thirds of the ratepayers for such a Union to be constituted), although the last of those which were established survived until 1869, the year in which the Salisbury and Alderbury Unions were amalgamated – the Alderbury Union, which combined the Close and the parishes to the south of the city, having been created under the 1834 Act.

Conditions in parish poorhouses were often unsatisfactory. The workhouse which was built in Downton in 1730 is remembered in an unfavourable light, whilst its equivalent in Salisbury would appear to have been a place of squalor and disorder. The report of the Poor Law Commissioners, whose publication immediately preceded the passing of the 1834 Act, complained that in parish poorhouses the inmates were often accommodated without any segregation on the basis of age or sex, and with the idle and dissolute living in the same quarters as the young and impressionable. The report went on to note, 'To these may often be added the solitary blind person, one or two idiots and not infrequently from among the rest, the incessant ravings of some neglected lunatic'. According to the Commissioners, enquiries about the failure to provide work for the able-bodied, suitable instruction for the children or appropriate supervision for the lunatics was met with the reply that the number of individuals involved were too few to justify the expense which would be incurred.

The report does, however, appear to have reflected popular prejudice, for after complaining that the parish poorhouse failed to segregate its inmates it went on to observe that the institution was 'a large almshouse in which the young are trained in idleness, ignorance and vice, the able-bodied maintained in sluggish, sensual indolence; the aged and more respectable are exposed to all the misery that is incident to dwelling in such a society without government or classification; and the whole body of inmates subsist on food far exceeding both in kind and in amount, not merely the diet of the independent labourer but that of the majority of persons contributing to their support'. The claim that disreputable individuals were living in idleness whilst enjoying a diet superior to that of the householders who were maintaining them is certainly suggestive of popular opinion, particularly as the report also included the evidence of witnesses who gave accounts of squalor and overcrowding in parish poorhouses.

In order to overcome the problems which they had identified, the Poor Law Commissioners recommended that paupers should be divided into four categories, the aged and those genuinely incapable of supporting themselves, children, able-bodied men and able-bodied women. They also recommended that each category should have its own workhouse, and that parishes should be combined into Unions so that existing poorhouses could be adapted for the purpose. In the event, on the borders of south-east Wiltshire and south-west Hampshire the Fordingbridge and Romsey Unions converted parish workhouses to meet the demands of the Act and the Alderbury and New Forest Unions built new establishments, although in every case the categories of paupers were segregated within the same building.

The New Forest Union had inherited four existing poorhouses at Fawley, Beaulieu, Eling and Bramshaw, but despite a lingering memory of the existence of the Bramshaw workhouse, no evidence of the living conditions of the inmates has survived. In April 1835 the vestry for the Hampshire part of Bramshaw passed a resolution stating

The New Forest Union Workhouse shown on the postcard by Mentop & Co. of Southampton, which was sent to Mrs R. Mayes of Downend, Bristol, with the message 'With best wishes for Easter 1906' but without a signature.

that 'a select vestry [i.e. one that was nominated rather than elected] be named to attend as such to the general concern of the Parish for the immediate management of the workhouse', a proposal which seems to have indicated that the ratepayers were aware of the provisions of the new legislation and that the management of the workhouse had hitherto been neglected. The minutes make no further reference to the subject, and on 29 February 1836 the *Salisbury Journal* printed an advertisement placed by the New Forest Poor Law Union (which had been formed in August 1835), inviting tenders for the construction of the Union Workhouse, potential bidders being advised that Mr Couchman, the master of the Eling Poorhouse, would show them the site for the new establishment. The New Forest Union was erected in Ashurst, constructed on a hexagonal plan with an administration block and accommodation blocks for the men, women and children radiating from a supervisory station that overlooked the whole of the interior. The workhouse was not a penal institution, but the design adopted by the New Forest Guardians resembled that of a model prison.

Certainly workhouses gained a reputation for harshness. Thomas Hardy, describing the Casterbridge Union as it was approached by Fanny Robin, conveyed this impression, although he did so with characteristic irony:

> Originally it had been a mere case to hold people. The shell had been so thin, so devoid of excrescences and so closely drawn over the accommodation granted that the grim character of what was beneath

showed through it, as the shape of a body is visible under the winding sheet. Then nature as if offended, lent a hand. Masses of ivy grew up, completely covering the walls and it looked like an abbey; and it was discovered that the view from the front . . . was one of the most magnificent in the county. A neighbouring earl once said that he would give up a year's rental to have at his own door the view enjoyed by the inmates from theirs – and very probably the inmates would have given up the view for his year's rental.[2]

Yet many of the features which made the institutions so notorious were found in the parish rather than the Union workhouse. It has often been noted that *Oliver Twist*, which has substantially coloured the popular view of the establishment, appeared in 1839, barely five years after the passing of the 1834 Act and no more than three or four years from the formation of Unions and the construction or conversion of workhouses, so that the novel portrayed conditions prevailing under the Old rather than the New Poor Law.

Union workhouses were more efficiently organised than the parish poorhouses which had preceded them, were better supported from the Poor Rate and were subject to inspection. Amongst the first entries in the earliest surviving minute book of the New Forest Union are the account of salaries paid to its staff on 17 April 1848, in arrears and for the quarter up to Lady Day (25 March). The list had at its head the chaplain, the Rev. Mark Cooper, who was clearly combining his parochial duties in Bramshaw with those that he performed at the workhouse and was receiving a payment of £12 10s 0d a quarter (£50 a year) as a stipend from the Union. After Mark Cooper came the master and matron G.H. and Jane Miall, who were, as was usual, man and wife and were paid 10 guineas and £7 10s 0d per quarter, whilst amongst the other staff employed or retained by the Union were a schoolmaster, T. Whitehorn, and mistress, J. Davis, who were paid £3 10s 0d and £3 15s 0d for the same period (£14 and £15 per annum) and who were both, like the master and the matron, provided with accommodation in the workhouse.

The census of 1841 showed that staff at the smaller Fordingbridge Workhouse comprised a master and matron (who were again a married couple) and a porter, although by 1861 they had been augmented by a resident schoolmistress. In 1881 the census return for the Alderbury Union Workhouse included not only the master and matron, William and Emma Wickes, but also a schoolmistress, an assistant mistress, a porter and his wife (who was described as a porteress and presumably shared her husband's duties), a nurse and a forty-six-year-old bachelor,

Frederick Talbot, who was listed as an 'industrial trainer'. In the same year Romsey Union workhouse had as its master and matron Thomas and Louisa Jerram, whilst their daughters, Mary aged twenty-seven and Susan aged twenty-six, were the assistant matron and schoolmistress. A third daughter Rosina, who was twenty-three, was organist, although the exact significance of this is unclear. One other member of staff, Lydia Taylor, aged fifty-seven, was the workhouse nurse. Her relationship to the master was given as servant, although this can hardly have been an accurate description of her status within the establishment.

The popular view of the diet of workhouse inmates has been influenced by *Oliver Twist*. Dickens, who wrote in the novel of the parish rather than the Union Workhouse nonetheless condemned the philosophy underlying the 1834 Poor Law by ascribing it to the Board who were responsible for administering the establishment. The Board discovered that the institution was 'a regular place of public entertainment for the poorest classes; a tavern where there was nothing to pay; a public breakfast, dinner, tea and supper all the year round; a brick and mortar elysium where there was all play and no work' – in response to which, and to deter idlers, 'they contracted with the waterworks to lay on an unlimited supply of water; and with the corn factor to supply small quantities of oatmeal; and issued three meals of thin gruel a day with an onion twice a week and half a roll on Sundays', until, driven by hunger, the workhouse boys drew lots to see who should ask for more, and thus introduced one of the most familiar scenes in Victorian literature.

Andover in the late 1840s did provide an actual instance of a workhouse in which the inmates faced starvation, and were reduced to fighting for marrow and scraps of putrid meat still attached to the bones which they were given to crush. On the other hand the harsh regime instituted by the master, Colin MacDougal, a veteran of Waterloo, and his wife, who was the matron, ultimately attracted the attention of the national press and led to an investigation by a Parliamentary Commission. Furthermore, the fact that the incident came to be known as the Andover Workhouse Scandal was an indication that, despite the intentions embodied in the 1834 Act, such conditions were regarded as outrageous.

On 4 September 1837 the Alderbury Union advertised in the *Salisbury Journal* for tenders, with samples, to supply foodstuffs and other items for the workhouse. Amongst the commodities required were bread and flour, both 'best seconds', salt by the hundredweight, flitches of home-cured bacon, legs and shins of ox beef, ox beef without bone and suet by the pound, breasts and necks of wether mutton, boiling peas, Irish salt butter, skimmed cheeses, rice, oatmeal, congou (a black china) tea and moist sugar. This list shows that inferior ingredients were being purchased for the pauper's diet. An ox was a working steer, fattened and slaughtered after its life as a draught animal was over, and ox beef must have been the cheapest available.[3] The other cuts were cheap and coarse, breasts and necks of wether mutton (a wether is a neutered ram) being examples of this, with much, if not all, of the meat being preserved in brine, as indicated by the purchase of salt in hundredweights. The paupers' meals must have been unvaried. Suet and rice suggest meat puddings and stews, with dried peas as the only vegetable and bread, bacon, boiled salt meat and skim cheese as staples. Moreover, whilst the actual paupers in the Alderbury Union Workhouse received better fare than their fictional counterparts portrayed in *Oliver Twist*, the purchase of quantities of oatmeal show that some gruel was being served although probably only to invalids.

There is no evidence to indicate the amount of food given to individual inmates, but despite its monotony the paupers' diet was superior to that of many labourers, whilst the workhouse inmates enjoyed one benefit not available to the cottagers – since they were given regular meals throughout the year and were not liable to experience the effects of the hungry gap in late winter and early spring, when the produce of the preceding season had been exhausted and the first crops of the summer had yet to be harvested.

The minute books of the Guardians of the New Forest Union show that in September 1848 tenders were being invited for the same foodstuffs as those purchased by the Alderbury Union eleven years previously, whilst they suggest that bread and flour were being bought for outdoor paupers, since the price of both commodities was given for the first and second districts.

Similar items continued to appear in the New Forest Union's accounts in December 1871, as they did in the comprehensive list of tenders to supply the Fordingbridge Union Workhouse and outdoor poor in the mid-1880s, although the Fordingbridge Guardians were also ordering treacle.

At the same time the Fordingbridge Union minutes do give an indication of the causes of the depression which was beginning to beset agriculture in the 1880s, and which would force many labourers off the land in the next decade, since they record payments to the Australian Meat Company and include a proposal made in 1884 'that inmates have Australian beef instead of Australian mutton'.

Yet if the food provided for the workhouse and outdoor paupers scarcely altered over a period of fifty years (and as the resident staff also had their meals found, they must have eaten the same diet), there was one significant addition to the tenders for the New Forest Union in 1871, since the guardians were purchasing wine, spirits and beer, with the same alcoholic liquors being procured by the Fordingbridge Union in the next decade. The Fordingbridge accounts for 2 March 1884 included payments for brandy at a guinea a gallon and gin at 12s 9d both listed as indoor with port and gin (outdoor) being purchased by the pint. Porter and ale were also being bought by the gallon with the words indoor and outdoor showing that the spirits, fortified wine and beer were intended for consumption by the paupers themselves. The reason for the procurement of alcoholic drink was indicated by a discussion which took place at a meeting of the Guardians of the Hursley Union near Winchester, reported by the *Romsey Advertiser* at the end of April 1904. Under a subheading 'Aged people like whisky', the newspaper reported that one of the Hursley Guardians, a Mr Bray, had queried an order for a gallon of whisky to be supplied to the workhouse. The *Advertiser* described the discussion which ensued, a debate in which Mr Bray's earnestness was contrasted with the flippant response of the clerk. The first answer to the query came from the master, who stated 'that the whisky was for the old inmates and that a gallon would probably last as much as six months', to which Mr Bray, giving an opening to the clerk, replied 'that he did not think that old people drank whisky' – an observation which elicited the response, 'My experience is that the older you get the more you like it (laughter).' Mr Bray then adopted a different line of argument by asking if the whisky was necessary, and on being told that it had been requisitioned on the instructions of the Medical Officer, went on to say that he, at least, did not think it was needed. This led the Medical Officer to enter the debate. 'I should not prescribe it should I not think it necessary', adding that he gave whisky regularly to a patient during an illness and this relieved him so much 'that he suffered much less than formerly', at which the clerk turned to the members of the Board and said, 'Please don't take that as a specific (laughter).' Further discussion for the matter was deferred.

Medicinal use would almost certainly have been the justification for the purchase of liquor by the New Forest and Fordingbridge Unions, although it is possible that ale and beer were provided for ordinary consumption, recalling Dickens's much earlier and ironic comment that the poor house was 'a tavern where there was nothing to pay'.[4]

In 1866 Mr W.H.T. Hawley, a poor law inspector, reported on both the Alderbury and Romsey Union Workhouses.[5] In the former he noted that the inmates (who would have slept in wards) had mattresses made of coconut fibre and beds stuffed with chaff, whilst in the latter the beds were stuffed with flock (scraps of cloth, wool and other fibres) and straw. Both workhouses provided washing troughs, with the Alderbury Union placing a trough in each ward and the Romsey Union attaching troughs to pumps, which presumably supplied the paupers with drinking water. Although the bedding was coarse it would probably have had an equivalent in the labourers' cottagers. As late as 1899 Horace Hutchinson and Rose de Crespigny observed that 'In the [New] Forest, the people sometimes use the dry beech leaves for stuffing mattresses.'[6]

Best yellow and mottled soap was being bought by the pound for use in the Alderbury Union Workhouse in 1837, whilst forty-seven years later the Fordingbridge Union was still receiving tenders for yellow soap. Washing soda also appeared in the tenders in both 1837 and 1884, although in the former year the Alderbury Union was procuring it by the pound whilst in the latter the smaller Fordingbridge Union was requisitioning it by the hundredweight. This may have reflected an increased awareness of cleanliness as the century progressed, and in turn might offer a possible explanation for the decline in infant mortality and increase in longevity over a corresponding period. The guardians at Fordingbridge additionally ordered mop heads and what were described as 'scrub brushes'. Mr Hawley commented in 1866 that in both the Alderbury and Romsey Workhouses the able-bodied women were made to undertake domestic work, washing, sewing and mending being specifically mentioned, and it was presumably they who were using the mops, scrubbing brushes and washing soda to maintain the cleanliness of the Fordingbridge Workhouse and the uniforms of the inmates.

On entering the workhouse paupers' own clothes were taken from them (when a new workhouse was erected in Fordingbridge in 1885 it included receiving wards with an adjacent bathroom, a clothing fumigation room and an inmates' clothing store, inmates being able to leave at any time provided they gave notice). Mr W.H.T. Hawley reported that in the Alderbury Union Workhouse, the men wore coats, trousers and waistcoats of fustian or army cloth (fustian was a coarse cotton twill and army cloth was serge), whilst the women had chambray (a cotton or linen fabric with white and coloured threads alternating) or cotton print dresses with appropriate underwear. In Romsey the uniform was similar, with the men and boys wearing fustian jackets and waistcoats and corduroy trousers and the women and girls being dressed in what were described by the poor law inspector as gowns and upper petticoats, all categories of paupers having a sufficient amount of underwear.

Tenders to supply the Fordingbridge Union with fabrics in 1884 suggest that much of the paupers' clothing was made in the workhouse itself. Flannel and calico were procured, together with striped linsey woolsey (a cloth manufactured from linen or cotton and woollen fibres), check linen, worsted and thread, and although no evidence of such a practice survives it is probable that some women inmates were given the task of stitching the garments required. Other items, women's and girl's stays, boys' but not men's clothes, hats for men and youths and straw hats for girls were bought in ready made. The workhouse uniform was similar, and in some cases superior to, the clothing worn by the labourers and their families. The memory of flannel and calico in the author's great-grandmother's shop in Redlynch, is an indication that cottagers' wives had to make their own underwear, and most village children attended school in clothes which had been repeatedly patched and darned and were handed down from older brothers and sisters. In instances where no other garments were available boys had to wear their older sisters' cast-off dresses. The workhouse boys in fustian, corduroy or, as at Fordingbridge, velveteen jackets were better dressed, but the workhouse uniform was irksome to the inmates and the need to wear it was humiliating. One small girl, whose mother was forced to go with her seven children into the workhouse when their father died of consumption, remembered being sent to the board school (a practice which became increasingly common after the 1870 Act took effect) and being ridiculed because she was wearing workhouse boots.

Items which were regularly requisitioned by Poor Law Unions – coffins – were invariably purchased in two sizes, one for adults and one for children. At Fordingbridge in the 1880s coffins were procured for under twelves and over twelves, the latter being exactly twice the price of the former. The stock of coffins retained by the Unions is a reminder that they were responsible for providing funerals for both indoor and outdoor paupers. Most clergy omitted to enter the workhouse as the place of abode of pauper parishioners who had been returned to their home villages for burial, although successive vicars of Bramshaw did record this information in the registers, noting those inmates who had been sent from the New Forest or, after 1869, Alderbury Union workhouses to be interred in the churchyard.

Pauper funerals would have been conducted with the minimum of ceremony or expense. In late November 1886 the Guardians of the Fordingbridge Union recorded in the minute book that a pauper, Agnes Chalk, was seriously ill in the Epileptic Hospital in Regent's Park. There is no indication of the circumstances in which she was admitted as a patient, but the clerk to the Union was instructed to write to the secretary of the hospital, 'requesting him in the case of a fatal termination to undertake the burial of her in London as economically and plainly as possible and that the Guardians would repay the cost of so doing'.

Another aspect of the conditions in the workhouse which tradition has remembered particularly unfavourably was the imposition of work on the able-bodied inmates. The tasks which the paupers were obliged to undertake have often been seen as pointless and soul destroying, continuously barrowing a pile of stones from one side of the workhouse yard to the other being sometimes cited as an instance of such purposeless labour. Evidence from the Alderbury, New Forest and Romsey workhouses is very limited, but where it does exist it seems to suggest that although the work given to the inmates was monotonous and often unpleasant it was not so pointless as tradition has claimed. Even in Andover Workhouse at the height of the scandal the paupers were crushing bones for fertiliser.

A complaint which came before the Board of Guardians of the New Forest Union in July 1848 provides an insight into the nature of the paupers' labour. The Board had been made aware, by the master of the workhouse, that the able-bodied men were not completing their allocated task of trenching a rod of ground a day. (A rod was 5½ yards, and presumably applied to the length rather than the width of the plot. Trenching is a form of double digging). A pauper, Charles Fry, was called before the Board of Guardians and insisted that he could not complete the amount of work allotted to him. 'Whereupon a deputation of the Board assisted by Mr Couchman [one of the relieving officers, and presumably the same Mr Couchman who was master of Eling Poorhouse before 1836] was requested to view the work an able-bodied man might fairly be expected to do and on their return they stated that they considered an able-bodied man if employed at task work would trench two rods a day.' There is no indication who the members of the deputation were and how well qualified they might have been to judge the amount of trenching a labourer on piece work – with the incentive of being paid – could have completed on a daily basis. Neither is it apparent what the purpose of trenching the plot may have been, although the site was evidently situated within the workhouse grounds. It is clear, however, that the Guardians were making some attempt at fairness in their view of the work which could be asked of the able-bodied paupers, and that they were only expecting such inmates to undertake tasks that would have been demanded of independent labourers outside the confines of the institution.

Mr Hawley's reports on the Alderbury and Romsey Union workhouses in 1866 recorded that the able-bodied paupers were engaged in harder labour than their predecessors at Ashurst eighteen years before. In the Alderbury Union workhouse the men were required to 'work at the pump, the mill, gypsum pounding and garden work', whilst their counterparts in Romsey broke stones. The object of the work undertaken at the pump is not known, whilst it is unclear what labour at the mill entailed.[7] Gypsum was used to lime the fields, and stone breaking (which has undertones of the prison yard) would have provided material for road-mending.

In *Far From the Madding Crowd* Thomas Hardy gave a suggestion that able-bodied paupers were employed in other ways. When Joseph Poorgrass was sent to Casterbridge Workhouse to collect the body of Fanny Robin he backed his wagon beneath a door, set 4 feet from the ground. 'The door then opened and a plain elm coffin was slowly thrust forth and laid by two men in fustian along the middle of the vehicle.' One of the men stepped onto the wagon, wrote, in chalk, upon the coffin lid 'in a large scrawling hand' and covered the coffin itself with a 'threadbare but decent' black pall, before handing Poorgrass the 'certificate of registration' and going back into the building. The fustian clothing suggests the workhouse uniform and the description of the incident implies that Hardy envisaged, or had seen, able-bodied paupers being employed as supplementary porters in the manner that he had portrayed (although it also indicates that they could write sufficiently well to inscribe 'Fanny Robin and child' on the coffin lid, albeit in a clumsy hand).

One aspect of the workhouse regime that has been remembered as particularly inhumane was the separation of married couples and parents and children. Albert Chevalier's music hall song 'Me Dear Old Dutch', which opened with the line 'We've been together now for forty years and it don't seem a day too much', took its point from the backdrop against which it was performed, which showed the gates of the workhouse. Yet whatever the popular perception, an examination of census returns suggests that the division of married couples only occurred relatively infrequently. The workhouse at Fordingbridge had thirty-seven adult inmates at the time of the 1851 census but of these twenty-seven were unmarried and four widowed, the remainder comprising the only three married couples in the institution. Romsey Workhouse, thirty years later, accommodated sixty adult inmates of whom thirty-four were unmarried, twenty-one widowed and five listed as married but without any spouse accompanying them.

The two workhouses were probably representative, with the majority of paupers having no immediate family to provide them with accommodation and support. Richard Jefferies indicated that this was the case in *Hodge and His Masters* when he described how his representative labourer's decline began to attract attention: 'Where were his own friends and relations? One strong son had enlisted and gone to

India and though his time had expired long ago, nothing had ever been heard of him. Another son had emigrated to Australia and once sent back a present of money, and a message written for him by a friend, that he was doing well. But of late he, had dropped out of sight. Of three daughters who grew up, two were known to be dead and the third was believed to be in New Zealand. The old man was quite alone . . .' Having become incapable of supporting himself, he was forced into the workhouse: 'muttering and grumbling, he had to be bodily carried to the trap and thus by physical force was dragged from his home'.

Children entering the institution were, according to popular memory, taken from their parents and brought up in isolation. The evidence from south-east Wiltshire and south-west Hampshire suggests that the segregation of adults and children was not always so rigidly enforced as tradition has claimed. In the 1851 census for the Fordingbridge Union Workhouse, parents – and often it was only the mother who was an inmate – were listed with their offspring. Whether this was because the entries were compiled from the Admissions Register (which has not survived) or whether families were not separated is unknown. Gilbert's Act allowed children to remain with their mothers until they were seven years old.

W.H.T. Hawley, reporting on the conditions in the Alderbury Union Workhouse, stated that the children were entirely segregated from the adults, whereas in Romsey the system was less strictly enforced: 'There are two schools in the workhouse, one for boys and the other for girls; but the children are not separated from the adult inmates further than having day rooms and dormitories exclusively appropriated to them.' The result must have been that some contact with their parents was maintained.

At the same time a significant number of workhouse children had surnames which did not occur among the adult inmates. In Fordingbridge in 1851 twenty-one out of forty-seven children fell into this category, whilst twenty-six of the forty children in the New Forest Union workhouse were in the same situation. A high proportion of juveniles must have been orphaned, abandoned or unable to be maintained by their parents.

It is difficult to establish the attitude of the inmates to the institution which they occupied. The stigma attached to the workhouse and its harsh reputation made it a place of last resort. George Sturt described Fred Bettesworth, his Surrey labourer, as saying 'I ent no workhouse man' when forced to approach the relieving officer with a request for medical assistance, but equally recorded that Bettesworth's neighbours were eager that his epileptic wife should be admitted to the institution because of the squalor in which they lived.[8]

Thomas Hardy, in his poem 'The Curate's Kindness', gives voice to an old man with a shrewish wife who was only reconciled to entering the workhouse because it would allow him to escape from his nagging spouse, but found that 'one young Pa'son' had intervened with the guardians to allow long married couples to remain together. The poem described the old man's attitude to the institution he was about to enter:

> I thought: 'Well I've come to the Union –
> The workhouse at last –
> After honest hard work all the week, and Communion
> O Sundays, these fifty years past.
>
> ''Tis hard; but,' I thought, 'never mind it;
> There's gain in the end:
> And when I get used to the place I shall find it
> A home, and may find there a friend.'

The ninth and penultimate stanza opens with the lines 'To go there was ending but badly; | 'twas shame and was pain' – a sentiment which probably reflected the view of the institution taken by its inmates.

Richard Jefferies, writing of Hodge's last days in the workhouse, indicated that it was the lack of independence and unvarying tedium of the regime which crushed the spirit of the old labourer: 'In the workhouse there is of necessity a dead level of monotony – there are many persons but no individuals. The dining-hall is crossed with forms and narrow tables, somewhat resembling those formerly used in schools. On these at dinner time are placed a tin mug and a tin soup plate, for each person, every mug and every plate exactly alike. When the unfortunates have taken their places, the master pronounces grace from an elevated desk at the end of the hall.'

Jefferies wrote that the food was superior to the diet the old labourer had eaten for many years, that the dormitories were clean, that there was a garden in which he could work (Mr Hawley in his report on Romsey Workhouse in 1866 noted that the aged and infirm inmates engaged in gardening), but none of it was familiar and none was his own: 'At home he could lift the latch of the garden gate and go down the road when he wished. Here he could not go outside the boundary – it was against the regulations.' The result was that the old man abandoned hope, 'ceased to exist by imperceptible degrees', and for all the benefits in the infirmary would rather have crawled under a hedge or a rick to die, an observation which probably reflected, like 'The Curate's Kindness', the labourer's view of the workhouse.

Chapter VIII
The Workhouse – Education, Health and Changing Attitudes

L ITTLE provision was made for pauper children before 1844. Many, like Oliver Twist, were apprenticed, although in most instances the apprenticeship was to husbandry or domestic service rather than a recognised trade. The Rev. Peyton Blackiston, the curate at Lymington, giving evidence to the Poor Law Commission of 1834, reflected the attitude of the gentry and clergy to the education of the lower orders – an attitude which had prevailed since the later eighteenth century: 'At this moment the generality of parochial workhouses in Hampshire do not supply any effective religious and moral instruction, the children cannot do even the coarsest needlework in a creditable manner nor are they practised in that kind of work, which as domestic servants they would be required to perform.' He added that before 1831 the only teaching which the children in the Lymington Poorhouse received was an hour a day's instruction in reading from the girl who cooked the meals. In that year a school was established, and 'an able woman was appointed to give instruction in reading and religious duties and to teach and superintend needlework'. The vestry had recently dispensed with her services, however, 'although her salary was only £10 per annum and her dinner'.

The curate clearly believed that pauper children should be taught to read but not to write (since the latter accomplishment would encourage them to look above their station), whilst religious and moral education would probably have entailed learning the church catechism. This included the Ten Commandments, the Apostle's Creed and the Lord's Prayer, and in response to the question 'What is thy duty towards thy neighbour?' required, as part of the answer, 'To keep my hands from picking and stealing and my tongue from evil speaking, lying and slandering. To keep my body in temperance, soberness and chastity' and 'To order myself lowly and reverently to all my betters', all of which would have been intended to instil in the children a sense of their place, and prepare them, with the teaching of needlework, for their role as domestic servants.

Attitudes to the education of the poor were nonetheless changing, and in 1844 legislation empowered the Poor Law Commissioners to provide schooling for workhouse children and to establish District Schools to cater for groups of workhouses. In the scattered rural Unions of south-west Hampshire and south-east Wiltshire the children were taught within the institution, as indicated by the presence of teachers among the staffs. The schools were subject to visits from HMIs, and as a result of one of these the guardians of the New Forest Union received, in July 1848, a letter from the Poor Law Board (which had replaced the Poor Law Commission after the Andover Workhouse scandal), which called for the resignation of Mrs Davis, the workhouse schoolmistress at Ashurst, 'as a report had been made to them by the Inspector of Schools that she was not competent to fill that office'. The guardians were evidently loath to dismiss her even so, and on 31 July another letter from the Poor Law Board was read, stating that 'after the explanation given by the Chaplain in his report, they would not insist upon Mrs Davis' resignation at present, in the hope that she would use diligence in qualifying herself in those respects in which she was reported by the Inspector of Schools to be deficient'.

The minute book did not elaborate on Mrs Davis's deficiencies as a teacher but she evidently failed to correct them, for the Guardians, having advertised for a replacement in September 1849, wrote to three applicants who had sent letters and testimonials, and of these 'elected' Miss Jane Vivian of Salisbury 'in the room of Mrs Davis'.

The evidence that the workhouse school was subject to inspection, that the master or mistress was expected to achieve a degree of competence or face dismissal and that candidates for a vacancy were required to provide testimonials and be subject to interview – a procedure which can hardly have been peculiar to the New Forest Union – show the extent to which expectations of the elementary education of pauper children had changed in two decades.

There was, even so, no indication that Miss Vivian or the other two applicants were certificated, and there is evidence from over a long period that it was often difficult for Unions to find suitable teachers. More than forty years after Mrs Davis's departure from the workhouse at Ashurst, the Guardians of the Fordingbridge Union appointed Miss Edith Mary Atkins as the mistress at their school with a salary of £20 a year. Fourteen months later, in March 1885, they too received a letter from an HMI, a Mr Clutterbuck, whose contents were not recorded in the minutes but which clearly led to Miss Atkins's resignation, since it was resolved in May 1885 'That the clerk give the schoolmistress a testimonial to the following effect, that the Guardians were satisfied with her general conduct but they would have been glad if the inspector's report on the school had been favourable but they hope that this might partly have arisen from her being there but a short time'.

Two teachers were appointed during the next month: Miss Axe, who had been employed by the Guisborough Union in North Yorkshire and seems not to have taken up the post, and Miss Thirza Reynolds, who was offered the situation on 29 May 1885 but had resigned by 26 June. Finally the Guardians invited Miss Susan (or according to the 1881 census Susannah) Bates, a workhouse teacher with the St Thomas Union in Exeter, to fill the vacancy – and no further reference to the matter appears in the minutes.

Sixteen years later, in 1901, the Guardians of the New Forest Union were facing a similar difficulty in finding a teacher, one candidate travelling from Manchester to be interviewed but declining the post, and the matron complaining that she had been obliged to give instruction to the children for twenty-four weeks.

Nothing survives to indicate the level of attainment amongst the pupils at the New Forest and Fordingbridge Workhouse schools but teachers whose competence failed to satisfy HMIs and frequent changes of staff, together with the status of the institution, which would have made it unattractive to more capable candidates, suggest that standards would have been lower than those in Board, National or British Schools.

Nor do the pupils themselves appear to have been particularly tractable. Entries in the New Forest Union minutes book made during the early 1870s record the administration of lashes to refractory boys. One entry dated 25 November 1872 noted the severe punishment imposed upon a particularly recalcitrant inmate: 'The master reported that a Boy in the House named "Osman" had wilfully and deliberately burnt his books by putting them on the fire. The boy was called before the Board and after being severely reprimanded and cautioned as to his future conduct, it was ordered that 18 lashes shall be inflicted on the delinquent for the offence.'[1]

An examination of enumerators' schedules indicates that workhouse children were often described as scholars well after they had attained the age at which most National or Board School pupils would have left to take up employment. In 1881, the year in which compulsory education was introduced for children aged between five and ten years, Fordingbridge Workhouse had five scholars among its inmates whose ages were between eleven and fifteen, its counterpart in Romsey had nine scholars of comparable age, and the larger Alderbury Union Workhouse had in its school twenty-three pupils aged between eleven and fourteen and a further six who were fifteen. Whether the older children derived any advantage from their continued schooling would, however, seem somewhat doubtful.

The minutes of the Board of Guardians of the New Forest Union for March and April 1872 recorded the arrangements made for the emigration to Canada of four youths from the workhouse, and in doing so indicated the attitude of the authorities to pauper children who had passed the age at which they could remain in the school. On 11 March 1872 the Guardians were informed that a Miss Goodenough, who was evidently well known to the Board, had offered to pay £10 towards the passage of George Hayter and William Sailes, who were both aged seventeen, and two fifteen year olds, Charles Woolfe and William Milligan. Six weeks elapsed before a second communication was received from Miss Goodenough, accompanied by a letter from a clergyman who was preparing to send the boys from Euston to Liverpool and was requesting 'that arrangements be made for forwarding them from their workhouse with a remittance of their passage money'. Since insufficient time was available to convene a meeting of the full Board, the chairman and the clerk had authorised the master to put the matter in hand and provided £22 to meet all expenses. Significantly there was no reference to any arrangements for the pauper emigrants' accommodation or employment when they arrived in Canada, and it would seem that the Guardians were more concerned that the youths should leave the workhouse than that provision should be made for them when they reached their final destination. Although the Rev. A. King was arranging to send the boys from Euston to Liverpool, his request that they should be forwarded from their workhouse as though they were freight seems to show something of his attitude to them.

Poor Law Unions provided medical assistance to paupers. In February 1836 the newly formed New Forest Union gave notice in the *Salisbury Journal* 'that the Guardians . . . will receive tenders from Medical Gentlemen, legally qualified to practice, stating at what sum they will contract for medical relief for each of the districts of the Union for six calendar months from 25 March next. Such contracts are to include all cases of sickness and surgery.'

Inviting tenders allowed the Board to secure the services of medical officers at the lowest possible salary, but the relationship between the New Forest Union and one of the surgeons which it retained does not appear to have been satisfactory. In September 1848 Mr Girdlestone, the Union medical officer for Lyndhurst and Minstead, was summoned to attend the meeting of the Guardians 'to explain a charge that had been made against him for non-attendance to a case of sickness'. He did not appear but instead sent a letter offering his resignation. A subsequent resolution that the resignation should be accepted, which was seconded by Henry Compton of Minstead Manor, suggests that the Board had other reasons for being dissatisfied with his services. By contrast George Nunn, who was also retained by the Union in 1848, was still serving as a medical officer in the mid-1870s, when he gave evidence at a number of inquests in the locality.

Workhouses usually had sick wards, Mr Hawley, the Poor Law inspector who visited the Alderbury Union Workhouse in 1866, noted that the institution had infectious wards for men and women; that whilst there was no paid nurse and although 'nursing is performed by the inmates . . . I have heard no complaint of its insufficiency'. At Romsey Workhouse, which was again without a paid nurse, he found that 'the nursing by night and by day is represented to be well performed'.[2]

Some workhouses had infirmaries where the poor received treatment whether they were inmates or not, although of the four unions in south-west Hampshire and south-east Wiltshire only Romsey had such an amenity. (The Southampton Workhouse infirmary was the predecessor of the General Hospital.) A pauper needing treatment nonetheless had to submit to a tortuous procedure. George Sturt, describing the experience of Fred Bettesworth in seeking to have his ailing wife admitted to Farnham Workhouse Infirmary, wrote that the old labourer had to give up a day's pay, walk 2 miles to obtain a certificate from the relieving officer, walk 3½ miles back to present it to the doctor, who attended the patient at his convenience and then provided another certificate which had also to be taken to the relieving officer so that he could issue an order instructing the master of the workhouse to arrange transport and finally admit the patient to the infirmary.[3]

Accounts of the workhouse infirmary portray it in a sympathetic light. Richard Jefferies described how Hodge was admitted there during his last weeks. 'In the infirmary the real benefit of the workhouse reached him. The food, the little luxuries, the attention were far superior to anything he could possibly have had at home.'[4] George Sturt wrote of a visit which Fred Bettesworth made to a friend in the recently completed Farnham Workhouse Infirmary in December 1901: 'He was almost enthusiastic over the whiteness of the sheets; the bees-waxed floor ("like glass to walk on") the little cupboards ("lockers they calls 'em") beside each bed; the nurse who "seemed to be a pleasant woman"; the daily attendance of the medical men; and other advantages.' All these things persuaded Bettesworth that the patients were "better off up there than what they would be at home". And out in the grounds "You'd meet two old women perhaps walkin' along together and then a little further on, some old men", which all appeared very satisfactory.'[5]

The absence of workhouse infirmaries attached to the Alderbury, Fordingbridge and New Forest Union Workhouses may have been due in part to the treatment available in Salisbury Infirmary, which was supported by public subscription and offered free attention to the poor without the stigma attached to the workhouse. W.H. Hudson in *A Shepherd's Life*, described the labourer's attitude to the Salisbury Hospital: 'The injured or afflicted youth, taken straight from his rough, hard,, life and poor cottage, wonders at the place he finds himself in – the wide, clean, airy, room and white, easy bed, the care and skill of the doctors and the tender nursing by women and comforts and luxuries all without payment but given it seems, out of pure divine love and compassion – all this comes as something strange, almost incredible. He suffers much perhaps, but can bear pain stoically and forget it when it is past, but the loving kindness he has experienced is remembered.'

The decision of the Wellow branches of the Oddfellows and the Hampshire Friendly Society to donate the collection taken at their parade service in September 1904 to Salisbury Infirmary was an indication of the hospital's importance (East and West Wellow were part of the Romsey Union), whilst the admission of the fatally injured ploughboy, Edward Reynolds, to the Infirmary in November 1864 reflected its significance to an earlier generation.

Although workhouse infirmaries treated the poor whether they were inmates or not, assistance from the Union was dependent, at least according to the law, upon a pauper's having a settlement. Settlements were introduced in 1662, when overseers were given authority to remove any stranger who arrived in their parish without the prospect of finding employment within forty days or of renting a property worth at least £10 a year. This was modified in 1697, when the Settlements Act permitted strangers to take up residence provided that they could produce a certificate from their native parish agreeing to receive them back if they applied for poor relief. Settlements continued to be required under the 1834 Poor Law Amendment Act although they were demanded by the Union and were probably only asked of candidates for admission to the workhouse.

Entries in the Guardian's Minute Books for the Fordingbridge and New Forest Unions indicate that this was the case, with one particular group of paupers featuring prominently in references to settlements – lunatics. The 1845 Lunacy Act had required county asylums to be built, and in an entry in the Bramshaw burial registers Alan Broderick recorded that Harriet Dibden of Nomansland Extra Parochial 'Died in the Idiot's

Asylum, Redhill, Surrey' and was buried in Bramshaw Churchyard on 19 October 1869 at the age of nine. The circumstances in which a nine-year-old child was admitted to the Surrey County Asylum when she was evidently a native of Nomansland are not known, but fifteen years later, in 1884, the Bramshaw registers recorded the interment of a thirty-eight-year-old man, James Goodenough, who had died in the Hampshire County Asylum in Fareham.

Census returns show that a significant number of what were usually, but incorrectly, defined as imbeciles[6] were, despite the existence of asylums, accommodated in workhouses. The inmates listed under this heading were drawn from a wider stratum of society than was usually the case. In 1881 the nineteen inmates of the Alderbury Union Workhouse who were listed in this way included eight who were recorded without any former occupation, three who had been agricultural labourers (one of them a sixty-two-year-old widow), two domestic servants, two bakers, a laundress, an auctioneer, a draughtsman and a banker. The youngest, a domestic servant, was twenty-two; the oldest, a former agricultural labourer, Aaron Hurst, who was a native of Whiteparish, was eighty-two; whilst two thirds of the inmates included in this category were under forty-five. One was married, two were widowed and the remaining sixteen were single. This suggests that pauper lunatics, in common with many other inmates, entered the workhouse because they had no immediate family to support them.

There is no indication of the accommodation provided for those who, in a contemporary phrase, were of 'weak intellect', but it would seem that they occupied the same wards as the other adults. There is, however, evidence from the minute books that Unions were often reluctant to admit imbeciles to their workhouses and sought to establish that they had settlements elsewhere. A typical instance of this occurred in 1900 when the case of William Arthur Dible came before the Guardians of the New Forest Union. The clerk to the Ringwood Union had written to the New Forest Board, alleging that William Arthur Dible (who was described as a lunatic) had a settlement in Lyndhurst, and had asked that he should be accepted without any formal procedure. The New Forest Guardians were evidently unwilling to agree and instructed the relieving officer for the Lyndhurst District to look into the question and report back to their next meeting. The investigation resulted in William Arthur Dible being accepted as the responsibility of the New Forest Union.

Sixteen years earlier, in February 1884, the Fordingbridge Guardians began a long correspondence with a variety of bodies which had the opposite outcome. The subject of the exchange of letters was Henry Hookey, a criminal lunatic whose offences were not specified. In

February Messrs Hore, Solicitors to the Home Office, approached the Fordingbridge Board to claim that Henry Hookey had a settlement in their Union. In response the Board instructed Mr Holloway, the relieving officer, to enquire into the matter. There is no record of the outcome of Mr Holloway's investigations, but two months later another letter was put before the Guardians, from Mr Ward, the clerk to the Wiltshire County Asylum in Devizes, stating that the Treasury had traced Henry Hookey's settlement to the Fordingbridge Union. The Guardians were again reluctant to take responsibility in the matter, the minutes recording that they had passed a resolution calling upon the clerk to write to Mr Ward and to inform him that they would only accept Henry Hookey on the usual justice's warrant. (The clerk was invariably a local solicitor, and probably gave advice on legal procedures.) Further correspondence must have ensued but only the resolution of the question, which occurred in July and August 1884, was recorded in the Minute Book. In July the Fordingbridge Board received a letter from Mr Hodding, the clerk to the Alderbury Union, concerning Henry Hookey's settlement. This again led to an investigation by Mr Holloway, and after that a second letter from Mr Hodding stating that the Alderbury Guardians had accepted Henry Hookey unconditionally.

Another case in which a pauper lunatic was treated very differently occurred in the following year, 1885. The Fordingbridge Union received correspondence from the Local Government Board and the Commissioners in Lunacy, complaining that an inmate of the workhouse, Ada Cox, had not been committed to an asylum. The clerk recorded that Dr Clifton, the workhouse medical officer, had expressed the opinion that the case need not be treated in an institution, and since Ada Cox's mother was anxious, with Dr Clifton's approval, to take her daughter home, she was ordered to be discharged from the workhouse.

Not all instances in which Unions pursued a settlement involved cases of lunacy. In March 1884 the Fordingbridge Board heard a letter from the clerk to the Wimborne and Cranborne Union in Dorset, agreeing to accept Emma Pope and four children. The reasons for Emma Pope's seeking admission to the workhouse are not known, but it is immediately evident why the Fordingbridge Union would have wished to confirm that her settlement was in the Wimborne and Cranborne Union and not in one of their own parishes.

In cases in which outdoor relief was given, paupers were not invariably removed to the place in which they had a settlement. Instead the Union in which they were residing paid relief and was then reimbursed by the Union of their settlement. As an instance of this, the Fordingbridge Union sent their counterparts in Romsey 36s 'for relief advanced to our settled poor in the quarter ending Michaelmas [29 September] 1887'.

One category of paupers who found shelter in the workhouse without having a settlement were vagrants. Tramps were accommodated for the night in the casual ward, which acted as the equivalent of a common lodging house. In July 1840 the burial register for St Peter's Church, Plaitford, recorded the interment of John Levi, an American vagrant, who had died in the parish at the age of sixty-six. That the curate Henry Lloyd, who conducted the funeral service, should have entered John Levi's name, nationality and age is an indication that he was well known in the locality, and although there is no evidence of his having sought temporary accommodation in any workhouse in the neighbourhood he must, nonetheless, have been buried at the expense of the Romsey Union.

In the 1851 census return for the Fordingbridge Workhouse only one vagrant appeared amongst the inmates, Jane Chambers – a single woman of twenty-five who was a native of Cork and whose status, profession or occupation was tramp. The succeeding entry was for Alice Chambers, who was less than a month old and whose birthplace was Fordingbridge. Although there is no evidence that Alice Chambers was born in the workhouse this seems likely to have been the case, and Jane Chambers' circumstances appear to illustrate a comment made by Richard Jefferies, advocating the establishment of lying in hospitals: 'A poor woman can go to the workhouse, but is it right, is it desirable from any point of view, that decent women should be driven to the workhouse at such times? As a matter of fact it is only the unfortunate who have illegitimate children that use the workhouse lying in wards.'[7]

A female vagrant was an exception, and it was usually male tramps who were accommodated in the casual ward. There is some evidence that their presence was not wholly welcome to Boards of Guardians. In 1872 the Board of the New Forest Union responded to the Pauper Inmates Discharge and Regulation Order which the Local Government Board had issued in the preceding November, and in doing so gave some indication both of the conditions in the casual ward and the attitude of the Union to its occupants. The response comprised four short paragraphs. The first stated that the casual ward should, in accordance with the Assistant Poor Law Inspector's recommendations, be divided by partitions, 2½ feet wide by 18 inches high, thus creating what were described as five separate sleeping places. This arrangement seems to have been usual in workhouse casual wards, although the recommendations suggest that before its adoption the vagrants slept randomly on the floor. The second was in direct response to the provisions of the new order which demanded that casual paupers should be required to pick oakum. Oakum was fibre obtained from old rope and used in caulking (sealing) ships timbers. Picking oakum was an occupation traditionally given to prisoners and workhouse inmates, although the evidence from south-east Wiltshire and south-west Hampshire suggests that it was only vagrants who were set this task. Fordingbridge Workhouse had an oakum account expressly for this purpose in the mid-1880s, and in 1872 the New Forest Union resolved to purchase oakum for tramps to pick.

The third paragraph of the 1872 minute suggests the attitude of the Union to vagrants, since it stated that the Board 'are still of the opinion that the dietary heretofore in force for casual paupers is ample and it is inexpedient to increase it'. It is not known what food was provided in the casual ward, but the tone of the entry suggests that whilst the Local Government Board had called for a better diet than the one supplied by the New Forest Union, the Guardians clearly had no intention of meeting their demands as improved conditions would encourage more tramps to apply to the workhouse. Another entry in the minute book written earlier in the month made the point even more explicitly: 'In several cases sturdy vagrants have applied for admission to the vagrants' ward and insisted upon having a fire provided for them and other comforts but on finding the master of the workhouse firm in resisting, for the present, any alteration of the regulations in force, they refused to remain and proceeded on their journey.' It would appear that sturdy (a word which had, in the Tudor period, been used of the able-bodied but in this instance probably meant professional) vagrants were aware of the Local Government Board's order, whilst the New Forest Union, in their determination to discourage them, were equally prepared to defy the regulations.

The final paragraph of the minute responding to the Order of November 1871 also included a resolution which led to a difference with the Local Government Board and with the assistant poor law inspector who was their representative. In January 1872 the Guardians of the New Forest Union had agreed 'That it is desirable to obtain a movable galvanised iron bath as an experiment in the Casual Ward', but a year later, in January 1873, they were read a letter from the Local Government Board, who complained that the assistant poor law inspector, Mr Murray Brown, had found that there was no bathroom for vagrants in the workhouse at Ashurst and consequently that tramps were not given a bath on admission. The letter also noted that vagrants were not set to work and were allowed to leave an hour earlier than the regulations demanded. In a further indication that the Union had failed to implement one of its own resolutions, the minute book recorded that the assistant inspector, who had attended the meeting of the Guardians, had recommended that some oakum should be purchased for vagrants to pick.

The Local Government Board was still complaining about the failure of the New Forest Union to give baths to vagrants in 1875. The Guardians were again read a letter quoting a further report which the Board had received from the assistant inspector, stating that 'whilst the requisitions for bathing vagrants relieving at the workhouse were supplied, the use of the bath was not regularly enforced and the attention of the Guardians was directed to the regulation contained in Article 5 of the General Order of the 22nd November 1871'.

Two and a half decades later, in 1901, an account of a meeting of the Romsey Board of Guardians which was printed in the Romsey edition of the *Andover Advertiser* also showed something of the attitudes of both the Poor Law Union to vagrants and of vagrants towards the authorities. The master of Romsey Workhouse had reported to the Board that two children named Anderson had been admitted, whilst their parents, who were tramps, were imprisoned for drunkenness. Twelve shillings had been found on the father, and the magistrates had suggested that the money should be paid to the Union – although it had not been forthcoming. The master then 'met the parents at the gate and told them. The mother was willing to hand over six shillings and he gave a receipt for this. The man said he should see the magistrates' clerk on the matter and subsequently a letter was received from the magistrates' clerk saying that the money should be refunded as no definite instructions had been given by the Bench and they could not do it. He had to return the six shillings.' Newspaper reports of the proceedings of the Guardians very rarely referred to inmates by name, and the editor and the journalist evidently shared the master's chagrin at the episode.

By the turn of the twentieth century attitudes to the workhouse had changed, an alteration evident from many sources. The *Andover Advertiser*, in common with much contemporary opinion, regarded 1 January 1901 as the opening day of the twentieth century. Its Romsey edition, printed on 4 January, included a regular column, 'In and around Romsey', which appeared under the *nom de plume* Tatler. On 4 January 1901 Tatler considered the advances made in a number of areas during the previous hundred years. One topic to which he gave particular attention was the workhouse, and in his paragraph contrasted the operation of the New Poor Law in its first decades with the manner in which it was being implemented in 1901:

The workhouses are no longer the places they were, Bumble is deceased and a paternal local Government Board, who took over the powers of the old Poor Law Board, well looks after the welfare of those who have to seek relief from the common fund. Everything is altered in the condition of life in the Poor House and the dietary and there is evidenced a liberality and a sentiment that does credit to present day ideas. 'The poor have you always with you', said One who himself had nowhere to lay His head and today we recognise its truth as did our forefathers but unlike them we regard poverty as a misfortune and not a crime; we pity instead of condemn; we readily assist instead of persecuting.

Tatler then quoted, at some length, the report of Mr Baldwyn Fleming, the poor law inspector for Hampshire, Dorset and parts of Wiltshire and Surrey. The passages from the report which attracted Tatler's attention were written as a refutation of the claim that the poor lived in the shadow of the workhouse. In pursuit of this argument the poor law inspector wrote that in his district in 1900 there had been 7,625 indoor paupers (those in the workhouse) and 25,634 receiving outdoor relief (in their own houses). He continued by claiming that 'if the life of the poor is one of hardship and application, how much more would it be so if no organisation existed for their kindly treatment and shelter where the necessities of failing powers call for means and resources beyond their own providing', and concluded that the provision made in the workhouse was to be regarded 'not as a shadow to be dreaded but as a fortunate fact to be thankful for'.

Evidence of a changing attitude to the workhouse and its inmates was seen at Fordingbridge in 1887 when, in order to mark Queen Victoria's Golden Jubilee, the paupers in the Union and the children were granted a holiday on 21 June (the date of the national celebrations), provided with a dinner and, in the case of the adults, with not more than one pint of beer each – if it was felt appropriate by a subcommittee formed to superintend the celebrations.

By the end of the century the Guardian's minutes and the local press were reporting the Christmas festivities which were being arranged for workhouse inmates. The minutes of the New Forest Union recorded that in both 1900 and 1901 the chairman had visited the workhouse on Christmas Day and had found the paupers enjoying themselves. In 1901 the entry had the somewhat ironic heading 'Christmas Day in the Workhouse', the irony lying in the clerk's perhaps unintentional use of the opening line of a poem written by George Sims, a crusading journalist, in 1879, which began, 'It is Christmas Day in the Workhouse' and went on to describe an outburst by a pauper during the Christmas lunch – who told how his wife had starved to death on the previous 25 December because the Union would not give her relief. In the New Forest Union minute of 30 December 1901 the chairman was recorded to have found 'that the fare provided by the Board was served in an excellent manner'.

The local press tended to report the Christmas festivities in the workhouses at much greater length than the Guardians' minutes, their accounts evidently being provided by journalists who had been invited to attend the pauper's treats. On 1 January 1904 the *Romsey Advertiser* described the events of Christmas Day 1903 in Stockbridge Workhouse, and used 10 inches of closely printed columns to do so. The newspaper also headed its account 'Christmas Day in the Workhouse' (and suggested that whilst George Sims lived on until 1922 his poem was already remembered only for its first line). The report included a description of the food provided, breakfast comprising bread, butter and ham with cakes and ale (which had appropriate echoes of *Twelfth Night*) at ten o'clock. These were followed by what the newspaper called 'the great midday meal', served to forty-seven inmates, who were given a menu of 'roast beef, roast legs of mutton, baked and boiled potatoes, savoy cabbage, Christmas pudding, blancmange, jelly, mince pies washed down with stout and mineral waters'. The meal was served, as was often customary in workhouses at Christmas, by members of the Board of Guardians, their wives, unmarried daughters and the staff. In the infirmary a different menu was provided by the nurse: 'roast fowl, potatoes, parsnips, brussel sprouts, puddings and sweets' (chicken presumably being considered more suitable for the sick and convalescent than beef and mutton). At tea the paupers were given plain and currant cake, jam tarts and cheesecake, and throughout the evening ale and mince pies were available.

Nearly half of the *Advertiser*'s report comprised a description of the decorations arranged in the dining hall by 'a painter down on his luck who had wandered into the casual ward' and who had festooned with evergreens the chandelier and the open rafters – the form of lighting was in contrast with the absence of a ceiling, although both were probably superior to their equivalents in the accommodation previously occupied by the inmates – and had hung pictures, amongst which was an oil painting placed over the fireplace that depicted 'a Stockbridge farm scene in snowy weather, the thatched barns and sheds, somewhat out of repair, being very realistic'. In a comment on the occupants of the casual ward, the newspaper remarked, 'How a man with the taste and ability displayed in the work, came to be on the road tramping from workhouse to workhouse, is one of the mysteries that so often meet the inquirers into the problem of our tramps.'

The account of the workhouse festivities was written in a style which was at once hearty and patronising, and it is evident that the paupers were expected to be appreciative of their Christmas treat. The vagrant artist was clearly aware of this, for at one end of the dining hall a painted shield bore the inscription written in bold letters, 'Best wishes to our Guardians. Good health to our Chairman', whilst at the close of the midday meal the chairman expressed his pleasure at again seeing the inmates and the hope that they had enjoyed their dinner (contemporary accounts often failed to make a distinction between lunch and dinner). The master responded by thanking the chairman and those who had served the meal, after which 'cheers for the chairman and all who assisted brought the dinner to a close'. Through the evening the paupers danced and sang to the piano, flute and mandolin (the last two instruments being played by the porter), and the newspaper concluded its report with a comment of a kind which was often made of entertainments provided for the lower orders: 'Altogether the day proved one which will long live in the memories of the inmates of Stockbridge Workhouse.'

The same tone was adopted in a report of the New Year at Andover Workhouse in 1911.[8] The first paragraph invoked the spirit of Oliver Twist, although the memory of the Andover Workhouse scandal seems to lie behind the wording:

> If Oliver Twist were alive today he would find the conditions much altered in the Andover Workhouse and instead of stern military training he would find discipline but of a gentler order for the times have changed and the people with them. No doubt Oliver had a little extra at Christmas – it might have been punishment – but there were no New Year treats and summer outings such as the present day inmates are accustomed to. People in the Andover Union look after the inmates in this respect as well as any workhouse in the country, and the glad and joyous looks at treat times speak only too approvingly of the care bestowed upon them.

Summer outings – often to the seaside – had become a common feature of the workhouse calendar by the early twentieth century, whilst the Andover New Year treat was similar in many respects to the Christmas festivities at Stockbridge Workhouse seven years previously. The inmates were provided with a bread and cheese lunch, at which the men were given a pipe and some tobacco and the women and children 'something extra', a dinner with a menu of bacon, parsnips, potatoes a pint of beer or porter and 'plum pudding ad lib', and tea which was served by the mayoress and four other local notables. The Christmas tree, decorated with fruit, was brought in, and each of fifty children present received 'something useful' from the 'lavish hand' of the mayoress. The Andover inmates did not dance or sing as their counterparts at Stockbridge had done, but were instead brought into the dining hall for a concert which began at seven in the evening and did not conclude until eleven. Several members of the Board of Guardians were in the audience, together with other members of Andover society. Concerts were a popular and frequently organised entertainment at the time, and the programme arranged for the paupers was fairly typical – with comic songs and sketches, drawing room ballads, instrumental solos and trios, a novelty item, whistling solos and dancing on the stage: 'the comic element was most enjoyed . . . and anything with a chorus met with manifest approbation'.

Closing remarks made by one of the Guardians, a Mr Page, at eleven o'clock provide an indication of the attitude of the middle classes to the workhouse inmates. Having thanked the performers he addressed the paupers: 'If they were all very quiet and did not make the least sound they would no doubt hear the ghost of Oliver Twist asking for more. After what they had enjoyed that evening he thought it would not be very difficult to have heard anyone present asking for more. He asked for cheers for everybody, which were heartily given.'

In the stratum of society from which the Guardians were drawn the inmates of the workhouse had become a good cause. The master of Andover Workhouse, in the round of thanks which followed the concert, expressed appreciation of the 'ladies and gentlemen' who had subscribed to the cost of the New Year and summer treats: 'These treats are not paid for out of the rates (hear, hear).'

In January 1904 the report on the workhouse festivities at Stockbridge noted that the Chairman of the Guardians had called for three cheers for a Mrs Norman who provided tobacco and tea for the inmates, whilst in January 1901 Mr R. Lyle, the master of the Alderbury Union Workhouse, reported that Mrs Robinson of Redlynch House had sent two boxes of fancy sweets for the children following an outbreak of measles. An entry in the Guardians' Minutes for the New Forest Union, which described the activities at the workhouse during Christmas 1900, recalled Richard Jefferies' observation that in the dining hall every pauper had a tin mug and a tin soup plate, all exactly alike. The clerk recorded that Mrs Studholme Wilson Cake and Dr N.T. Shepherd had donated approximately four dozen earthenware drinking cups, which would mean that the tin mugs formerly used in the workhouse could be done away with.

One indication of the way in which attitudes to the workhouse had changed was in its use as a subject for picture postcards. From 1902

A coloured postcard of Romsey Workhouse sent to Mrs Tucker of Woolston, Southampton, by Amy who wrote 'My last resource' under the photograph. Members of the staff stand on the edge of the lawn with croquet mallets and balls in front of them and male and female inmates on benches behind.

the Post Office had permitted cards to have a picture on the front and both the address and the message on the back (hitherto the address alone was allowed to be written on the rear). Postcards, which only required a ha'penny stamp and could, if posted early, be delivered on the same day, now came into widespread use. Enterprising photographers, newsagents and stationers issued numerous cards showing views, street scenes, buildings and significant events in their locality, and among these were depictions of the Union workhouse. Several views of Romsey Workhouse were sold, including one which showed, somewhat bizarrely, the staff with croquet mallets and balls on the grass in front of them and with benches of aged paupers looking on. The card, which must have been produced with the co-operation of the authorities, was perhaps intended to show happy and contended paupers, but whilst the middle classes had come to see the workhouse as a haven for the aged poor, the labouring classes perceived it to cast a shadow which survives in popular memory even today.

Chapter IX
Work – Labour in the Fields

A LTHOUGH small farmers relied upon casual labour at the busiest seasons of the agricultural year, some labourers travelled considerable distances on foot in pursuit of the higher wages paid on large farms at haymaking and harvest. Charles Dovey walked from Sherfield English, 5 miles west of Romsey and on the borders of Hampshire and Wiltshire, to Alton in order to obtain casual employment as a reaper. Recently married and in need of income, he slept in barns and outhouses and worked very long hours in order to earn the extra shillings which such labour provided. George Sturt described how Fred Bettesworth walked, as a young man, from Surrey to Sussex in pursuit of the same object,[1] whilst Richard Jefferies wrote in an essay published in *The Open Air* in 1885 of Roger the Reaper, a representative itinerant harvester who slept on the bare boards of a vacant cowshed (the cattle being kept in the fields in August) with only a few sacks for bedding. Rising very early, he made his way into the harvest field oblivious to everything except the extra wages which he could earn. Sustained only by a breakfast of dry bread, an onion and tea, together with vast quantities of watery beer (and Jefferies described the weak ale supplied to the reapers as 'the vilest drink in the world'), he laboured for fourteen hours under the blazing August sun and undertook tasks which required neither skill nor concentration. Yet, even as Jefferies wrote, machinery was coming into the harvest fields and making the itinerant reaper redundant. Charles Dovey's work in Alton was undertaken in the 1860s, before the depression on the land and the increasing mechanisation of agriculture, and in Jefferies' essay Roger's work was restricted by the use of the reaping machine, although not yet by the reaper-binder. He cut by hand the corners of the field inaccessible to the mechanical harvester, but otherwise his work consisted of gathering bundles of straw and twisting them into a rough rope, which he used to tie the sheaves, constantly stooping and bending as he did so. He would then be sent to another field to pitch sheaves into a four-wheeled wagon, lifting them to a considerable height with a two-pronged pitchfork. The process of tossing them onto the wagon strained his stomach muscles, his arms and his shoulders, even as bending to tie the sheaves had strained his back. At the end of the day his recreation was to go to the alehouse and drink away part of his wages before returning to the cowshed with uncertain steps and, after a supper of bread, bacon and another onion, to his sacking bed. Jefferies portrays Roger as a young, unmarried man who is nonetheless provident enough to use a pound to purchase a pair of stout winter boots, and return to his parents' cottage with half a sovereign in his pocket. The essay contrasts the circumstances of Roger and his father, who by dint of constant work had, like H.M. Livens's match faggoter, acquired a cottage and a degree of independence. It is unclear how far Roger and his father were drawn from life, but they contrast the circumstances of a thrifty and far-sighted labourer of the 1850s and 1860s, when agriculture flourished, with those of a field worker in the 1880s after depression had begun to make conditions on the land more severe and independence more difficult to achieve. (In the same way, in *Lark Rise* Flora Thompson wrote of two elderly hamlet dwellers, Sally and Dick, who lived in greater comfort than most cottagers, supported by a capital of £75 which Sally had inherited from her father and which she and Dick had augmented through the frugality with which they lived. Flora Thompson described them as survivals from a more favoured era, although perhaps significantly she noted that Laura, who represented her younger self, visited her childhood home on the eve of the First World War and found that the roof of Sally's cottage, which had with the £75 been part of her legacy, had fallen in, whilst the once well-kept garden was an unkempt waste.

Richard Jefferies claimed in 1874 that some agricultural labourers enjoyed a higher standard of living than many of their fellows. In particular he identified older labourers who had two or three bachelor sons living at home and contributing to the income of the household as those who could live in modest comfort, remarking that 'it is not unusual in such cottages to find the whole family supping at seven (it is in fact dining) on a fairly good joint of mutton, with every species of common vegetable'[2] (although this could only have applied in the summer and autumn, as vegetables would have been far more scarce in late winter and spring).

An examination of the enumerators' schedules for the parishes on the North Eastern boundary of the New Forest and the borders of Hampshire and Wiltshire at the time when Jefferies was writing suggests that such households were rare. Few parents had sons over the age of twenty living at home, whilst the presence of daughters who were more than twelve or thirteen was virtually unknown. A typical example of a farm worker's family is found on the 1881 census return for Whiteparish, where in the hamlet of Cowesfield Henry Gwyer (whose father had been the tenant of Landford Farm when the plough boy Edward Reynolds was fatally injured in the threshing engine) was occupying 240 acres with his younger brother Charles and elder sister Ellen, who was presumably keeping house for her two brothers. Henry Gwyer was employing three men and two boys with the carter, Edward Mundy, living with his wife Jemima and seven children in one of two cottages which appear to have been attached to the property. The eldest of the seven, Tom, was eighteen and a carter like his father, whilst a second son, Fred, was fourteen and a ploughboy. Of the remainder, three were girls aged between twelve and three, whilst a third son was ten. The census gives no definite indication of the standard of living enjoyed by Edward Mundy and his family, although a farm worker with a specific area of expertise, such as a carter, commanded higher wages than an ordinary agricultural labourer, and the fact that his eldest daughter was still at school when she might have gone into domestic service suggests that some extra income was available.

According to Richard Jefferies carters, who did not merely drive the four-wheeled wagon but were responsible for all the work with horses including ploughing, were the first men on the farm each morning, coming to feed (or bait, as Jefferies puts it) their teams as early as half past three. It was a matter of the greatest pride that the team should be in prime condition and of the utmost importance that they had a precise amount of food – which they were to be given well before they commenced work.

Jefferies also described the youthful under-carter, referring both to his responsibilities, which often seemed beyond his years, and his lack of stature: 'Frequently teams of powerful horses drawing immense loads of hay or straw may be seen in the highway in the charge of a boy who does not look ten years old judged by town standards but who is really fifteen. These short, broad, stout, lads look able to stand anything and in point of fact do stand it, from the kicks of the carter's heavy boot [and carters were noted for their rough treatment of the ploughboys who worked with them] to the long and bitter winter'.[3]

If the carter was early to work the milker was only a little later in commencing his day. In Tess of the d'Urbervilles the period which Tess spends in the Valley of the Great Dairies (the Frome Valley) is an idyllic interlude in her short ill-fated existence, but in Jefferies' account the milker's life (and he claimed that by the 1870s women had ceased to milk) was less pleasant, particularly in the winter. The milker began his task at four o'clock in the morning and worked until half past five. He carried the buckets of milk suspended from a pair of yokes to the dairy, drew water for the dairy maids – and in winter when his sacking apron became wet icicles would hang from its fringes. Breakfast followed at six, after which he joined the ordinary routine of the farm until three, when the afternoon milking began. This was completed at half past four, after which the dairy would be cleaned and the dairy maid assisted in her heavier tasks. The day closed after fourteen hours, at about six in the evening. Jefferies claimed that whilst a milker's work might be less unpleasant in summer, in the darkness of a winter morning it was far from idyllic: 'To put on coarse nailed boots, weighing fully seven pounds, gaiters up above the knee, a short greatcoat of some heavy material and to step out into driving rain and trudge wearily over field after field of wet grass with the furrows full of water, then to sit on a three legged stool, with mud and manure half way up to the ankles and milk cows with one's head leaning against their damp, smoking hides for two hours, with the rain coming steadily drip, drip, drip – this is a very different affair.'[4]

The cowman – the fogger as Jefferies called him[5] – had equally disagreeable work in winter. Climbing to the top of a rick covered in snow and hung with icicles, he had to cut 'a great truss of hay' with a hay knife, remove it with a particularly heavy pitchfork made for the purpose, tie it with a horse hair rope and carry it on his back 'for perhaps half a mile through the snow, the furrows of the field are frozen over but his weight crashes through the ice, slush into the chilly water. Rain, snow or bitter frost, or still more bitter east winds, harsh winds as he most truly calls them – the fogger must take no heed of either for the cows must be fed.'[6] Having attended to the animals and breakfasted on bread, cheese and beer, the cowman had to muck out the yard and barrow away the manure before being put to the ordinary work of the farm.

Richard Jefferies wrote of the, often extensive, farms of the north Wiltshire downland where considerable numbers of men were employed. In the south-eastern corner of the county, near the boundary of the New Forest, a large farm comprised 200 acres, practised mixed agriculture and employed at most eight or nine men and two or three boys, with the result that the number of labourers undertaking the type of work described in the *Toilers of the Field* would have been limited, and on the numerous small farms the family that held the tenancy would have undertaken these tasks themselves, a circumstance which, whilst it might not have made them any less unpleasant, would have affected the attitude of those who undertook them.

A distinction was sometimes made between agricultural and general labourers, agricultural labourers being those with a specific skill such as the carter, the dairyman or the shepherd, whilst general labourers, although not without skill, were engaged in the routine activities of the farm. Enumerators' schedules often list general and agricultural labourers, although it is not always evident how the terms were used, general labourers sometimes referring to men who worked on a purely casual basis, turning their hand to any kind of employment which became available, whilst agricultural labourers were those with permanent positions on farms.

One group of labourers whose presence on the land has largely been forgotten is women. Flora Thompson wrote, in *Lark Rise*, of women labourers employed in the fields in the 1880s, although the evidence of enumerators' schedules suggests that they had become a rarity by that date. In the parish of Landford in 1851 there were eight field women, but by 1861 there were none. In Lockerley in 1861 seventy-seven general and agricultural labourers were resident in the parish, but of these only one was a woman; whilst in Whiteparish twenty years later one twenty-three-year-old woman, Ann Wassall, the daughter of a shepherd, was listed as an agricultural labourer.

According to Flora Thompson, the women field workers of the 1880s were the successors to a large body of unruly and loose-living female labourers whose unsavoury reputation deterred the majority of village women from undertaking agricultural work. The evidence from Landford in 1851 suggests that the eight women labourers were the widows, wives and daughters of ordinary farm-hands. Some field women were very young. Harriet Russell, the daughter of Hannah Russell, the pauper washerwoman living in West Wellow in 1851, was listed as an agricultural labourer although she was only twelve years old, and in Landford the youngest woman labourer recorded in the same year was thirteen. By contrast the oldest was sixty-five.

Flora Thompson wrote that most of the six women who engaged in field work in Lark Rise – Juniper Hill in Oxfordshire – were themselves the respectable wives of farm workers whose children had gone from home and who welcomed the independence they gained from their 4s a week wages. The women worked separately from the men, often in different fields, and were engaged in lighter tasks: weeding, hoeing, stone picking, trimming turnips and mangelwurzels and on rainy days, repairing sacks under cover.

Richard Jefferies writing in 1874, also described the work undertaken by women.[7] Like Flora Thompson over sixty years later, he listed stone clearing (removing flints from hay meadows to ensure that they did not cause damage during haymaking) and hoeing, but added couch-gathering (collecting couch grass broken into fragments by the plough and piling it up to be burned: in his novel *Desperate Remedies*, published in 1871, Thomas Hardy wrote: 'The couch-grass extracted from the soil had been left to wither in the sun; afterwards it was raked together, lighted in the customary way, and now lay smouldering in a large heap . . .' Jefferies also noted that the women beat clots with a short fork on pasture. Clots were cowpats, and beating them scattered the dung to increase its effectiveness in the soil, whilst avoiding the bare patches which it would leave on the grass if it remained where it had fallen. In *The Toilers of the Field* he described the dress of the field women, referring to clothing which recalled the workhouse uniform: 'It used to be common to see women dressed in a kind of smock-frock; this was worn in the days when they milked, and it is still occasionally worn. Now they generally wear linsey dresses in the winter and cotton in the summer . . . They wear boots nailed and tipped much like the men but not so heavy, and in rough weather corduroy gaiters.'

According to Flora Thompson, the gaiters were made from old trouser legs, although one field woman, Mrs Spicer, wore her husband's corduroys in their entirety.

Contemporary paintings depicting women engaged in agricultural work show them to have worn the hem of their skirts around their ankles – allowing greater freedom of movement but showing their large boots. These, with their big hands, emphasised the fact that, despite their picturesque appearance, they were not ladies.

The field women participated in haymaking and harvesting, but at these seasons most of the women of the village would be involved in gathering the crop. Jefferies claimed that the hayfield brought the sexes into closer proximity than any other season and made the women, whether married or single, the butt of innuendoes and crude behaviour to which they responded in kind. (In one sketch, 'A True Tale of the Wiltshire Labourer', Jefferies has a tipsy mower trying to steal a kiss from a pretty girl, although he implies elsewhere that the liberties taken involved far great impropriety.)

Harvesting saw whole families at work together, because farmers paid piece rates and everyone employed could contribute to the income of the household. Jefferies wrote in 1874 that the labourers' wives and elder daughters reaped beside their husbands and fathers, whilst the younger children gathered the corn into stooks (or hiles as they were known in the dialect of the New Forest) and performed other small tasks. Reaping was particularly hard for the woman worker:

> The standing corn, nearly as high as the reaper, keeps off the breeze, if there is any, from her brow. Grasping the straw continuously cuts and

wounds the hand, and even gloves will hardly give perfect protection. The woman's bare neck is turned to the colour of tan, her thin muscular arms bronze right up to the shoulder. Short time is allowed for refreshment; right through the hottest part of the day they labour. It is remarkable that none, or very few, cases of sunstroke occur. Cases of vertigo and vomiting are frequent, but pass in a few hours. Large quantities of liquor are taken to sustain the frame weakened by perspiration.[8]

Much of this paragraph indicates that women's work in the harvest field would have been regarded as unladylike. Drinking small beer and being tanned and bronzed by the sun would all have been considered unbecoming. A pale skin was regarded as desirable, and the village women's sunburnt arms and necks, which indeed imply that they worked in their petticoats, since a dress would have left only their hands and faces uncovered, would have marked them out as members of the labouring classes.

Yet for all the arduous nature of their work the women did not receive their wages. If they were single their money was added to their father's pay and if they were married it was included with their husbands. Nor did the effort of the day end when the reaping was completed, for the woman harvester had to return to her cottage, which could be as much as 2 miles distant, carrying her gleanings on her head and, in some instances, nursing her latest child.

Flora Thompson regarded gleaning – or leazing as she called it – as a pleasant activity, a hard but sociable task, undertaken in the agreeable surroundings of the August countryside. In a favourable season two or more bushels of corn could be collected to be threshed at home and then delivered to the miller who ground it, retaining a percentage as remuneration and returning a sack of flour which would be displayed on a chair in the living room for the admiration of visitors. Flora Thompson was, however, writing fifty years after the scenes and events which she described, and her account is often suffused with nostalgia. Furthermore her mother, as the wife of an artisan rather than a farm labourer, was unlikely to have taken part in gleaning and experienced its hardships at first hand. Richard Jefferies, the son of a small farmer, wrote as a contemporary, describing the rural life of his day without any illusions about its harshness. His view of gleaning was somewhat different: 'Gleaning – poetical gleaning – is the most unpleasant and uncomfortable labour, tedious, slow backaching work, picking up ear by ear, the dropped wheat, searching among the prickly stubble.'[9]

Babies were taken into the fields during haymaking and harvesting, and often left in the care of one of the older girls, whilst in *Hodge and*

His Masters Jefferies wrote that the farmyard, the road and the fields were the playground of the labourers' children, who wandered between the feet of the carthorses, along the slippery banks of streams, amongst the livestock and in the vicinity of the traction engine with impunity. The death of William Curtis of Hamptworth, kicked or trampled by his father's horses, and of Tinny Lovell indicated that they were potentially fatal hazards. At the same time, though, they prepared children for work in the fields. By the middle of the nineteenth century the offspring of the labouring classes were being given some schooling but as log books (which were introduced in 1862) indicate, the opportunity to earn even very small sums led to pupils being withdrawn from their classes and sent to the fields and woods. Headteachers frequently complained that attendances were low because pupils were involved in haymaking or in minding livestock (the summer holidays coincided with the harvest and indeed were generally known as 'harvest holidays'). The Revised Code, introduced in 1862 in an attempt to raise standards in elementary education, required children to achieve a certain level of success in tests which were set nationally. Teachers were paid according to their pupils' results, and frequent absences were reflected in their salaries. Harry Churchill, the headmaster of Landford School from 1859 to 1877, frequently expressed his frustration in the log book and his thankfulness that haymaking and other busy seasons in the agricultural year had come to a close. He was nonetheless sufficiently aware of the importance to parents of the small sums of money which children could earn to acknowledge it indirectly in one entry in his log. Acorning was a near-forgotten activity which saw pupils going out to the woods and hedgerows to collect acorns, which could be sold to the farmers for a few pence and fed to the pigs. On 2 November 1868 Harry Churchill wrote in his log book, 'Am rejoiced to find that acorning has ended for this season and that nearly all of those absenting themselves on that account have returned to school this morning' – although he added that it had been 'a most bountiful harvest, such as one as the oldest inhabitants have no recollection'.

At the time that Harry Churchill was writing most of his pupils would have left school before they were eleven. Nearly twenty years earlier the census of 1851 showed that there were ten Landford inhabitants (from a population of just over 250) who were aged between eleven and fifteen and were in full-time employment. Of these three were ploughboys, two were thirteen-year-old girls who were agricultural labourers, two assisted their father on his 12 acre smallholding, one was a broom-maker, one was a farm servant and one, a girl, was working with her mother, who was a laundress.

Richard Jefferies' description of the youthful under-carter leading teams drawing heavily laden wagons is an indication that by their mid-teens boys were expected to take the same responsibilities as the men, although one task which was frequently allocated to boys was bird scaring. In *Once There Was a Village School* Elizabeth Merson wrote that one of her informants, identified only as a Bramshaw man born in about 1900 and still alive in 1979 when the book was published, recalled long hours spent in the fields periodically banging a tin in order to scare birds. W.H. Hudson, whose study *A Shepherd's Life* was published in 1910, recorded cycling through the Ebble Valley and seeing a solitary boy in a wide expanse of ploughed fields. The boy, who was aged about twelve or thirteen, ran a quarter of a mile carrying a 'queer heavy looking old gun' to stand staring at Hudson as he rode by. When the boy was asked why he had run such a distance to merely look and say nothing he replied, 'Just to see you pass' – evidence of the unrelieved monotony of his working day.

An instance of the dangers inherent even in bird scaring were illustrated in an item printed in the *Salisbury Journal* on 3 December 1864 under the heading 'Gun Accident'. The item recorded how a youth, Arthur Dibden, who was about fourteen years old, had been sent 'bird keeping' (scaring) with a gun and powder flask by his employer, Mr Neal of Parsonage Farm, Bramshaw. 'The lad incautiously threw some powder on a piece of burning wadding when the flask exploded. His hand was dreadfully shattered and part of his clothes were burned. He is now progressing favourably but it is feared the amputation of some of his fingers will be necessary.' It is unclear whether the boy was taken to Salisbury Infirmary or whether the amputation was to be performed at home by the local surgeon, but the incident shows how, as with the death of Edward Reynolds a fortnight before, such accidents were taken for granted.

The fatality to Edward Reynolds was also an indication that agriculture in the second half of the nineteenth century was in transition, and that hand labour was giving way to machinery. At the inquest into the death of the Hon. Henry Nelson, who was fatally injured in a riding accident in Landford in 1863, Martha Moody, who had been attending a turnpike gate through which the deceased had passed, said he had told her that his mount was disturbed by a horse-driven threshing engine on a nearby farm. It is unclear whether the threshing machine which caused Edward Reynolds's death was driven by horse or steam power, but permanent fastenings for the belts which drove the machinery are still in place, though long disused, at Manor Farm, Landford, where the accident occurred.

The increasing variety of equipment available to the farmer was not only creating new hazards to employees and others; it was also reducing the amount of labour required on the land. Writing of the role of field women in haymaking, Richard Jefferies commented in 1874 that 'Before the haymaking machines and horse rakes came into vogue, it was not uncommon to see as many as twenty women following each other in échelon, turning a "Wallow", or shaking up the green swathes left by the mowers.'[10]

Louis Hatch, in his memoir *Hamptith*, recalled being taught to tie sheaves by a woman neighbour, who must herself have acquired the technique when large bodies of female labour were required in the harvest field, their role having been supplanted by the reaper binder. The effect of the reaper binder was noted much earlier, in 1879, by Richard Jefferies who observed that whilst gleaning remained an important activity for the cottage women, 'Reaping by machinery has made rapid inroads and there is not nearly so much left behind as in former days . . . the cunning of the mechanitian has invaded the ancient customs; the very sheaves are now to be bound with wire [it was in fact twine] by the same machine that reaps the corn. The next generation of country folk will hardly be able to understand the story of Ruth.'[11]

Yet ancient practices did not become extinct as rapidly as Jefferies implies. Flora Thompson wrote in *Lark Rise* that the labourers of the 1880s still undertook much farm work by hand, and did not regard machinery as anything more than a toy. One biblical method remembered to have been used by small farmers on the Hamptworth Estate immediately before the First World War was broadcast sowing, a skilful sower being able to distribute the seed as evenly as a mechanical drill. In his short novel *Green Ferne Farm* Jefferies described the technique employed by a middle aged labourer: 'Now watch his steps; regular as clockwork. See his hand springs from his hip and describes an exact segment of a circle – no a parabola, I suppose – every time, so as to make the seed spread itself equally. That's higher than science – that's art, art handed down these thousand years.'

Agriculture in Victoria's reign retained a continuity with the past, but the innovations made in the late nineteenth and early twentieth centuries steadily eroded that link and ushered in a very different rural society.

Chapter X
Work – The Artisan, The Shopkeeper and The Servant

A T the time of the 1881 census much of the population of Whiteparish was living in the centre of the village, whilst the larger farms and substantial houses were situated in more outlying areas. As a result the majority of the inhabitants of the middle part of the parish were artisans, shopkeepers or labourers. The column in the enumerators' schedules headed 'rank, profession or occupation' listed twenty-eight different forms of employment apart from labouring, and of these the work of the blacksmith was most directly involved with agriculture.

The population of Whiteparish included four blacksmiths (one of whom was occupying the Fountain Inn without any suggestion that he was a licensed victualler), and it was by no means uncommon to find two or three smithies in one parish. The hamlet of Earldoms, immediately to the south of Whiteparish, had two forges, and there were

The Street, Whiteparish, before the First World War. The notice on the right-hand side of the photograph reads 'King's Head Yard. Accommodation for Cyclists'.

two in Plaitford in 1861 and 1871. One of these was in the hands of the Tutt family, whilst the other was owned by the blacksmith, Charles Perman. The Tutt family had been the proprietors of their forge for several decades: the census of 1841 listed John and William Tutt as blacksmiths in the parish, and whilst William Tutt died in 1844, John was described as a retired smith in 1871 – the forge then being worked by his son and grandson, both named Edwin. By 1881 the Tutts' smithy had gone, perhaps in the aftermath of the elder Edwin's departure for Leatherhead or of his suicide in 1875, and only Charles Perman's forge remained. A poem of seventeen stanzas entitled 'A Forest Hamlet' and describing Plaitford, whose author is know only by the initials FSHE, was printed on a quarto sheet, probably in the 1890s, and included the line 'As Perman's anvil loudly rings'.

In April 1901 the Romsey edition of the *Andover Advertiser* printed a paragraph describing Charles Perman's funeral which referred to him as 'one of the oldest inhabitants aged 85 in the parish of Plaitford', yet he was not a native of the village and according to tradition came there in response to a newspaper advertisement. Memory recalled that George Pearce, a blacksmith on Plaitford Common who had died in 1845, had left a widow, several children and the forge which had provided the family with their livelihood. As her husband had worked on his own, the widow Martha Pearce advertised for a smith and received a reply from Charles Perman, who was living in West Knoyle where he was born. Charles Perman walked to Plaitford in pursuit of the situation and was first employed by and afterwards married Martha Pearce, becoming the proprietor of the smithy. Charles and Martha Permain had one daughter, Maria, but one of Martha's children by her first marriage, who had become a favourite with her stepfather, remembered in later life that when she was particularly unhappy, he would say 'Come into the cubby hole' and draw her between his knees, the smell of his corduroys, which must have been impregnated with the acrid fumes of burning hoof, remaining with her all her life.

The number and proximity of smithies in relatively small villages is an indication of the number of working horses on farms (although the parish of Landford, which lies between Earldoms and Plaitford, had no forge, so horses would have been brought from there to one of the neighbouring parishes to be shod). Individual farmers seem to have favoured particular smithies, Marian Harding recalling that her father Frank Curtis always took his horses to Frank and Billy Hutchings, Charles Perman's grandsons who inherited his forge. At the same time the blacksmith undertook other forms of ironwork, on occasions repairing damaged farm machinery.

The wheelwright, who built and repaired four-wheeled wagons and other farm vehicles, also relied upon agriculture for part of his livelihood. On the other hand farm wagons continued in working order for decades. Richard Jefferies wrote that they outlasted their original owner and often his successor as well, so that the wheelwright also worked as a carpenter and joiner and frequently, as was the case with Walter Hood at West Wellow, Charles Young in Bramshaw and Oliver Kendal in Landford, as the village undertaker.

In 1881 Whiteparish had only one resident who was listed as a wheeler (a frequent abbreviation for wheelwright). The enumerator described him as a 'Carpenter and Wheeler', but the first trade was struck out. He was Harvey Lovell who, with his wife, Hannah, a former schoolteacher seven years his senior, and their six-month-old daughter Jessie, was living on the farm occupied by his aunt, Mary Harnett, a widow who, at the age of sixty-four, worked 69 acres with the two men and two boys whom she employed. It is not recorded whether Harvey Lovell had a wheelwright's shop on his aunt's farm or whether he was employed elsewhere, the latter being perhaps more probable. If this was the case Whiteparish farmers who had work for a wheelwright would have been obliged to look for a tradesman in a neighbouring village.

The author's grandfather, Frederick Ings, was apprenticed to a wheelwright and carpenter in Redlynch at the age of twelve in 1902. He remembered being sent to Ringwood, where among other tasks he was set to plane doors – which was particularly heavy work. He cycled from Redlynch to Ringwood and back, but returned so weary that he was unable to pedal his machine, instead supporting himself on the frame and pushing it home. His employers did not retain him after he had served his time, and in common with many other village youths he joined the army for what was then known as seven and five, seven years with the colours, serving with the regiment, and five as a reservist. His first posting was to Jamaica in 1907, and he was subsequently stationed on one of the Solent forts. Due to join the reserves in the autumn of 1914, he spent the whole of the First World War on the Western Front as a wheelwright in the Royal Artillery, and finally ended his period in the services with the British forces occupying Cologne after the war. The rest of his working life was spent as a builder, the wheelwright's trade dying out as horse-drawn vehicles were supplanted by motor transport.

Agriculture created employment in other fields. One of the stanzas in FSHE's poem 'A Forest Hamlet' referred to a drover, Daniel Cull:

Think not old Daniel Cull's forgot
He's driven the cattle years and not

Will we relent a thought to lend
His good wife Hannah's many a friend

Daniel Cull lived in a mud-walled cottage just across the county boundary in Landford. In 1851, when he was sixteen, he and his eighteen-year-old sister Ellen were described as orphans and as drovers. Ellen Cull subsequently married a carpenter, and by 1881 had long been Mrs Giles and the carrier to Romsey, her eccentricities being remembered in the 1950s. Her brother continued to be listed in successive censuses throughout the second half of the nineteenth century as a drover, presumably driving cattle to and from markets in the locality rather than further afield, memory claiming that he penned them in a disused sand pit overnight and then drove them to market or to a new owner on the following morning.

Another craft which principally depended upon agriculture was hurdle-making. Hurdles were produced by interweaving split hazel stems between uprights. Small areas of ground not otherwise worth cultivating were sometimes maintained as hazel coppice, the stools being cut every seven years, thus allowing them to regenerate. The 1851 census for Landford included an entry listing William Hull as a hurdle-maker, whilst the 1861 return for Plaitford included two hurdlers, Charles Moody and George Dunn. William Hull, who was a widower and deaf and dumb, was found dead in his mud-walled cottage in 1866, an inquest returning, on the evidence of Mr Nunn, the surgeon, a verdict of death by strangulated hernia. Hurdlers disappeared from the census returns after 1861, and in 1879 Richard Jefferies wrote that hurdles were no longer made by individuals but were manufactured by master carpenters from the towns, who employed a number of men in this work and undercut the village maker.[1] The hurdlers whose hut Edward Thomas found near Timsbury, littered with cigarette ends, were perhaps employed on this basis, as were the purchasers of concessions on areas of coppice which were remembered to have been auctioned annually at the King's Head in Redlynch.

Although the parish of Landford was largely agricultural in the nineteenth century, and whilst most of its population, which never exceeded 278 (a peak which it reached in 1861 and which was far below the 486 recorded in Whiteparish in 1881), were engaged either in farm work or domestic service, it did have a number of besom-makers, who were absent from its larger neighbour and from Plaitford. The makers of besoms were all members of two branches of the same family, the Moodys, who had been represented in the parish since the late seventeenth century. In 1851 there had been six broom-makers in the village, the largest single group of workmen after farm labourers and the various categories of domestic and outdoor servants. One, Dan Moody, who was listed as a farmer of 70 acres and employer of two labourers, nonetheless called his house Broom Hall, and when he made his will in 1858, naming Isaac Fielder, the relieving officer, as one of his executors, bequeathed 'my tools and stock in trade of a broom maker' to two of his sons whilst also leaving a small legacy to Martha Perman, another of his ten children. The 1850s saw besom-making in Landford at its height. By 1881 it had declined, with only two besom-makers and one broom dealer remaining in the parish. In Redlynch the trade continued until well into the twentieth century, again largely in the hands of one family, the Newmans, whose brooms were distributed over a wide area.

The developing railway network allowed goods to be carried over much greater distances than hitherto; milk, as an instance, being transported into the large towns. Thomas Hardy portrayed Tess and Angel Clare taking milk to the station in a significant development in their ill-fated relationship, whilst Richard Jefferies complained that so much milk was sent into the towns that village women could not find enough for their children. By the reverse process, bulky and heavy commodities were brought into rural areas, coal becoming much more readily available. Coal dealers appeared even in rural parishes, whilst the Salisbury coal merchants, Clark and Lush, established a depot at Downton station.

Forestry was an occupation which saw little change through the Victorian period and into the twentieth century, the woodmen listed in successive census for many parishes continuing to work with the axe and cross-cut saw. Richard Jefferies, who commented that the woods were a scene of activity throughout the seasons, noted that amongst the tasks undertaken in woodland was rining, stripping the bark from oak trees after they had been felled, oak bark being used in tanning. Horace Hutchinson and Rose de Crespigny, in *The New Forest, Its Traditions, Inhabitants and Customs*, had also listed rining as one of the sources of casual employment for the forester, the tannery at Downton probably purchasing bark collected in the Forest.

The sawyer would have converted timber into planks and, like the woodman, appeared in the enumerators' schedules for most rural parishes during the nineteenth century. The first entry in the 1881 census return for Whiteparish listed a sawyer, George Hayter, who was living in what is still known as The Street with his wife, widowed daughter – a servant out of place – and an eleven-year-old girl, Emily Pritty, a native of Standlynch on Lord Nelson's estate, who was described as a 'scholar and boarded out pauper'. George Hayter was sixty-nine and evidently still working, probably as a top sawyer in a saw pit.

The traditional method of planking tree trunks was in a pit with a cross-cut saw. The top sawyer stood on the log or on a board at right angles to it whilst the bottom sawyer, who was usually a younger and less experienced man, was in the pit itself – being showered with sawdust as he worked. Pit sawing was a slow and laborious process. It was not only agriculture which was being affected by mechanisation, however, and by the later nineteenth century timber was increasingly being planked with a circular saw driven by a stationary engine (or, as on the Hamptworth Estate, in a timber mill powered by water).

The sawyer was principally involved in preparing timber for use in building, and a conspicuous feature of the population of rural parishes in the nineteenth century was the increasing presence of building workers. This was especially true of bricklayers. In Landford in 1851 there was one carpenter and, more surprisingly, a father and son working as a plumber and glazier and a glazier and painter. At the same time there were no bricklayers. In 1881, when the population of the parish was still largely employed in agriculture or service, there were three. The rise in the number of bricklayers is first seen in 1861 when Silas Moody, who a decade before had been a besom-maker, was listed as a bricklayer and broom-maker. (It was by no means unusual in the nineteenth century, for a cottager to follow a succession of different occupations. Silas Moody's nephew Reuben was, at various times, a bricklayer, a master tailor, a turnpike keeper, a grocer and the postmaster of Landford.)

Brick had been used in the construction of manor houses and farmhouses since the turn of the seventeenth century, but by the 1860s landowners were erecting estate cottages and agricultural buildings that used the same material, worker's dwellings, barns and other outhouses having the year of their construction frequently built into one wall in blue brick. This usually occurred in the 1870s and '80s before the onset of the depression on the land. Brick buildings required not only bricklayers but also brickyards. Local production of a heavy material avoided the expense and difficulty of transportation over long distances.

Literature has portrayed brickmakers as squalid ruffians, the brickmakers in *Bleak House* and at Hoggle End in *The Last Chronicle of Barset* being examples of this, although the evidence from rural communities in the nineteenth century suggests that such a portrayal is inaccurate and that employees in brickyards were indistinguishable from other residents. The 1881 census for Whiteparish includes entries for a 'Redware Potter', an annotation in another hand adding helpfully 'brick and tile', whilst Shadrach G Rose was described more explicitly as a brick- and tile-maker. Percy Hatch, the long-standing verger and sexton, remembered John Pointer, the foreman at the Brook Brickworks on the southern perimeter of Bramshaw, who was not a churchman but a Wesleyan Methodist, as a man of great sincerity who lived by the highest principles. The Brook Brickyard was one of many in villages where suitable clay was available. Often the only surviving evidence of local brickworks is to be found in place names such as Kiln Lane in Redlynch or Brick Kiln Cottages on the Hamptworth estate, although bricks and tiles bearing the impression of the Rockingham Clay Works are still found in the vicinity of West Wellow. The Rockingham Clay Works, which also produced pottery and, briefly electrical insulators, was an important manufacturer in the locality for thirty years from the early 1870s until the supply of suitable clay was exhausted in 1902, transporting bricks and other goods by steam traction engine and wagon.

Although a significant number of villagers were employed in occupations which did not involve work on the land, agriculture impinged upon their livelihoods as it did upon that of the bricklayer erecting cottages and farm buildings. Bootmakers appear on the census returns for many parishes, Isaac Fielder's brothers George, Ezekiel and Isaiah being examples of these, whilst in Whiteparish in 1881 there were a bootmaker, a boot and shoemaker and a shoemaker. Richard Jefferies claimed that labourers preferred to patronise the village bootmaker who knew their particular requirements in footwear, although they would have a long wait for the finished article. Reg King, who with his brother Stan opened a shoemaker's in Landford Post Office in the early 1930s, recalled a request from an old farm labourer for a pair of working boots. On being presented with a pair which were made from thick leather with heavy hobnails, the old man refused them, with the comment, 'I doant want they, they's Sunday boots, I want boots for working in.' If the bootmaker produced footwear for the fields, the shoemaker (and it is evident from the entries in enumerators' schedules that there was a distinction between the two) probably made lighter articles for women. He may have enjoyed the patronage of farmers' wives and daughters, but Richard Jefferies claimed that farm servants and dairy maids imitated the style, if not the quality, of the squire's daughters' clothing, wearing chignons and kid gloves and carrying parasols when arrayed in their finery. He also commented, 'the girl must have a "fashionable" bonnet, and a pair of thin tight boots, let the lanes be never so dirty or the fields never so wet'. The shoemaker's trade perhaps owed something to this trend, of which Jefferies so evidently disapproved.

The baker, like the shoemaker, was almost universally represented in rural parishes, confirming Jefferies' observation that cottagers'

The bakery at Bramshaw, before 1913. The name of Charles Lauriston Hall, who had succeeded his father-in-law William Domoney as proprietor, is painted above the door.

wives had ceased to bake bread, although he noted in *Wildlife in a Southern County* that the farmer's wife would occasionally do so (the inglenook fireplace which was found in old farmhouses was sometimes accompanied by a bread oven). The baker sold both bread and cakes, although Percy Hatch, recalling his experiences as errand boy in William Domoney's shop in Bramshaw, remembered that standards of hygiene were not high. The leaves would be swept off the surface of the rainwater butt – which would not have been used for drinking – and the currants, which had been placed in a large sieve, were dipped in it to wash them. At the same time the baker, who had to be on the premises in the early hours of the morning, would interrupt his work to shave, and then use his shaving brush to glaze the buns with sugar water.

Yet whilst the village baker was a nearly universal presence, the bakery was not of itself sufficient to provide a living, and was generally accompanied by a grocer's. In 1851 Alexander Moody of Landford had been a besom-maker, an occupation he followed with his brothers Samuel and Silas (who was twenty-five years his junior). A decade later (when Silas was a bricklayer and broom-maker and Samuel was still making besoms) he had become the proprietor of a grocer's shop. He continued to be described as a grocer in 1881 when he was seventy-two, but by 1887 he had been succeeded by his son Reuben. Although no bakery is recorded in the shop until Reuben's son, Gabriel, came into the business early in the twentieth century, an arrangement with Reuben Moody to supply food for a tea, which was provided by a collection made among the parishioners and held to mark Queen Victoria's Golden Jubilee (the Landford gentry had provided a lunch for the villagers), suggests that bread and cakes may already have been made upon the premises.

The final decades of the nineteenth century saw another significant development, the establishment of post offices in rural parishes. Whilst village post offices offered an expanding service, the role of postmaster (or mistress) was often combined with another – sometimes unlikely – trade. Initially rural post offices provided little more than premises for receiving and dispatching letters, but they went on to become post, money order and telegraph offices. In Landford the post office was established in about 1870, with two successive schoolmasters also acting as postmaster (having sufficient education to perform the duties which this entailed, but without the social status to baulk at the position). A hatch was set into the porch of the school house to allow for the easier conduct of post office business, but in 1893, with the appointment of a new headmaster, the post office was transferred to Reuben Moody's grocer's shop, the electric telegraph following in 1895.

At Fritham the post office was located in a farmhouse, Augusta Hickman, the farmer's wife, acting as postmistress, whilst Kelly's County Directory for Hampshire, recorded in 1895 that there were two post offices in Lockerley, one on The Green, where James Richard Price, a tailor, was the postmaster, and another on Butts Green (which Edward Thomas passed on his cycle ride from London to the Quantocks in 1913). There the postmaster was Tom Williams, a coal dealer. By 1898 the two post offices were in the hands of Jacob Peach, a shopkeeper and baker, and Louis Annetts, a carpenter and undertaker, whilst at Awbridge the postmaster, George Frederick Hurst, was a builder.

Landford only had a grocer's, but Whiteparish, a larger and more populous village, had a number of shops, among them a butcher's, where the proprietor was also the farmer of 10 acres, the smallholding probably providing some of the meat that was offered over the counter.

Amongst the other Whiteparish shopkeepers recorded by the 1881 census was Richard Drake, a native of the village, who was a draper and grocer. Since drapery was listed first, it was presumably the principal part of the business, which was prosperous enough to allow Bethiah Drake, Richard's daughter, to work as his assistant and for his eldest son, Joseph, to be a pupil (apprentice) teacher. Both were children of a first marriage, since Anne Drake, Richard's wife, was twenty-eight whilst he was forty-seven, and Bethiah and Joseph were respectively twenty and seventeen.

The drapery business may have offered opportunities to the husband and wife who were listed as a tailor and tailoress, and the two dressmakers who were also resident in Whiteparish in 1881. The tailors and seamstresses were likely to have taken orders from farmers and perhaps cottagers' wives, but it is also possible that they undertook piecework for the larger drapers in Salisbury and Romsey. In 1851 Caroline Roud of Sherfield English had been a shirt-maker and must have worked in this way. Fifty years later, on the death of Queen Victoria, the Salisbury drapers Blooms, and Clark and Lonnen, and their counterparts in Romsey, Henry Guard, Sharland Brothers and E. Williams, offered an extensive range of mourning. Sharlands of Romsey advised their customers, in their advertisement in the *Andover Advertiser*, that 'owing to a large demand, orders for mourning should be placed at once'. This was doubtless a ploy to secure trade, but the demand for mourning clothes could only have been met if drapers had called upon the casual assistance of the large numbers of seamstresses in the locality (especially as Williams claimed to provide 'dress making in all its branches').

There was another respect in which village shops provided work, since they often employed errand boys. Percy Hatch went from being Saturday boy at Domoney's shop to become the telegram boy at Bramshaw post office. On one occasion he was called upon to deliver a telegram to Sir William Mather (of the Manchester engineering firm

A card bearing the imprint 'Fielder, Post Office, Bramshaw', from where it was dispatched as an improvised greeting on Christmas Eve 1906.

Mather and Platt) who was occupying one of the large houses in the village. Finding Sir William Mather in the gardens, Percy Hatch delivered the telegram, at which the great engineer absentmindedly put his hand into his waistcoat pocket and produced a 5s tip, an unexpected windfall which was still remembered seventy years later.

If agricultural labourers constituted the largest single group of workers in rural parishes, domestic servants and outdoor staff were second in number, becoming more numerous as the Victorian period advanced. Richard Jefferies commented that many village girls began work as farm servants, where ample food caused their scrawny bodies to fill out and to become plump and comfortable, whilst Flora Thompson described how cottagers' daughters began work in what they called a 'petty place' before graduating to a larger establishment. This practice led Richard Jefferies to complain that farmers' wives had to train clumsy young women, only to have them move as they became useful. Evidence from enumerators' schedules suggest that in the parishes of south-west Hampshire and south-east Wiltshire young men were usually employed as farm servants, since they would have been able to undertake heavier work in the fields or the yard. Furthermore wages for servants employed in this way could be very low, one Landford girl commencing as a scullery maid at Bramshaw Vicarage early in the twentieth century at half a crown a week (£6.50 a year).

Even where there was a big house in a village it did not necessarily employ local residents in any numbers. Broxmore House in Whiteparish had an indoor staff of twelve, but of these only two page boys and an under-housemaid had been recruited from the village. On the other hand domestic service could offer opportunities. The author's great-aunt, Florence Mary Ings, was sent to New House in Redlynch to be trained by Mrs Matcham's maid in the skills required of a lady's maid (a position which young women who would not otherwise have considered service were prepared to accept). Among the tasks which Florence Ings was given was to sew aprons with large pockets, which 'Granny' Matcham would fill with bread which she fed to the horses. Having attained the age of eighteen, Florence found an advertisement in the *Lady* for a lady's maid in Paris, applied for the situation and in 1901 left Newhaven for Dieppe, knowing nothing of France and no word of the language. Arriving at the station in Paris she was met by an Italian groom who spoke English and was taken to her new place of work. Here the mistress was capricious, and whilst she had English maids she also tired of them, dismissing them after a few months and employing others. Finding herself in the French capital without a situation, Florence Ings was undaunted and went on to another post, ultimately spending three years in Paris, where she came to understand French but never to speak it fluently. She then went on to Germany, Switzerland and Ireland, before returning to England in the period immediately preceding the First World War. In Germany she worked for the wife of an aristocrat, and on one occasion encountered Herr Baron who, having good English, asked where she came from. On being told Redlynch, he replied that he knew the village, having been shooting on the New House Estate whilst staying a Broadlands. Florence Ings's employment abroad restricted the opportunities available to her younger sister Nellie. Their parents did not approve of their eldest daughter's travels, and found Nellie a situation with Mrs Robinson at Redlynch House before securing her a place at Hedgerly Park near Reading, where she worked as a scullery maid, recalling towards the end of her long life that she and another scullery maid were not permitted to eat with the other servants but had to take their meals in a room akin to a cupboard beneath the stairs.

Both Florence and Nellie Ings remained in domestic service throughout their working lives (neither married), Florence as a housekeeper (in which capacity she encountered among others Arthur Conan Doyle and H.G. Wells), Nellie as a cook.

Domestic service has come to be seen as demeaning, but to many young women in the nineteenth and early twentieth centuries it offered desirable employment. Evidence of this was provided by the case of Annie Thorne, a single woman of West Tytherley who was committed for trial by Romsey magistrates in September 1903 on a charge of 'unlawfully concealing the birth of her illegitimate male child at West Tytherley on August 30th'.[2] The evidence as reported in the *Romsey Advertiser* contained some bizarre features. The offence had been committed at West Tytherley Rectory, where Annie Thorne had been working as a kitchen maid for two months. The first witness called was Rose Henbest, the cook, who testified that she shared a room with the prisoner and had never heard her admit to her condition. The accused had fainted on the morning of 30 August and struggled to do her work. On Tuesday 1 September Rose Henbest had gone to make Annie Thorne's bed and found the mattress soaked in blood. On the basis of information from another servant, Susan Blake, who evidently lived out, she went to the privy and, looking down it, thought she saw a baby, an impression she sought to confirm by calling the coachman and having him strike a match. She then confronted the accused who admitted, somewhat implausibly, 'The child was born on Saturday night,' adding that she 'woke up and found the child in bed'. Susan Blake was called, and testified that she had elicited from the prisoner the information that the dead infant was in the privy, an admission which she passed

West Tytherley Rectory at about the time that Annie Thorne attempted to dispose of her dead infant in the privy.

on to Rose Henbest. The bench then heard evidence from Dr Cusse of Broughton, who testified that he had examined the prisoner with her consent and, telling her that he believed she had recently given birth, received the reply that she had done so two or three years before. He had returned to the Rectory the next day, and with the coachman retrieved the dead infant from the privy. Washing the body, he conducted a post mortem and established that the child had not been still born. Again confronting Annie Thorne, 'She told him that the baby lay in bed an hour after it was born and that it was dead when she found it. She got out of bed and put it behind her box and that on the Monday morning she put it down the privy.' Dr Cusse then stated that the child might have been born between the sheets and suffocated, or that Annie Thorne might have been unconscious and lain on the infant with the same effect.

Mrs Henry Wood, in the sensational novel *East Lynne*,[3] has one of her characters, the wife of a prosperous provincial solicitor, say that her husband was certain that the vast majority of young women whose infant children died smothered them with the sheets. The Romsey magistrates seemed in 1903 to be accusing Annie Thorne of infanticide, but committed her on a lesser charge because they could not prove the more serious one. The prisoner's own testimony was entirely implausible and suggests panic, whilst the allegations if true would show the lengths to which she would go to remove a burden which could blight her future prospects. The conduct of her fellow servants, who must have known of her condition, indicate that they would have been prepared to abet her in concealing the birth if she had sent the child away (although they could hardly have ignored the actual outcome, and it seems improbable that Rose Henbest was unaware of the confinement until she made Annie Thorne's bed). Notable, too, is the fact that the rector and his wife did not know that their kitchen maid was so near to giving birth. Francis Girdlestone, the rector of Landford, in compiling a list of communicants in the mid-1870s, included one of his maids (whom he clearly knew only by her Christian name) as Emma, and nothing more. The case of Annie Thorne indicates that middle- and upper-class employers were virtually oblivious of their servants, particularly if they only moved from the kitchen to the attic storey and were rarely if ever seen in the family.

Chapter XI
Nonconformity

DISSENT was a significant element in rural society during the Victorian period and in the early twentieth century, and the growing extent to which the activities of nonconformists were reported in sympathetic local newspapers is evidence of their increasing importance as the nineteenth century progressed.

Nonconformity long predated the reign of Victoria, having its origins principally in the English Civil War and the Clarendon Code, a series of Acts passed in the immediate aftermath of the Restoration, which set out to punish the Puritans by excluding them from the Church of England and from public office. Protestant dissenters gained some freedom of worship under the Toleration Act, which rewarded them for supporting William and Mary in the Glorious Revolution of 1688 and permitted them to hold services unhindered, provided that their meeting houses were licensed by a magistrate or the archdeacon or bishop of the diocese. The Act remained in force until 1852, although it was increasingly disregarded in the years preceding its repeal.

The surviving meeting house certificates issued in Wiltshire have been catalogued[1] and show that two-thirds of the licences dated from after 1790. Through much of the eighteenth century the principal nonconformist denominations were the Baptists and Congregationalists, although the greatly increased activity of the dissenters from the end of the century onwards is in part attributable to the Methodist Revival which John and Charles Wesley had begun as a movement to reinvigorate the inert and often lax Anglican Church of their day. Methodism could not be contained within the Church of England, however, and by the close of the eighteenth century it had become a denomination in its own right, going on to be the sole form of nonconformity in many rural parishes.

The close of the eighteenth and the early decades of the nineteenth century saw two other developments which influenced the increase in dissent. One was the effect of the French Revolution and the Revolutionary and Napoleonic Wars, upheavals which encouraged radicalism among the labouring classes, whilst the other was the increase in population and the emergence of self-sufficient squatters who found in nonconformity an expression of social class. Richard Jefferies wrote that the labourers felt a proprietorial interest in the chapel which they had built themselves, which they supported and where they worshipped with their social equals, the squires and tenant farmers attending the parish church.

Initially Methodism in south-east Wiltshire and along the northern boundary of the New Forest took the form of cottage meetings which, whilst they adopted the name of the Connexion[2] (as the denomination is known in Methodist terminology), probably did not have any affiliation with the church itself. In successive months in 1816 cottages in Nomansland and Landford were licensed as Methodist meeting houses, although the congregations which met in the dwellings of James Winter and Samuel Moody both seem to have been short lived, in the latter case because Samuel Moody and Alexander (his eldest son, the besom-maker) moved to the neighbouring hamlet of Hamptworth. Without central organisation and leadership such cottage meetings almost inevitably collapsed, and indeed it was not until the 1830s and 1840s that Methodism began to emerge as an enduring presence in the villages and hamlets along the Forest edge.

This development was due, at least in part, to a schism which occurred in the Methodist Church in the first decade of the nineteenth century. In 1805 a group of Methodists in the Potteries began to hold open air camp meetings which were addressed by a number of speakers. Camp meetings originated in America and were frowned on by the Methodist leadership, who expelled their organisers, with the result that by 1812 a new connexion, the Society of Primitive Methodists, had been formed. The original Methodist Church adopted the surname of the founder, and as Wesleyans remained the largest single branch of Methodism (by 1900 there were seven separate Methodist denominations), the Primitives being the second most numerous connexion.

Wesleyan Methodism drew its support from farmers, local businessmen, shopkeepers and artisans, whilst the Primitives attracted members of the labouring classes. Deriving their name from the last sermon delivered by John Wesley, in which he referred to the practice of the primitive – original – Methodists, they claimed to be following the authentic tradition of the founder, and insisted that all their churches should hold open air meetings once a year. Primitive Methodism was also fervently evangelistic, seeking to establish new congregations or societies. In south-eastern Wiltshire and south-western Hampshire the Wesleyans had chapels in villages where much of the property was in the hands of an estate which provided opportunities for tenant farmers, shopkeepers and artisans, whilst the Primitives established congregations in hamlets where there were large numbers of squatters. At West Wellow, which was substantially owned by the Embley Estate, the property of the family of Florence Nightingale, the Methodist church was Wesleyan, but in the hamlet of Canada Common, which lies within the boundaries of the parish but had a strong sense of being a separate community and was originally settled by squatters, the Methodist congregation was Primitive.

The distinction between Wesleyan and Primitive Methodists is also illustrated by a comparison between the trustees appointed to the Wesleyan chapel at Bramshaw in 1865 and those who took office at Newtown Primitive Methodist Church in 1867. Although the Bramshaw trustees included a shoemaker and a carpenter, they also numbered two brothers, Benjamin and Martin Hoddinott, who were substantial tenant farmers on Lord Palmerston's Broadlands Estate, together with Henry and Samuel Pope, the former having a farm on the Embley Park Estate and the latter occupying Copy Hall, Winsor, on the edge of the New Forest. Among the other trustees were William Newman Petty, a builder from West Wellow whose business was sufficiently well established to allow him to erect Wellow Board School in 1875, and John Prince, a coal and guano merchant, whose premises were in Chervil Street, Romsey, and who had a depot at Romsey station.

Although none of these men was likely to have been a worshipper at Bramshaw Wesleyan Methodist Church, instead representing the local leadership, they did indicate the social standing of the connexion. The Newtown trustees were drawn from the congregation and from artisans and labourers, comprising a small farmer, a bricklayer, a cordwainer, strictly a leather worker but in fact a bootmaker, a general dealer and cordwainer, a thatcher, a carpenter, a builder (Samuel Collins of Awbridge), a house-painter, three labourers, William Moody, the former farm labourer who tradition states was evicted from the Embley estate for becoming a local preacher, and John Wright, the Primitive Methodist minister from Romsey.

The social divide between the Wesleyan and Primitive Methodists led to antagonism between the members of the connexions, which persisted after the union between them in 1932 and has not been entirely forgotten today.

The Wesleyan and Primitive Methodist Churches were organised on a basis which had evolved during the lifetime of John Wesley, with the congregations or societies being grouped in circuits, each with a superintendent minister and, in larger circuits, assistant ministers, who with a body of local preachers took the services in each chapel, each circuit issuing a quarterly plan listing the preachers who would lead the acts of worship on every Sunday in the three month period.

The circumstances in which dissent was introduced to rural parishes along the northern border of the New Forest are almost entirely unrecorded. The Ecclesiastical Census of 1851 had required the representatives of each church, chapel or meeting to provide the date on which their place of worship had been erected, but the vast majority of congregations would have begun meeting in a cottage, and precise details of these initial gatherings did not have to be included.

The Bramshaw Wesleyan Society is known to have built its first chapel in 1839, but nothing is recorded of their activities before that date. The original trustees, unlike their successors in 1865, were resident in the village, although they were representatives of the artisan rather than the labouring classes and included two blacksmiths, James and George Weeks, who were probably father and son – since George was only twenty-two, whilst James was presumably the same Mr Weeks who in 1831, according to the vestry accounts for the Hampshire part of Bramshaw, received 3s 6d for repairing the stocks and a further 1s 6d for providing three locks to secure them.

In *Nomansland, A Village History* H.M. Livens provides an account of the evangelisation of the hamlet by the Primitive Methodists. According to Livens, two strangers came across The Green (whose boundary marked the border between Hampshire and Wiltshire), approaching a man who, with his wife and little daughter, was standing at his cottage gate. The strangers asked for the house of a Mr Boyce, whom, they had been told, would be sympathetic to their cause and, finding that the cottager they had approached was Mr Boyce himself, went on to explain that they had come to Nomansland with the intention of conducting services, a proposition which was greeted with enthusiasm. As a result 'the kitchen of the old thatched cottage was placed at the disposal of the evangelists as occasion required. Thus was the Good News brought into Nomansland by Messrs. Brewer (a travelling preacher from Southampton) and Tutt (the Plaitford Blacksmith) which was destined to direct the feet of not a few into sweeter and worthier ways of life, and to set stars of hope shining in dark and troubled minds.'

Livens wrote that one of the informants who recalled the early days of Primitive Methodism in the hamlet was 'an aged dame, the same with the lass at the garden gate when the preachers came over The Green', who also recalled the construction of the first mud-walled chapel in the settlement, remembering that some of the most unruly youths participated in the erection of the building, yellow clay adhering to their boots after they had puddled it into the walls of the structure. *Nomansland, A Village History* dated the visit of Messrs Brewer and Tutt to about 1848 and the building of the first chapel to 1856. Neither date agrees with the Ecclesiastical Census, which recorded that the chapel was built in 1845, six years before the survey was taken and sufficiently close to the event to be accurate. Yet whilst Livens's chronology is unreliable, the details of his account, allowing for the fallibility of memory, is probably substantially correct. The visit of Messrs Brewer and Tutt must have taken place in the early 1840s, since William Brewer is known to have been serving as a Primitive Methodist minister in the Southampton Circuit at that time. Mr Tutt is presumably John Tutt, whilst the description of William Brewer as a travelling preacher is correct, although it seems likely that Livens was unaware that it was used of ministers and not of lay members. (As recently as the 1990s former Primitive Methodists on the Romsey Circuit spoke of ministers still holding office as travelling, whilst even today a minister approaching retirement asks for 'permission to sit down'.) An oral tradition which was still circulating in the 1970s identified the first members of the Primitive Methodist society in Nomansland as part of the Boyce family, whilst, assuming memory to be accurate, the fact that William Brewer and John Tutt came seeking a Mr Boyce whom they expected to be a sympathiser and probably found him waiting to meet them, suggests that the Primitives had been active in the hamlet before the arrival of the two evangelists.

The efforts of Primitive Methodists to secure converts is evident from the third instruction to preachers printed on a Romsey Primitive Circuit Plan for the Spring Quarter of 1888: 'It is desirable that Preachers planned should stay to Sabbath Prayer Meetings and watch for souls.' Nothing is known of the manner in which the Tutt family came to be active in the connexion, but Plaitford, which, with its large squatter population, should have been fertile ground for Primitive Methodism, in fact saw several invariably unsuccessful attempts to form a congregation. On three occasions, in the 1880s, 1890s and 1920s, services were held in Manor Farm, and in the earlier instances briefly included on the Romsey Primitive Circuit Plan, but in each case the acts of worship were discontinued within a few months. Greater success accompanied an attempt to found a society in Ampfield, a chapel being built in 1895 and continuing in existence until early in the Second World War, whilst the Woodfalls Primitive Methodist Circuit succeeded in establishing what would have been described as a cause at Sherfield English in 1909, the initial services being held in a tent.

Accounts of the manner in which cottage meetings were conducted are only provided by printed sources. According to Livens, the services which began in the summer following the visit of William Brewer and John Tutt were held, as far as possible, in the open air, taking place 'in the lea of [Boyce's] faggot rick on the Green just opposite his gate'. In adverse weather the acts of worship occurred in the kitchen of Boyce's cottage. Outdoor meetings would have been considered more desirable as they offered an opportunity to appear to the wider community. One of Livens's informants, a Mrs Mussell, recalled in 1910, "We had a curious old thing for a pulpit . . . like the seat of a chair with an enormous high back and a board on the top for a book, and my mother would lay a white cloth on it'. Flora Thompson described cottage meetings at some length in *Lark Rise*, writing that a spotless living room was cleared of furniture to make way for long, hard, backless benches with a table in front, on which stood a lamp, a glass of water and a large Bible. A seat for the preacher was placed behind, and if he was late a Sankey and Moody hymn was sung unaccompanied, extempore prayers offered in which the deity was made aware of the least of the intercessors' troubles, whilst on occasions one of the worshippers would give a testimony, confessing to trifling offences as if they were the grossest sins. Yet if their faith was 'simple and crude, [they] brought to it more fervour than was shown by the church congregation, and appeared to obtain more comfort and support from it than the church could give. Their lives were exemplary.' Memory seems to have been in error in at least one detail of Flora Thompson's account, since the different branches of the Methodist Church had their own connexional hymn books. Equally, and as in so many aspects of her narrative, she seems to invest the scenes she describes with a glow of nostalgia which purges late Victorian rural life of some of its harshness. Richard Jefferies, in contrast, described a little cottage room where ten, fifteen or twenty fervent worshippers were packed to suffocation. Livens in his pamphlet described how Boyce's kitchen 'was liable to become so thronged of an evening that the fervent saints could scarcely find air enough to breathe', whilst on a remarkable occasion, as she recalled at the opening of the wooden Mission Hall which she had built in Landford in 1899, Lady Ashburton attended a meeting in one of her tenant's houses at which the windows had to be opened because of the heat, and immediately resolved to build the congregation a place of worship.

Evidence of the preaching in dissenting places of worship is again found either in literature or else is anecdotal. Flora Thompson distinguished between preachers of the word and those who rambled for an hour to no purpose, and between the ill-educated but fervent

Landford Wood Mission Hall, with Landford Wood Farmhouse in the background. The photograph has traditionally been titled 'The Opening', although there is no evidence to support this. Lady Ashburton is believed to be seated seventh from the left, whilst the bearded man in the back row has been tentatively identified as R.W.S. Griffith, the superintendent of the Schultze Gunpowder Works at Eyeworth.

preacher who gained a rough eloquence in holding forth upon the power of the blood and the 'self seeking poseurs' who occupied the pulpit to satisfy their own egotism. Jefferies also recognised the effectiveness of some cottage preachers, describing how a man who had been labouring in the fields during the heat of a summer day 'may be found exhorting a small but fervent congregation in a cottage hard by'.[4]

Yet Jefferies implies that it was not only the Bible which was expounded by the cottage preacher but also *Foxe's Book of Martyrs*: 'Though he can but slowly wade through the book, letter by letter, word by word, he has caught the manner of the ancient writer, and expresses himself in an archaic style not without its effect' whilst 'His congregation approve his discourse with groans and various ejaculations'.

Jefferies remembered having heard a preacher describing, 'in graphic if rude language', how a martyr was dragged to the place of execution along footpaths and over stiles, at each of which the victim was offered his life in return for a recantation but invariably refused and was at last taken to the stake in the middle of a field. Recognising that the episode had some basis in history, Jefferies nonetheless noted that 'the preacher made it quite his own by the vigour and life of the local colouring in which he clothed it, speaking of the green grass, the flowers, the innocent sheep, the faggots and so on, bringing it home to the minds of his audience to whom faggots, grass and sheep were so well known'. The congregation entered into the description, not merely responding with 'groans and ejaculations' but also working themselves 'into a state of intense excitement as the narrative approached its climax, till a continuous moaning formed a deep undertone to the speaker's voice'.

Anecdotal evidence describes the same crude style of preaching. One Primitive Methodist local preacher, active in the Romsey Circuit in the late nineteenth and early twentieth centuries, George Light, a brickmaker from Tytherley, was remembered to have randomly punctuated his sermons with a cry of 'sudden death sudden glory', whilst Percy Hatch, who occasionally attended Bramshaw Wesleyan Church in his boyhood, recalled that at least some of the preachers who occupied the pulpit there were similarly rustic. One speaker had walked to his appointment at Bramshaw, and spontaneously announced to the congregation, 'I did come across the common and they vuzz bushes was blowing and they was lovely' (vuzz being furze or gorse). Another, holding forth upon the Valley of the Shadow of Death, warned his hearers, 'It'll be so dark in they old Valley of the Shadow, there won't be nar a lantern, nar a candle nar any kind of light at all. In fact it'll be so dark in they valley, thee won't see thee's hand in front of thee's veace' (face). 'Nar a', in the now largely extinct dialect of Wessex, meant 'not any', and recalls what was reputed to be the Dorset girl's prayer to St Catherine, asking for assistance in finding a husband: 'Ar a one better than nar a one, St Catherine'.

An indication of the earnestness of many local preachers is provided by the census returns, which from 1861 onwards often give the preacher's voluntary office with his or her occupation. George Hayter, the Whiteparish sawyer, was listed in this way in 1881, whilst Hannah Sillence, the daughter of the (Anglican) parish clerk at Landford was described as a local preacher and washerwoman in 1861, when she was nineteen. As a further indication of her zeal she donated £8 10s 2d to the fund for the building of Landford Primitive Methodist Church in 1867, a very substantial sum from her very small wage which was probably collected in pennies and ha'pennies.

One insight into the mentality of rural nonconformity was provided by Heywood Sumner when he recorded his conversations with the centenarian 'Old Tame', who had been "called away', as he put it, from mowing to hear the Lord summon him beside 'a girt dog's tomb'.[5] Typically he fell back for ten years, returning to his 'old sinful ways' but received a second call when he was in Bramshaw Church. Listening to the parson, and thinking 'I shan't get much good out of ee', he heard the Lord's voice speaking to him out of the wall, 'This is no place for ee', and so he left the church – never to enter an Anglican place of worship again, instead joining the Wesleyans. Heywood Sumner found him tiresomely aware of the wiles of his enemies, and of the way in which, by divine aid, they had been put to confusion. He also recorded that he found the old man writing texts and wrapping them around pebbles, which the children of the keeper at Boldrewood dropped in the road to Minstead and Emery Down. Old Tame argued that someone would read the papers, and that the texts would find their mark just as David's sling stones had in striking down Goliath.

Yet if some Wesleyan preachers were as unpolished as their Primitive counterparts, provision made for them at Bramshaw showed that others enjoyed a greater degree of affluence. At the rear of the chapel are a stall and feeding rack provided for the preacher's pony, whilst a small area of grass near the entrance was the place where, by tradition, he parked his trap. Primitive Methodist preachers usually had to walk to services, with the churches often being at a considerable distance from one another. At one extremity of the Romsey Primitive Circuit were Romsey itself and Newtown, and at the other Sway near Brockenhurst and Wooton in the vicinity of Lymington. Amongst the preachers planned for Wooton and Sway in the spring quarter of 1888 one was from Nomansland, one from West Wellow, two from Cadnam and one from Winsor. To fulfil their commitments any one of these men would have made a round journey of 25 or 30 miles, whilst oral tradition recalls an anonymous preacher who walked from his home village to Sway to conduct two services and lead the prayer meeting which followed evening worship, and then walked back through the night to arrive home in time to feed his team the following morning.

Although the conviction of the Primitive Methodist local preachers is immediately evident, the claim made by H.M. Livens that their efforts led many people in Nomansland into 'sweeter and worthier ways of life' and 'set stars of hope shining in dark and troubled minds' is less easily supported. In *Nomansland, A Village History* an account is given of 'a wild, swaggering fellow, a heavy drinker and cruel to his wife', whose sister had tried, unsuccessfully, to reform him. At length he agreed to sign the pledge if she would do so, and in consequence, and having promised to abstain from strong drink, he 'became quiet in his ways, gentle tempered and obliging'. Having been illiterate, he set out to teach himself to read, sitting at home in the evening 'spelling out a chapter of the Bible word by word and letter by letter'. Livens concluded: 'This humble follower was a happy illustration of how the laborious life of a peasant, saved from fury and confusion may end in the joy of a childlike trust in the all sufficing God.' The entries in the baptismal and burial registers for Bramshaw give a different impression, as do the columns of the local newspapers. The *Salisbury Times* recorded, in one week in 1898, the conviction of Frank Judd of Nomansland, who was fined 10s and costs for trespassing on the Hamptworth Estate to snare rabbits, and the prosecution of a single woman, Martha Tucker, who was summonsed for assaulting her neighbour Kate Bryant, and after contradictory evidence was bound over to keep the peace for six months. The item in the paper concluded, 'Defendant thanked the bench and said she would be pleased to do so.'

One cause that was energetically, although not exclusively, pursued by nonconformists was temperance. The *Salisbury Times* for 25 January 1901, besides reporting the death of Queen Victoria, noted activities in the city which would have aroused the interest of its Free Church readership. The unfavourable response of the Home Secretary[6] to a 'delegation of reformers' who were calling for legislation to reduce the 'drink traffic' by buying up and revoking licences provoked the comment, 'This recent exhibition of Tory opposition in Temperance Reform ought not to discourage campaigners.' In the same edition the newspaper gave an account of the annual meeting of the Wilts Temperance Council, whilst giving a report under the heading 'Temperance Teaching' that indicated one of the principal objectives of the movement, converting the young to their cause: 'Under the auspices of the Salisbury and South Wilts Temperance Association the children attending a number of schools in the city and county have had the evil psychological effects of alcohol pointed out to them by Mr Frank Atkins.'

The activities of the Free Churches reported in other areas of the local press reveal the same preoccupation. On 6 November 1902 the *Romsey Advertiser* gave lengthy coverage to a meeting of the town's Free Church Council, held in the Abbey (Congregational) Hall. Among the speakers was the Rev. F.B. Meyer, who had been elected to Lambeth Borough Council and who argued 'that every publican who put up for election on a town council should be opposed and the same remark applied to a brewer. No publican or brewer should be nominated for the office of deacon in any church but they must have all the officers clear of any complicity in the trade.' A previous speaker at a meeting whose agenda was not primarily concerned with temperance had complained that £186 million was spent annually on drink, whilst only £25 million was expended on religion, with £7 laid out on liquor for every £1 outlay on religion.

Nor was it only in large gatherings that temperance was a major theme; it impinged upon most Free Church events. The Romsey edition of the *Andover Advertiser* reported the West Wellow Primitive Methodist Sunday School Anniversary which was held on Whitsunday 1898, and included a summary of the address given by the Sunday School Superintendent: 'He urged all to rescue the young from the evils of the world, especially from the drink curse.' The desire to rescue the young from the evils of drink was particularly evident in the extent to which the children's temperance society, the Band of Hope, had branches in rural chapels. Yet whilst temperance was such a preoccupation, the evils of drink were found even among nonconformists. Percy Hatch remembered being frightened by William Barter, a builder and Wesleyan Methodist who had been responsible for the construction of the Bramshaw Chapel. He recalled the apprehension he felt when, as a small boy, he had to avoid the builder who was staggering drunkenly from one side of the road to the other and calling for another quart. Reuben Moody, who became the grocer and postmaster in Landford, was also remembered to have consumed excessive quantities of alcohol. The husband of one Primitive Methodist local preacher and the father of another, he was nonetheless the subject of an anecdote which has survived in various forms. In its most colourful version it is claimed that he was alone in the post office with his daughter Jessie, when she, who was upstairs, heard him fire his shotgun in the kitchen. Filled with apprehension, she came down to find the old man standing before the end of the Welsh dresser with a triumphant expression on his face and a great hole in the dresser itself. Turning to his daughter, he announced, 'I did get er,' and on being asked what he had got replied, 'They girt pink mouse.'

Nor did the young regard temperance meetings purely as a source of edification, since they and many other activities held at the chapels also provided amusement. A former member of Newtown Primitive Methodist Church, whose childhood home had overlooked the chapel, remembered watching with eager anticipation the lighting of the lamps on Band of Hope evenings in the winter, as the Band of Hope provided one of the principal recreations of the week.

Indeed, there was an element of entertainment in many nonconformist activities. Most important occasions were accompanied by a tea, whilst the West Wellow Primitive Methodist Sunday School Anniversary in 1898 illustrated the combination of earnestness and amusement which often characterised such occasions. The Whitsunday services were separated by a service of song, which would have used a text published in pamphlet form by a tract society and combining narrative, dialogue and musical items. Such services were presented regularly over several decades, the participants usually being children. On Whit Monday a tea was followed by a meeting at which four local preachers delivered an address together with the circuit minister, and at which the Sunday School superintendent gave a report. Between these items came songs and recitations, whose titles, 'A Bunch of Flowers' and 'Trouble at Amen Corner', suggest that they had a comic as well as an edifying character.

In February 1903 Joseph Griffin and his wife retired as the headmaster and assistant teacher of Plaitford National School. A presentation was made at the school and George Curtis took the chair. A Wesleyan local preacher, he included among his remarks the observation that 'No Free Churchman need fear to send his children to a church school if conducted as the Plaitford School had been'. Education was a contentious issue among nonconformists, since they were often obliged to send their children to National – Church of England – schools, where they feared their offspring would be inculcated with Anglican dogma. This issue came to a head as a result of the 1902 Education Act, which abolished nondenominational School Boards and provided for the support of sectarian schools from the rates. Asked at the meeting of the Romsey Free Church Council for his opinion on the matter, the Rev. F.B. Meyer argued that National and nonconformist British Schools should be self-supporting (there were British Schools at Romsey and at Downton). Other free churchmen adopted a more radical course, and responded by passive resistance, refusing to pay the rates rather than contribute to the support of Church schools. On 4 April 1904 the *Romsey Advertiser* carried a report on the sale of goods belonging to W. and J.W. King, a father and son from Nomansland. Having withheld their rates, they had a sewing machine, table, half a dozen 'small chairs' and two easy chairs sold by Dutch auction. The reaction showed the depth of feeling among dissenters. The goods were offered in two lots at 6s 6d each, purchased by Mr J. Moody of Landford (who was almost certainly John Moody, a farmer and Primitive Methodist local preacher), who would very probably have returned them to their owners. Immediately afterwards a meeting on the Green adopted a motion proposed by the Rev. H. Rose of Cadnam and seconded by John Moody, which denounced the 1902 Education Act, and was followed by a second meeting in Nomansland Primitive Methodist Chapel at which Mr R. Bellamy, Mr W.H. Payne, Mr J.W. King and Mr J. Lampard, who had auctioned the goods, all gave 'stirring addresses' with the Rev. H. Rose in the chair. Mr Rose was the minister at a Cadnam Congregational church, Robert Bellamy was

Nomansland Green from a postcard produced by Barber of Wellow, a local photographer.

a Baptist and a colporteur brought to Fritham by R.W.S. Griffith, the superintendent of the Gunpowder Works at Eyeworth, W.H. Payne was secretary of Fritham Free Church and chief clerk at the Powder Mill, and John Willis King was a Primitive Methodist. The Kings may have been making a gesture of defiance, but it was one which demonstrated the common hostility of nonconformists to the Act.

If many nonconformists viewed the Established Church with suspicion if not hostility, members of the Church of England were equally antipathetic to dissenters, whom they usually viewed with contempt. The Rev. Alan Broderick, the High Anglican Vicar of Bramshaw wrote on the flyleaf of the baptismal register an undated note: 'The cottage lectures were tried and discontinued as having a tendency to lessen the difference between the service of the church and dissent.'

Decades later Percy Hatch surreptitiously attended Bramshaw Wesleyan Church. His father, learning of his truancy from the parish church, thrashed him with a trouser belt. By an irony Albert Hatch, like his father Henry, fell out with the parson of the day, and himself became a regular worshipper at Bramshaw Chapel.

Chapter XII
The Natural Result of the Spread of Education

WHEN Queen Victoria came to the throne in 1837 elementary education in the villages on the north-eastern boundary of the New Forest and beyond was organised on a voluntary and piecemeal basis. In some parishes there were adequate elementary schools but in many the only provision was a dame school, which offered very little instruction even in reading and writing. In 1783 the Rector of Landford, Henry Eyre, had stated in his returns to Bishop Barrington's visitation questionnaire that there was a charity school in his parish for sixteen poor children who were taught reading and working (the same curriculum which Peyton Blackiston had noted as provided at Lymington workhouse school fifty years later). Francis Girdlestone, the rector of Landford from 1871 to 1885, looking back to the early nineteenth century, again commented upon the existence of a dame school in the parish, whilst one small girl from a Methodist family who attended such a school in Awbridge in the middle of the nineteenth century recalled the instruction to have been so limited that she had learned to read by following her Bible during chapel services.

Landowners were, nonetheless, coming to recognise that village children should receive an elementary education, and began to take responsibility for its provision. As early as 1812 George Eyre of Warrens House in Bramshaw had built a school for the boys of the parish, followed in 1819 by a second for the girls. Countess Nelson did the same in Landford in 1842, donating the site for the school, whilst Alan Broderick recorded, on the flyleaf of the Bramshaw baptismal register, that a school had been established in Nomansland in 1865, George Morrison, the owner of the Hamptworth estate being another landowner whom tradition maintains made a site available.[1]

In Bramshaw, Landford and Nomansland the schools were supported by the National Society (who had made a grant to meet the cost of the building at Landford). The National Society, whose full title was the National Society for Promoting the Education of the Poor in the Principles of the Established Church, was an Anglican body. Squires who gave the land on which schools were built expected the pupils to be taught that they should be dutiful members of the Church of England and learn to order themselves lowly and reverently before their betters. (Lady Ashburton, when she founded what was known as Melchet Court School, later Sherfield English School, in 1874, secured the appointment of the evangelical Francis Mowlem as headmaster, and clearly intended that he should seek converts on her Hampshire estate.) The National Society had been founded in 1811, but a year earlier the nonconformist British and Foreign School Society had come into being, establishing British Schools – which were usually located in larger centres of population and attracted the support of dissenters. A British School (attended by the author's great-grandfather, James Ings) was established in what is now the Memorial Hall in Downton, British Schools making a significant contribution to elementary education by adopting the Lancasterian System. This was developed by a Quaker, Joseph Lancaster, and involved the use of monitors, older pupils who taught the younger children under the supervision of a qualified master or mistress. Being inexpensive, it was widely employed by National and other elementary schools.

Although there had been government involvement in elementary education, notably in the introduction of the Revised Code with its limited curriculum and invidious system of payment by results, which was instituted in 1862, it was not until 1870 that Gladstone's first Liberal administration actively promoted the provision of elementary schooling. In that year the Forster Act as it was known, after the Secretary for Education of the day, W.E. Forster, divided the country into School Districts, each with a Board authorised to build schools in parishes where no adequate alternative was available. The Michelmersh School Board was responsible for the erection of schools at Awbridge and West Wellow, both being, like all their counterparts, secular and non-denominational, although a subsequent amendment, the Cowper Temple Clause, allowed the option of teaching Religious Knowledge. (School Boards were the first public bodies to give women the right to vote for and to sit as members.) As most parishes in south-west Hampshire and south-east Wiltshire had National Schools which had been opened before the 1870 Act was passed, Board Schools were only infrequently built – and in Wellow, William Nightingale, the father of Florence and owner of the Embley Estate, provided the site. In some areas, instead of complementing the alternative options, the Board Schools came to rival and ultimately to supersede them, a situation which led Horace Hutchinson and Rose C. de Crespigny (who herself became a manager of Bramshaw Boys' School in 1906) to write in *The New Forest, Its Traditions, Inhabitants and Customs*, 'The old voluntary schools . . . still hold their own in most of the Forest villages, though here and there the board school has supplanted them.'

Rose de Crespigny had become a school manager under the provisions of the 1902 Education Act, which made the County Councils responsible for elementary education, Board Schools becoming Council Schools and National and other voluntary schools receiving support from the rates. It was this which led to opposition from nonconformists.

Yet whilst elementary education was established in most parishes by the middle decades of the nineteenth century (West Wellow Board School had replaced an earlier establishment in unsuitable buildings), and although most village children received at least two or three years' instruction, they were not always amenable to schooling. In her history of Bramshaw School Elizabeth Merson recorded that the original boys' school had been burnt down by its pupils. A converted cart shed with wooden walls and a thatched roof, it was destroyed in about 1850 when a group of boys were putting lighted paper up the chimney and a stray spark ignited the thatch. Percy Hatch, who had known one of the culprits, claimed that the boys were not floating pieces of burning paper up the chimney but were in fact, like Osman, the pupil in the New Forest Union Workhouse School in 1874, burning their books. The schoolmistress, whom Elizabeth Merson identified as Miss Titheridge, evidently had little control over her pupils.

Perhaps significantly, the first schoolmistress at Nomansland was, according to Livens, Miss Mary Tidridge. His account suggests that the headteacher in the hamlet had a thankless task, the older boys throwing stones and bottles at the school door and on occasions breaking windows. The schoolmaster had his gate removed, a post was put in his path to trip him up, or he was 'clotted', pelted with clods or turfs. Indeed, Livens claimed that 'more than one person who had the doubtful privilege of being appointed teacher at Nomansland, had to retire from the post with wandering wits',[2] a claim which probably owed more to bragging than to any actual events. On the other hand Harry Churchill, the headmaster of Landford School from 1859 to 1877, recorded in his log book the undisciplined behaviour of some of his pupils who, amongst other misdemeanours, broke down the school fences and drove two heifers up and down the turnpike road which ran past the building. Desperation was evident in the punishment imposed upon Martin Luther Moody (one of the fourteen children of Reuben Moody and his wife Martha, the stern-faced Primitive Methodist preacher), who was tied to the leg of the headmaster's desk for swearing.

Harry Churchill with pupils probably of the Upper Standards, photographed outside Landford National School in the early 1870s. The picture is one of several which otherwise show the church or the major houses in the village and were included in a loose-leaf journal kept by successive Rectors of Landford.

John Newey, Harry Churchill's successor, imposed discipline by the vigorous use of the cane, and since he left Landford in 1890 to become the first male headteacher at Nomansland and was still in office in 1910 when Livens wrote his pamphlet, having presumably subdued his unruly pupils by the same methods that he had used in his previous post, the claim that several masters at Nomansland School went out of their minds seems all the more implausible.

Flora Thompson in *Lark Rise* wrote of the experiences of one schoolmistress, Matilda Annie Higgs, whose too liberal approach to her pupils led to a collapse in discipline and her early departure.

On 2 June 1906 the headmaster of Bramshaw Boys' School, Reginald Bowditch, proposed the toast 'The Army, Navy and Reserve Forces' at the annual luncheon for the men of the Bramshaw branch of the Hampshire Friendly Society, the chairman, the Rev. J.W. Godden, the vicar of the parish adding that 'they were very pleased to welcome Mr Bowditch for the first time. He did valuable work . . . educating the children in a very interesting way. He was pleased to think the children were taking great interest in his instruction, and he was sure the parents of the parish would do their best to back him up. (applause).'[3] Reginald

Bowditch had been appointed headmaster in the preceding year, with his mother as assistant teacher. His predecessor, who had occupied the position for thirty-three years, had been an autocrat, and the vicar's comment that the children were now being taught in a very interesting way suggests that the new headmaster employed far more advanced methods. At the same time the parson's hope that the parents would give him their support suggested an element of uncertainty, which proved to be justified. *Once There was a Village School* records that two young men from Bramshaw were brought before the magistrates in August 1907 and bound over to keep the peace after they had assaulted Reginald Bowditch. The headmaster, who was an enthusiastic amateur boxer, had evidently responded in kind as 'one of the defendants was badly knocked about'. Elizabeth Merson includes an extract from a letter written by the Rev. John Godden to Mary Eyre, the wife of Briscoe Eyre, the squire in October 1907, indicating that Reginald Bowditch had taken to carrying a revolver and would not give it up. His resignation followed the next year.

Yet despite the difficulties which were encountered by teachers and although, according to Flora Thompson in *Lark Rise*, parents fell into two camps, those who regarded anything more than the most basic schooling as superfluous and those who welcomed elementary education as a means of advancement, teaching in village schools was not without effect. Levels of literacy are difficult to establish, although one indication is given by the marriage registers, the bride, bridegroom and two witnesses having to sign each entry or at least make a mark. In Bramshaw, between 1837 and 1865, 391 individuals signed the register whilst 111 made a mark. Between 1866 and 1888, the year in which a mark was made in the register for the last time, there were 239 signatures and 20 crosses. Thus in the first half of Victoria's reign just over a fifth of the individuals whose names were found in the registers did not sign the entry, whilst in the third quarter it was only one in twelve. The proportion of signatures in the Bramshaw marriage registers is high. In Plaitford between 1837 and 1865, 148 individuals were married or witnessed a marriage, 87 signed their names and 71, only a little under half, made a mark. On the other hand between 1867 (there were no weddings in 1866) and 1888 there were thirty-eight marriages and at all but three of these the bride, bridegroom and witnesses all signed their names (the bride and bridegroom at one wedding in 1867 and one of the witnesses in each of two others in 1871 being the exceptions).

At St John's Church, Lockerley, 380 individuals were married or witnessed a marriage between 1843 and 1868, and of these 106 men and 104 women made a mark in the register, whilst 70 women and exactly 100 men signed the appropriate entry. When in 1831 Moses Pearce, one of the co-owners of the allotment leased to the trustees of Newton Primitive Methodist Church, married Anne Finch, who was fourteen (the law then permitted girls to marry at twelve and boys at fourteen) in the presence of Jesse Finch and Sarah Landon, only the bridegroom signed his name, but when in 1855 Moses Pearce's eldest daughter, Mary, married George Moody, the bride alone made a mark.

Such evidence has to be approached with caution, however: entries in a marriage register indicate that individuals could sign their names but nothing more, whereas literature suggests that literate members of the labouring classes would in certain circumstances make a mark rather than a signature. In *Bleak House* Esther Summerson, convalescing in rural Lincolnshire after a bout of smallpox, goes into the parish church at the close of a marriage service to see a girl who had been one of the most adept pupils at the village school place a mark in succession to her new husband and then explain, 'He's a dear good fellow, miss, but he can't write yet – he's going to learn of me – and I wouldn't shame him for the world.' Flora Thompson, recalling her childhood in the 1880s, noted that many cottagers had a sufficient level of literacy to meet their needs but some, who could sign their names, made a cross on a document because they felt abashed to be seen to do otherwise.

In Plaitford the entries in the marriage register list only labourers and artisans (although the proportion of labourers declined significantly as the century progressed), whereas in Bramshaw some of the signatures in the register were made by individuals who had been fully educated, among them Mark Cooper's daughter, Emma Caroline, who married a military surgeon in 1855. Yet despite these qualifications, and although an examination of the registers in only three parishes can hardly permit any conclusions to be drawn, it does indicate that there had been a substantial increase in literacy in the final third of the nineteenth century. Evidence of the effect of the growth of elementary education and the ever greater numbers of villagers who could read and write is found in a number of sources. In 1862 John Wise included in *The New Forest, Its History and Scenery* a chapter headed 'Folklore and provincialisms'. What Wise called provincialisms were in fact dialect words and phrases whilst, writing of the folklore of the Forest, he remarked, 'No one is so superstitious, because no one is so ignorant as the West Saxon,' and went on to list a number of folk remedies and traditions which he claimed were current in his day. At the same time he argued that a belief in sprites and fairies, in St Swithun's power to control the weather or that the man in the moon had been banished there for stealing firewood in the Forest would not be openly admitted. 'But I do say that these superstitions are all, with more or less credit held in different parts of the Forest, although even many who believe them the firmest would shrink, from fear of ridicule, to confess the fact. Education has done something to remove them; but they have too firm a hold to be easily uprooted.'

Wise also noted that old women of the Forest went 'gooding' on St Thomas Day (21 December), and children would beg for food and drink (shroving) on Ash Wednesday. Richard Jefferies recorded the practice of 'gooding' in north Wiltshire during the next decade, but de Crespigny and Hutchinson wrote that this activity, together with shroving, had been abandoned by 1899, whilst they commented that although Wise claimed that fairies and the sprites, Puck and Lawrence, who in the one instance misled the forester and in the other made him idle, were still part of current belief in 1862, this was far from being the case at the end of the century: 'You are but laughed at if you ask for them.'

In the same way, and whilst acknowledging that many 'provincialisms' survived in 1899, the two authors claimed that a large number had dropped out of the foresters' vocabulary. They noted a saying, mentioned in *The New Forest, Its History and Scenery*, 'Eat your own side speckle band' – which applied to greedy people, and referred to a story of a girl who shared her breakfast with a snake and reproved him in this way for taking too much. De Crespigny and Hutchinson made the comment, 'One has heard it but it is scarcely known now.' They attributed the decline of the dialect to the growth of schooling. 'This is the natural result enough of the spread of education and increased communication.'

One means of communication which increased through the Victorian period and did so because of the spread of education was the postal service. The penny post had been introduced in 1840 and the growth of rural post offices and the increasing range of services which they offered, even if only as an adjunct to another business or premises, could not have taken place if villagers had not been literate enough to engage in correspondence.

Another source of opinion and information which expanded with the rise of literacy was the local press. In *Hodge and His Masters* Richard Jefferies wrote of what he called 'the old newspaper', which was bought by every farmer and carefully studied by each member of his family who could find references to topics which aroused their interest, whilst 'The squire, the clergyman, the lawyer, the tenant farmer, the wayside inn keeper stick to the old weekly paper, and nothing can shake it. It is one of the institutions of agriculture.' According to Jefferies, the editors of such publications would receive advertisements and notices from bailiffs, keepers, farmers, auctioneers and solicitors' clerks. Clergymen would come to the office with news of 'a cottage flower show, a penny reading, a confirmation or some such event', and tenant farmers studied the editorials which both reflected and influenced their opinions. Jefferies concluded that, 'These old established papers, in fact, represent property. They are the organs of all who possess lands, houses, stock, produce; in short of the middle class.'

The labourers did not buy the newspaper but encountered it in the public house, where they would read it or, if illiterate, hear its contents discussed by those who were not; whilst by the time that *Hodge and His Masters* was written at the end of the 1870s the situations vacant column had become important to farm workers. 'The carter and the shepherd look down the column . . . as they call at the village inn for a glass of ale or if they cannot read ask someone to read it for them.'

The *Salisbury Journal*, which had commenced publication in 1729, was an example of the kind of local newspaper which Jefferies was describing, and the material it included in its columns tended to reflect the bias of its readership. Yet whilst Jefferies suggested that the weekly paper was so secure in its position that any attempt to establish a rival was bound to fail, the abolition of stamp duty on newspapers in 1861, which coincided with the increasing level of literacy, meant that new titles did emerge, catering for a different, more popular readership. The *Salisbury Times* which first appeared in 1868 was an example of such a newspaper, whilst the publication of the Romsey edition of the *Andover Advertiser* at the very end of the nineteenth century and its transformation into the *Romsey Advertiser* in 1901 was a reflection of a similar trend.

The *Salisbury Journal* was closely printed during the Victorian period in a very small type, and with an austere style which was reflected even in its advertisements, whilst the *Salisbury Times* appeared in larger print and with advertisements which were illustrated with line drawings and had a lighter touch. Typical amongst these was one promoting the products of a Salisbury tobacconist, 'Support Local Industry by Smoking Steven's Shag', the same long S forming the initial letter of the last three words, whilst Elias Baker, a magic lanternist, whose premises were in Fisherton Street in Salisbury, included an elaborate drawing of a lantern with two lenses in his lengthy advertisement. The reportage in the newspapers also differed, the editions which appeared after the death of Queen Victoria illustrating this. The *Salisbury Journal* which was circulated on 26 January 1901 appeared with every column surrounded by a black border. Its editorial, which was headed 'The Queen', began in a literary style, with a quotation from Tennyson, and wrote exclusively of the deceased monarch, although not without introducing a comment on the war in South Africa (which the paper claimed to have 'hastened her end') and delivering side thrusts at 'the mistakes her ministers and people made' and the nation's 'greed for gain and lust for revenge', whilst patriotically supporting the war itself. At the same time the newspaper carried such items as the results of the Archbishop's Examination for Admission to Christian [i.e. Anglican] Teacher Training Colleges and an account of the second of three lectures on 'The Continuity of the Church' given in St Edmund's Schoolroom by the Rev. W.H. Dawson, 'who at the commencement of his remarks made a feeling allusion to the death of the Queen'.

The *Salisbury Times* which appeared on 25 January also carried a leading article on the Queen's death, and one which claimed that the nation was stricken with grief, although 'there are some consolations in our grief for the end came like a celestial benediction on a beauteous life'. The *Times*, however, reported on temperance meetings and on Mr H.C. Messer's 'capital' exhibition of 'photos, cameras etc.'. (Horace Messer was a Salisbury photographer, and his exhibition was in the United Free Methodist Church in Milford Street). The paper also carried an account of the Wesley Guild Meeting at Church Street Wesleyan on 19 January which had taken as its subject 'Economy'. Another Guild Meeting, advertised as taking place on 25 January, was to be a lecture by Mr Theodore Brown 'on the work of our comic draughtsmen, supplemented by lightning sketches of political celebrities'. Whether Mr Brown's lecture took place or not is unrecorded but it may have been postponed, since the *Salisbury Times* noted on 1 February that 'the nation is still mourning the Queen consequently engagements have been few'. The leader on 1 February was headed 'Education in Sarum' and complained, 'It is a sign of decadence rather than of progress, that the subject of education ceases to be engrossingly interesting.'

Both the *Journal* and the *Times* reported on the services conducted in the city churches, although the *Journal* covered the acts of worship at the Cathedral, St Thomas's, St Martin's, St Mark's, St Mary Magdelene Mission Church in Gigant Street (which was attached to St Mark's), St Edmund's and St Osmund's (Catholic) Church, including extracts from the sermons delivered by their clergy, whilst services conducted in the city's free churches were dismissed in seven lines, with only Salisbury Baptist Church, where the pastor, the Rev. A.J. Edwards 'payed an eloquent tribute', being specifically mentioned. The *Salisbury Times*, by contrast, printed a lengthy account of the Bishop, John Wordsworth's, sermon in the Cathedral and of the address given by the evangelical Vicar of St Paul's, Edgar Nembhard Thwaites, who two years earlier had taken the chair at the inaugural meeting at Lady Ashburton's Mission

Hall in Landford, but otherwise and apart from St Mary Magdalene's Mission printed reports from Fisherton Primitive Methodist, Salisbury Baptist, the United Free Methodist, Church Street Wesleyan and St Osmund's Churches.

The *Salisbury Times* had identified a new readership distinct from the middle-class subscribers to the *Salisbury Journal*, made up of small businessmen, artisans and others who were literate, leaned towards nonconformity and had a very active interest in the temperance movement and in education – many free churchmen seeing schooling as a means of advancement.

Yet whilst the *Salisbury Times* was aware of the potential new readership, its reporting of local issues was largely concerned with activities and events which took place in the city. The *Romsey Advertiser*, in contrast, found its readers in rural areas. In 1904 it proclaimed that it circulated in Romsey and fourteen of the surrounding villages, although it printed reports from numerous others and by 1906 had extended the area in which it was distributed to the northern boundary of the New Forest, with Cadnam, Copythorne, Winsor, Brook, Bramshaw, Fritham, Nomansland and Bartley among the twenty-five villages and hamlets listed at the head of the first page. The paper, like its Salisbury counterparts, was printed with black borders around the pages as it reported the death of Queen Victoria but also noted, albeit briefly, the memorial services held in the outlying villages. In one instance it recorded that 'The news of the Queen's death was received at West Wellow at about ten o'clock on Tuesday night. The knell at the church was tolled also the next morning and evening. On Monday there will be a special service at the Mission Room, Canada and also at other places of worship in the district.'[4]

News of significant events reached rural communities without the local newspaper, although it often came by word of mouth and with exaggeration and rumour and publications such as the *Advertiser* must have supplied additional details which would otherwise have been unknown. Weekly papers also reported events abroad. During 1904 and 1905 the readers of the *Romsey Advertiser* were able to follow the course of the Russo-Japanese War in a series of lengthy articles. Whilst items from across the country were described in a column headed 'General News', it is, however, the page which covered events in the paper's catchment area which is perhaps the most significant in illustrating the increase in literacy. The regular reporting of nonconformist and particularly Primitive Methodist activities is especially revealing. Accounts of Sunday School anniversaries printed the names of children who took part, and descriptions of camp meetings listed the speakers (one at Nomansland in 1898 being followed by a 'fellowship meeting' where 'earnest testimony, prayer and praise were indulged in for three hours'). A report of a public tea and service held in the same chapel after the Romsey Circuit Quarterly Meeting included a summary of a sermon by the superintendent minister on the means of gaining converts, which contained a number of aphorisms including 'Kindness and charity which thinketh no evil should be evinced even in exposing the sinfulness of others' and 'The man who exposes your sins is your friend not your enemy'.

Primitive Methodism, drawing its support from the labouring classes, had many members who earlier in the century would have been illiterate or at best only able to read haltingly, and it is noticeable that whilst the trustees who were responsible for chapel buildings and the Quarterly Meeting of the principal officers of the circuit both elected secretaries, it was the minister who (in the Romsey Primitive Circuit at least) took the minutes. By the late 1890s a local newspaper could assume that part of its readership would not only be interested in accounts of Primitive Methodist activities and their participants but could also read several inches of closely printed type describing them.

The *Romsey Advertiser* provided another indication that the ability to read and write had increased among the labouring classes, since by the early years of the twentieth century it was printing serialised stories. In January 1904, as an instance, 'Of Royal Blood, A Story of the Secret Service' was appearing in weekly instalments, whilst readers were informed that on 5 February 'will be commenced in this Paper a Powerful romance by Esther Miller entitled "What was HER SIN?"'. Esther Miller has long been forgotten and the stories which the *Advertiser* was serialising had no enduring literary merit, but they did demand fluency in reading and that their probably principally women readers should have some leisure time.

Elementary schooling was not the only source of education in rural communities during Victoria's reign and in the earlier twentieth century. Talks and lectures were given in rural as well as urban communities. The Band of Hope gave talks to children, Mr A. Jolliffe, the area secretary, who came from Portsmouth, frequently addressing the pupils at village schools on subjects such as 'The Action of Alcohol on the Human System'. These talks had a very narrow range of subjects, but the temperance movement recognised the value of a medium which had first appeared in the middle of the nineteenth century and achieved widespread popularity by its close, the magic lantern. The Band of Hope had its own extensive collection of magic lantern slides. Some titles suggest that they were purely propagandist. 'An Evening at the Gin Palace' being typical, but others, whilst extolling the virtues of temperance by illustrating the lives of national figures such as W.E. Gladstone or General Gordon (the latter was the subject of a lantern lecture by Mr Jolliffe given at Fritham Free Church in 1909), or the heroic work of groups like the lifeboatmen, did offer some instruction.

Nor was it only bodies such as the Band of Hope which appreciated the value of the magic lantern. At the turn of the twentieth century Elias Baker's advertisement in the *Salisbury Times* began 'Lectures and Entertainments, Magic Lantern' and 'offered 20,000 slides to select from, Religious, Temperance, Educational and Amusing'. A lanternist like Elias Baker may have supplied the slide series shown at Lockerley in January 1901 by the Rev. H. Creighton of King's Somborne, a 'lantern lecture on the Boer War in the schoolroom. The attendance was very good, the subject well treated and the audience appreciative.'

In 1874 Richard Jefferies had written of the reading-room that 'it has been tried but usually fails to attract the purely agricultural labourer. The shoemaker, the tailor, the village post master, grocer and such people may use it; also a few of the better educated young labourers, the rising generation; but not the full-grown labourer with a wife and family and cottage. It does good undoubtedly; in the future, as education extends, it will become a place of resort.'[5] Jefferies was defending the public house when he wrote these words, arguing that it was a labourer's only source of recreation. Reading rooms, which as their name implies contained shelves of books, providing a place where they could be read and where members could meet, had little value to labourers who were at best barely literate. His comment about the rooms' future importance was prescient. In 1898 the Romsey edition of the *Andover Advertiser*, under the heading 'A Grand Gift', recorded that 'a large and enthusiastic meeting' with the vicar in the chair heard that Mr Archibald Coates of Embley Park was planning to erect a Reading Room and Institute in West Wellow. The building was to 'be capable of accommodating over 200 persons with partitions for reading room, library, games & c, a bar for coffee, cocoa and tea and apartments for a caretaker'. The meeting, according to the newspaper, heartily thanked the munificent Mr Coates, and elected a managing committee before closing with 'ringing cheers' for the benefactor. The reading room, which was to serve as a village hall for decades and had amongst its other amenities a three-seater privy, was built quickly and opened in October without, according to the *Andover Advertiser*, any formalities. The newspaper commented: 'It is an innovation that will no doubt prove welcome to the villagers during the long winter evenings, proving not only a means of recreation but also of instruction; providing literature that is not only light, to be read and thought no more of but that which must stimulate a certain amount of mental effort and appeal to the intelligence and understanding.' The reading room was meant to be morally improving as well as educational, the bar for coffee, cocoa and tea clearly being intended to counteract the influence of the public house. The same was true of the much smaller reading room in Nomansland, built in 1910 with H.M. Livens (whose pamphlet was published in order to raise funds for the project) as one of its principal instigators. Despite Livens's claim that Primitive Methodism had been a means of bringing sweetness and light to the hamlet, the behaviour of the members left much to be desired, to the extent that a notice had to be posted warning that anyone gambling, using obscenities or consuming alcoholic liquor on the premises would have their membership suspended.

The Wellow Reading Room was clearly intended to be used for other public functions, and even the Reading Room at Nomansland which had very restricted space was the venue for courses for adults which were sponsored by the county council. One was a 'butter school', although exactly what this would have entailed is not clear.

As the nineteenth century drew to its close, evening classes became increasingly widespread in rural communities, allowing those who attended to acquire an education extending beyond the limited curriculum available at elementary schools. Scattered references to these classes were made in the local press, among them night schools held on Lady Ashburton's estate at Melchet Court. The subjects offered were not recorded, but they are remembered to have been attended by the older youths, to have been conducted by the headmaster of Sherfield English National School and to have received the patronage of Lady Ashburton herself and of her son in law, Lord Northampton.

Other activities which were intended to improve techniques in horticulture and which enjoyed the patronage of the gentry were flower and produce shows. One, a 'Cottage Garden Show', as the *Romsey Advertiser* described it, was held by the Whiteparish Horticultural Society in the grounds of Melchet Court in August 1903. The Society drew its support not only from Whiteparish and its accompanying hamlets Cowesfield and Broxmore but also from Melchet, Sherfield English, Landford, Earldoms, Hamptworth, Plaitford and Wellow, whilst vice-presidents included Lord Nelson, Mrs Crossley of Landford House, and Mrs Wigram of Landford Lodge. Mr Hall, the head gardener at Melchet Court, arranged a display in the show tent whilst the judges were Mr Thirlby, the head gardener at Broadlands, and Jimmy Budd from Lockerley Hall. Classes for both flowers and vegetables were available, with begonias, dahlias of various types, asters, gladioli and sweet peas being shown. The season had been unfavourable, and dahlias (which thrive in wet conditions) were the feature of the day, although the fact that half hardy annuals were being exhibited rather than cottage garden flowers was an indication that the fashion for bedding out which had been taken up by the big country houses from the middle of the nineteenth century had now reached the cottage. The vegetables too included varieties which were not traditionally associated with the cottage garden, whilst honey was also judged. Mr R. Bungay of Wellow showed a section from one of his hives, which aroused considerable interest amongst the visitors.

(Henry Bungay remembered that his father, George, had kept bees and that he and his younger brother, Hubert, had annoyed them by throwing stones at the hive. He recalled how his father had lain in wait behind a hedge when the two boys were tormenting the bees, and sprang out to catch and belabour them with his trouser belt.)

The Whiteparish Horticultural Society was nonetheless aware of social distinctions. Section one of its show contained open classes, whilst section two was for day labourers only. Nor was the event confined to exhibiting garden flowers and produce. 'The Whiteparish Brass Band was in attendance and played a number of selections. In an adjoining field were roundabouts, swinging boats, shooting galleries, coconut shies, Aunt Sallies and other forms of amusement and as there was dancing in the evening the public had no difficulty in passing a pleasant time.'

Melchet Court from an F.G.O. Stuart postcard franked August 1904, showing the Pleasure Grounds with displays of carpet bedding.

The 'magnificent hall' at Melchet Court had been the scene of another event in 1898, which offered its audience an opportunity to hear classical music.[6] The occasion was a concert 'under the immediate patronage of Lady Ashburton' with the object of providing 'funds for prizes for scholars attending the Melchet evening schools'. The programme was largely made up of popular ballads, Alfred Gay singing 'The Death of Nelson' and a comic song, 'Doom, Doom, Doom'. 'The story as unfolded by Mr Gay caused rounds of merriment and had to be repeated.' Francis Mowlam, the headmaster of Sherfield English School who had arranged the concert, showed due deference, expressing 'the great disappointment he and he was also sure the audience also felt at the inability of Lady Ashburton and Lord Northampton to be present'. If the audience was disappointed to be denied the presence of their aristocratic patrons, it is to be wondered how they received 'The pianoforte solos, "Bridal Procession" (Grieg) and "In A Troika" (Tchaikowski)' which were given by Miss Alice Ivemy. Miss Ivemy, who came from Southampton, was evidently one of the performers whose contributions were of a very high order (there is evidence that some amateur musicians of the day were close in standard to professionals), but it is probable that the large audience preferred 'Doom, Doom, Doom' and 'Jarge's Wedding' to salon pieces by leading composers.

Chapter XIII
Mobility

THE opening years of the reign of Queen Victoria coincided with the final flowering of the coaching era. South-eastern Wiltshire and south-western Hampshire were not crossed by any of the great coaching roads, but the route from Southampton to Salisbury and from Salisbury to Bristol and Bath nonetheless saw regular coach traffic, with forty coaches a week running between Salisbury and Southampton and back in 1839 and forty-one from Salisbury to Bristol.[1] Among these was the 'Red Rover', which gave its name to a public house in the parish of West Wellow that was situated beside the turnpike road along which the coach passed. The Red Rover was never more than a village inn, however, and The Shoe at Plaitford played a more significant role in the coaching period. Equidistant from Salisbury and Southampton, it was ideally placed to serve as a posting station where coaches could change horses for the next stage of their journey, and the inn was substantially enlarged and a coach house and stables built for the purpose.

Henry Bungay recalled in old age having been told that Queen Victoria had once stopped at The Shoe and taken a glass of milk, although he doubted whether this was true. Another fuller, and perhaps more authentic, version of the tradition was included in a publication which appeared in 1998 and drew upon an item in a West Wellow parish magazine which had been published in 1903.[2] In this the vicar of the day, the Rev. G.C. Elton, noted the death of one of his oldest parishioners, Mrs Harriet Alsop. Harriet Alsop had been born at The Shoe in 1816, the daughter of the landlord, James Cocks, and remembered that the then Princess Victoria and her mother, the Duchess of Kent, had once taken tea at the inn whilst their horses were changed. The anecdote suggests that in the early decades of the nineteenth century the road was still of some importance, but evidence from enumerators' schedules and other sources shows the decline of the tavern as a posting house and consequently of the coaching trade which supported it. In 1841 James Cocks was a widower living with a single daughter (several of his children had already predeceased him, and the headstones which mark their graves in Plaitford churchyard are perhaps indicative of the inn's prosperity). He employed an ostler, to attend to the horses, and four male and three female servants. The more comprehensive return of 1851 showed him to have been both an innkeeper and a farmer of 63 acres with four labourers. He was continuing to employ an ostler (his nephew) together with a housekeeper and a twelve-year-old servant girl. The resident staff also included a seventy-year-old gardener (the produce perhaps being sent to Salisbury or Southampton for sale) and two agricultural labourers, who were described as servants, with another four who were lodgers, the distinction between the lodgers and servants being unclear.

In 1861 James Cocks was still innkeeper and farmer at The Shoe, although his staff had declined to five and he appears to have been in failing health, since his employees included a sick nurse, a seventy-three-year-old widow named Elizabeth Hutchings. Of the remainder one was his niece Maria Cocks, who was his housekeeper, another was a cook and a third a thirteen-year-old girl, whom the enumerator described as 'waitress, inn servant'. The presence of a cook and a waitress suggests that there must still have been some passing trade, as does that of a 'horsekeeper', seventy-one-year-old William Smith. The number of agricultural labourers had diminished to one, Michael Hood, who had been amongst the lodgers ten years earlier.

James Cocks died in 1863, and a tablet commemorating both him and his long-deceased wife Margaret, was erected in St Peter's Church, Plaitford. His successor, Sam Edwards, had by 1871 only one employee, a fifteen-year-old cow-boy, whilst in 1881 he had none – although his two eldest daughters, Rhoda who was twenty-one and Bessy aged sixteen, were still living with their parents and may have assisted with the trade of the inn.

There is no evidence from census returns to suggest that horses were kept at The Shoe or that meals were regularly served there after 1861, but FSHE, in the poem 'A Forest Hamlet', included three stanzas about the inn, the second of which reads:

> In olden times 'The Shoe' has thrived,
> Before the railway was contrived,
> When landlord Edwards owned the steed,
> That ran the mails with rapid speed.

FSHE's memory did not extend to James Cocks, whilst the London and South Western Railway had reached Salisbury in 1847, sixteen years before Sam Edwards became landlord of The Shoe. On the other hand

*A Barber postcard of the Shoe Inn and the former Sarum to Eling turnpike road
(now the A36) in the opening decade of the twentieth century.*

the allusion to his owning 'the steed, that ran the mails with rapid
speed' is perhaps significant. The development of the railway network
westwards was long interrupted after 1847, and it was not until 1856 that
a line connecting Salisbury with Warminster and therefore with Bristol
was opened, although this ran on the GWR's broad gauge track. In the
following year a direct line from Salisbury to London via Andover was
completed, and in 1859 this was followed by a railway to Yeovil which
would ultimately extend to Exeter. The broad gauge line to Bristol was
converted to the standard narrow gauge in 1874, but it would seem likely
that the coaching trade along the Southampton to Salisbury and Bristol
road persisted into the 1860s, even though it has left no evidence in the
census.

The coach house and stables at The Shoe were still standing in
the early twentieth century, although they had long ceased to fulfil their
earlier function. Marian Harding remembered that in her childhood
the rooms which had once been occupied by the stablemen (who had
probably combined the position with that of agricultural labourers)
accommodated an elderly widow, Mrs Harrison, who worked as a
seamstress and had made two best frocks for the young Marian Curtis
and her elder sister Dorothy.

The road along which the Red Rover and other coaches ran
between Salisbury and Southampton and beyond was a branch of the

Sarum to Eling turnpike. Turnpike roads had their origins in the second half of the seventeenth century, but their heyday coincided with that of the stagecoach. Turnpike trusts were initially established by individual Acts of Parliament, although the procedure was facilitated by a General Turnpike Act in 1775. Trusts were allotted sections of road for a period of twenty-one years (although this was usually extended). They were required to maintain them, and in return and in order to meet the cost were permitted to put up barriers, usually in the form of a bar which was supposed to resemble an infantryman's pike – hence the name. The bar was accompanied by a cottage for the toll-keeper, who was responsible for collecting the fee payable by each vehicle or traveller on horseback, the toll varying according to the mode of conveyance and with separate charges for herds or flocks of livestock.

The Sarum to Eling Turnpike was constructed in the 1750s and had three branches. The principal one ran from Lopcombe Corner in Winterslow to Salisbury and then on to Redbridge on the outskirts of Southampton, with secondary branches from Landford to Totton (which like Redbridge was then in the parish of Eling) via Bramshaw, Cadnam and Netley Marsh, and from Whiteparish to a point 4 miles beyond Romsey.

Turnpikes were unpopular, and traditions exist of farmers taking detours to avoid gates, although local traffic and vehicles travelling to or from church or funerals were usually exempt from tolls. At the same time honest and efficient trusts, and the Sarum to Eling turnpike was among these, went to considerable lengths to ensure that the highway for which they were responsible was well constructed and maintained in good order. One of the last turnpike trusts to be constituted took responsibility for the route from Cadnam (where it formed a junction with the Sarum to Eling Turnpike) to Fordingbridge in 1832. The lengthy stretches of straight road and the ditches on either side still indicate the way in which the turnpike was built. Turnpike trusts and toll roads declined with the coaching trade, and there is evidence which suggests that the Sarum to Eling Trust had abandoned its branch roads before it was finally dissolved in 1871. The main route was still in use in 1863 when the Honourable Henry Nelson, the son of the Dowager Countess Nelson, paid his toll to Martha Moody (the wife of Reuben Moody, the future grocer and postmaster in Landford), who was keeping the gate at Earldoms and who was the last person to speak to him before he was fatally injured falling from his horse. On the other hand, whilst Harry Churchill, the headmaster of Landford School, noted in October 1863 that pupils playing around the toll bar, which with a toll-keeper's cottage was situated beside the school, would be subject to punishment,[3] neither the census return of 1851 nor that of 1861 show a resident toll-keeper, so the gate may have been left unmanned even though the toll-house continued to be occupied (the school closed for a fortnight in 1867 because five children who lived there were suffering from scarlet fever).

The impact of the railway on the life and activities of the cottagers living in proximity to the northern boundary of the Forest is difficult to judge. The London and South Western Railway line, which ran from Salisbury to Southampton, passed through Romsey, Dean and Dunbridge, whilst a branch line which was begun in 1864 when Countess Nelson of Trafalgar House (the daughter-in-law of the Dowager Countess and sister-in-law of Henry Nelson) cut the first sod, ran from Downton to West Moors and was ultimately extended to Bournemouth. Countess Nelson also opened the station at Downton in December 1866, although there is little memory of regular rail travel by villagers. The author's great-aunt Florence Mary Ings' recollections included a Sunday School outing to Bournemouth which must have taken place in the early 1890s and entailed a journey by rail. She recalled that the superintendent, engaging in horseplay, chased one of the young women teachers into the sea, where a pink stain began to appear on her white skirt as the dye from her red flannel petticoat ran in the salt water. Other memories suggest that Sunday School treats were usually less ambitious, involving a trip into the New Forest on a horse-drawn wagon with a picnic tea or games or a tea and games in a field near the chapel. W.H. Hudson wrote in *A Shepherd's Life* in 1910 of the number of people travelling to Salisbury on market days. These included 'Hundreds and hundreds . . . coming by train, you see them pouring down Fisherton Street in a continuous procession, all hurrying marketwards', although how many of the railway passengers came from villages and hamlets situated at a distance from the stations at Dean, Tisbury, Downton and Breamore can only be a matter of speculation. Far more significant in terms of journeys from the villages to the towns was the carrier's wagon. Hudson also described cycling into Salisbury on a fine market day and overtaking 'the early carrier's carts on the road, each with its little cargo of packages and women with baskets and an old man or two', together with 'the half gypsy, little "general dealer" in his dirty, ramshackle little cart, drawn by a rough, fast travelling pony'. In Salisbury itself Hudson saw 'The carriers' carts drawn up in rows on rows – carriers from a hundred little villages on the Bourne, the Avon, the Wylye, the Nadder, the Ebble and from all over the Plain each bringing its contingent'.

The 1903 edition of Kelly's County Directory for Wiltshire listed ninety-seven villages served by carriers, and whilst Hudson wrote only of the villages of the river valleys and the plain, Kelly included those who came from the south of the city, among them Boyce of Nomansland, who left the William IV at 3.00pm on Tuesdays and Saturdays and Herrington and Webb from Redlynch, the former departing from the Wheatsheaf on Tuesdays, Thursdays and Saturdays and the latter from the William IV on the same days, both leaving at 4.00pm. Carriers from the parishes on the south-eastern border of the county also travelled to Romsey, the destination of Mrs Giles, the Landford carrier. Remembered for wearing a coal scuttle bonnet when such headgear had long passed out of fashion, her meandering journey to the town could take six hours, often involving detours to drop passengers or deliver parcels of groceries which had been ordered by different cottagers and she had purchased on their behalf, conveying at the same time items of news and gossip from along her route.

Evelyn Hart, the daughter of a middle-class Salisbury family, who was born in 1892 and later became deputy headmistress of South Wilts Grammar School, wrote in her memoir *Before I Forget*, which she completed immediately before her death in 1983, of a journey to Stapleford by carrier's van which she undertook at the age of about five. The van had wooden benches for passengers on either side and an overhead rack for parcels. Evelyn Hart sat over a block of ice, which began to melt and form a puddle beneath her feet, and she remembered the expression on the faces of a fat woman and her son as they glanced at the water on the floor. She also noted that the men stepped out of the vehicle when it went uphill to lighten the load, whilst shoes were fitted to the wheels to slow its progress on the declines.

The carrier's wagon endured long after the demise of the stagecoach (although coaches survived in remote areas until the end of the century), but by the time of Evelyn Hart's journey to Stapleford other modes of transport were beginning to emerge. The bicycle had developed during the latter part of the nineteenth century with the introduction of pneumatic tyres (although on roads surfaced with flints these were susceptible to punctures) and gears. Many cycling clubs with their own uniforms were established, whilst bicycles were cheap enough to be widely available as a mode of conveyance.

At the same time as the bicycle was becoming common, another form of transportation which would ultimately contribute to the transformation of rural society was beginning to emerge. The 1903 edition of Kelly's Directory for Wiltshire included in its commercial section an entry for 'Logan E.J., Cycle and Motor Engineers, Fisherton St'. The motor car was starting to appear on the roads, although it was greeted with a surprisingly unfavourable reaction even amongst some of the well-to-do.

A choir supper held at Nether Wallop at the very turn of the twentieth century included among the songs and recitations which followed the meal an evidently comic song, 'The Motor Car', whilst on 17 April 1903 the *Romsey Advertiser* printed a letter from Samuel Page of Wimborne who complained, after cycling from Wimborne to Romsey on Easter Sunday and following a route through the New Forest, that whilst he had enjoyed his expedition, 'for the cyclist such rides are fast losing their charm owing to the fast increasing number of motors we now meet on our roads'. Samuel Page had ridden from Wimborne to Ringwood on empty roads, but proceeding to Romsey via Picket Post and Stoney Cross had met no fewer than nine motor cars: 'These cars were without exception travelling (I have no hesitation in saying) not less than twenty-five miles an hour. Without exception they were monopolising the whole of the road.' One coming at speed around a bend in a narrow road near Ower forced him to drop, with his bike, into the ditch to avoid a 'smash up'. He counted himself fortunate to be riding only 2 feet from the left-hand verge. He went on to complain that 'The road through the Forest which was a most enjoyable ride, these motorists have rendered almost impassable for a cyclist, the speed at which they travel, scattering as it does, all the dust from the roads and sending it in clouds over the fields and hedges, leaving only the sharp grit to cut our tyres and worry the cyclist'. Despite this, he concluded that the motor car was 'one of the best inventions of late years when sensibly controlled'.

A few weeks previously the *Romsey Advertiser* had printed an item with the heading 'Landford' and sub-heading 'A Motor Car Case', which reported an action in the King's Bench Division brought by Mrs Crossley of Landford House and Mr and Miss Furse against the Imperial Motor and Cycle Works, whom they accused of failing to stop a motor car in accordance with the regulations issued by the Local Government Board. The case, in which each party accused the other of negligence, illustrated the antagonism felt in some quarters to the new mode of conveyance. The incident which led to the action had occurred to the south of Bramshaw church. On 16 April 1902 Mrs Crossley was driving a wagonette and pair of horses with two companions. They encountered a car being driven by a 'servant' of the Imperial Motor and Cycle Works, who owned the vehicle. According to Mrs Crossley the car made the horses restive, so she raised her hand (in accordance with the Local Government Board's ruling) to tell the driver that he must stop. He ignored the warning, the horses became uncontrollable, snapped the traces and bolted. The three occupants of the wagonette were thrown out and Mrs Crossley broke two ribs and suffered severe bruising. As a result she claimed £355 in damages for the depreciation in value of the horses, the repairs to the carriage and the cost of a trip to Switzerland on the advice of her doctor.

The Imperial Motor and Cycle Works responded by saying that it was not they who were negligent but Mrs Crossley, 'who was driving a pair of spirited horses, which she handled so unskilfully that in attempting to turn them they ran into a hedge', the harness broke and the animals bolted, the car and the wagonette coming no nearer to one another than 40 yards. The jury were evidently unimpressed by Mrs Crossley's arguments, found that neither party was negligent and awarded damages of £20 to Mr and Miss Furse.

The local press continued to print reports of often quite minor road accidents, but in February 1911 they covered, at considerable length, the first fatality involving a motor car on the road from Salisbury to Southampton, and in doing so indicated how unfamiliar motoring was to much of the public. The victim of the accident was a student at Salisbury Theological College, William Coope Walke, the son of a former Vicar of Redlynch, Nicholas Piccolo Walke, whom Florence Ings remembered to have been an eccentric who rode a pony which he charged into any knot of boys that he saw. The Rev. Nicholas Walke had died at the end of the nineteenth century and his son was living in Cornwall at the time of his death. He was the passenger in a car driven by Douglas Bunbury Sullivan, who had studied at the same theological college for two years. According to evidence given at the inquest (the jury included J.W. Harding, the future father-in-law of Marian Harding), Annie Jane Hawksworth, the wife of a school attendance officer, had cycled from Southampton to Plantation Road, West Wellow, to visit a friend and had just started out on her homeward journey at about 5.15pm when, on turning into the main highway, she saw an approaching motor car and took action to avoid it. The driver in turn swerved and the car went out of control, smashing a pillar box and hitting a telegraph pole. William Walke was thrown out of his seat and hit his head with such force that he was killed instantly. Douglas Sullivan claimed that he had lost control of the vehicle because a tyre burst, but much of the evidence was taken in an effort to establish the speed at which the car had been travelling. Mrs Hawkesworth was called and gave a lengthy account of her part in the accident, which concluded when she replied to a juror that the car was exceeding the speed limit of 20 miles per hour.

William Mansbridge, a labourer from Wellow, saw the car pass from his cottage gate and claimed that it was travelling at 60 miles per hour. He had remarked to his wife, 'That car will be in Salisbury in fifteen minutes if there is no obstacles in the way' and that 'nothing could get out of its way in safety'. Motor cars were so infrequent that he remembered seeing the vehicle going in the opposite direction earlier in the afternoon. Asked if he had any experience in estimating the speed of motor cars he replied, 'Well a few years ago I was on the railway and I have been on an engine when I have travelled the rate of 60 miles an hour. That is the estimation I gave and I consider the car was travelling as fast if not faster.'

Other witnesses testified to the same effect. George Pointer, a coal merchant, also claimed that the car was travelling at 60 or 70 miles per hour. He too was asked if he had any experience on which to base his judgement: 'Well I don't know that I have sir, but I have never seen one go as fast as this one did.' 'And I suppose you see a good many pass the road don't you?'. 'Yes Sir.'

William Macintosh, 'a gentleman' from Chatmohr, a property in East Wellow, was summoned because he had been the owner and driver of motor cars for some years, and having seen the one which was damaged in the accident could give an account of the position of the controls. He estimated that the vehicle could reach a speed of 50 or 60 miles per hour but was probably at half that speed at the time of the crash. Another witness, Albert Mitchell of Mitchell Brothers, a garage in Romsey, finally stated that the car's top speed would have been 40 or 50 miles per hour under favourable conditions.

The jury retired for fifteen minutes before giving their verdict. The 'Romsey Advertiser' recorded the foreman's pronouncement: 'We find Mr Walke's death was caused by extensive fractures to the skull, and that Mr Sullivan was driving at the time at a speed exceeding twenty miles an hour.' The coroner replied, 'And that of course will amount to a verdict of manslaughter.' On the strength of this Superintendent Littlewood of the Romsey Police arrested Douglas Sullivan, although in the event charges were dropped and he never stood trial.

The impact of the accident is apparent from the lengthy reports in the local papers, and from the erection of a wooden cross placed at the scene of the fatality and provided by the people of Wellow. (A tablet was also placed in the chancel of St Mary's Church, Redlynch, although this made no reference to the motor accident.) With the positioning of the cross folklore comes into play, for tradition claims that flowers were placed at its foot by an unseen hand who was presumed to be William Walke's fiancée. Similar claims were made for Airman's Cross, the monument to the victims of the first fatal crash involving members of the Royal Flying Corps, and for other sites, including the grave of T.E. Lawrence at Moreton in Dorset.

Yet despite hostility and fatal accidents the advance of the motor car was inexorable. The 1903 edition of Kelly's Directory for Wiltshire which had listed E.J. Logan as a cycle and motor engineer also included an entry listing Burden Brothers of the Canal, Salisbury, as motor manufacturers. Burdens, who had been watchmakers, went on to make the Scout motor car, and by 1906 were advertising their vehicles in the Romsey newspaper. The advertisement, which was severely plain, largely comprised a testimonial from W.W. Ord, a Salisbury doctor who had purchased a Scout motor in November 1905, which had given every satisfaction: 'The car runs very quietly especially on the top speed, in which it can climb most of the hills about here. For the first 1,000 miles the petrol consumption worked out at 22½ miles per gallon, which, considering that the engine had not been run at all previous to delivery, seems to me very good.'

With the increasing numbers of motor vehicles, outlets for petrol also increased. By 1914 E. Dunning of Cadnam on the north-western boundary of the New Forest was advertising as a 'Cycle Manufacturer and Motor Engineer' and was able to supply tins of 'Motor Spirit', whilst his bill-head showed an open-topped car with a party of passengers, women prominent amongst them. Dunnings nonetheless described themselves as agents for 'Royal Enfield, Fleet, Star, Gloria, Sunbeam etc' – all of whom were cycle manufacturers.

Edward Thomas, writing of his cycle ride from London to the Quantocks at Easter 1913, passed through Salisbury on a Sunday morning when the city was virtually empty, but he recalled his previous visit on a wet Tuesday evening and in doing so described the variety of vehicles, pedestrians and animals travelling to outlying parishes. The market was over:

> . . . clergy with wives and daughters were cycling out past a wagon for Downton drawn by horses with red and blue plumelets; motor cyclists were tearing in, a tramp or two trudged down towards the bridge. In the city itself the cattle were being driven to the slaughter house or out to the country, a spotted calf was prancing on the pavement, one was departing for Wilton in a crowded motor bus, a wet, new born one stood in a cart with its mother, a cow with udders wagging was being hustled up the Exeter Road by motor cars and pursued at a distance by a man who called to it affectionately as a last resource; another calf was being held outside a pub whilst the farmer drank; black and white pigs were steered cautiously past plate glass; and in the market place Sidney Herbert and Henry Fawcett on their pedestals were looking out over the dark wet square at the last drovers and men in gaiters leaving it, and ordinary passengers crossing it and a few sheep still bleating in a pen.

In this passage Edward Thomas was approaching the small output of poetry on which his reputation now largely rests, but he was, for all that, capturing a point at which long-standing modes of transport, represented by the farm wagon in the traditional Wiltshire colours of red and blue and the animals being driven through the streets, were juxtaposed with motor-cycles and cars. This juxtaposition was perhaps most clearly evident in the calf being taken to Wilton on a crowded motor bus.

The Scout Motor Company ultimately failed. Producing individual cars to order, it was unable to adapt to mass production, suffered a set-back when much of its machinery was requisitioned during the First World War and sent to France, and never resumed full production after the close of hostilities, finally going into voluntary liquidation in 1921. The progress of motor transport went on nonetheless. The streets of Salisbury were surfaced with tar in 1908, whilst the road from Salisbury to Southampton was treated in the same way in 1917 to accommodate the progress of military vehicles from the Plain to one of the main ports of embarkation to France. By the 1920s the Co-op bakery at Downton was making deliveries by Model T Ford van. The Victorian era, which had begun with the stagecoach and saw the advance of the railway network, was followed by the emergence of motor vehicles – which would substantially contribute to the demise of a rural society whose roots lay deep in the past.

Chapter XIV
Transition

IN January 1901 the Rev. Edgar Thwaites, the Vicar of St Paul's, Salisbury, addressed his congregation on the death of Queen Victoria, telling them that 'The Golden Age is past, the greatest woman in the world is gone, the Victorian era is past.' Victoria had been on the throne for sixty-three years, and only the oldest of her subjects could remember the period before her accession. The final decades of the reign had seen her become an object of reverence, perceived to be the embodiment of the values of the nation. As a result her death was greeted with a sense of loss which was apparent from the extent to which the population went into mourning. At the same time there is evidence from many sources that the period from the 1880s onward witnessed an increasing awareness that society and the world were changing in ways which led to a sense of unease, an awareness which seems to be evident in the words of the Vicar of St Paul's.

The first forty years of the Victorian period had been seen as an epoch of largely uninterrupted progress. Britain had been the foremost industrial power, acquiring immense wealth through the policy of free trade which had allowed the passage of goods in and out of the country without restriction, the empire had extended over vast tracts of the globe creating markets and providing raw materials, whilst the Royal Navy made the nation and its interests virtually unassailable. By the close of the nineteenth century these advantages were slipping away. The United States and Germany had exceeded Britain in industrial output and whilst they could, thanks to Free Trade, export their products to British markets without paying tariffs, they imposed heavy duties on goods imported into their own countries. The struggle to overcome the Boer irregulars, and in particular the successive defeats during 'Black Week' in December 1899, had exposed significant military weaknesses, whilst Germany was building a fleet which was seen as a threat to Britain's maritime supremacy. How far these concerns were noted in cottage homes is uncertain, but there is evidence that change was also being felt in rural society.

Thomas Hardy believed that he was witnessing the passing of the ancient order on the land – a sense which also sent composers and musicians, some of whom were or would become very eminent, to visit workhouses and elsewhere in search of folksongs only remembered by the oldest inmates. Flora Thompson wrote at the close of *Lark Rise* that hamlet dwellers came to see Queen Victoria's Golden Jubilee as a watershed, 'before the Jubilee' being said in the same spirit that 'before the war' would be in the 1920s, whilst even at a very local level FSHE suggested in 'A Forest Hamlet' that the passing of the generation during which Sam Edwards had been landlord of The Shoe in Plaitford had marked the close of an era. The fifth stanza of the poem read:

> Ah joins the church in sacred ground
> Beneath whose surface, sleeping sound,
> Faces we can call to mind
> We look only there to find.

The twelfth verse opened with the couplet, 'Fresh faces crowd the olden spot; | The old ones wane and soon forgot.'

Although very little is known of FSHE (tradition ascribes the initials to a woman who lived in London but was a frequent visitor to Plaitford), it is evident that she had first known the village in the later 1860s or 1870s and was writing in the 1890s, a period during which the rural population had both declined and changed in character. In 1871 there had been fifty-six households in Plaitford and 220 inhabitants. A decade later there were forty-one households and the number of inhabitants had decreased to 171. This drop in population occurred earlier than in many parishes in the vicinity and the fact that Plaitford's population fell at least a decade before those in other parishes is significant. A limited geographical area and a high proportion of inhabitants subsisting on the wages earned from casual labour, the sale of produce and other erratic sources of income made the village especially vulnerable to the effects of depression, and the cottage unfit for habitation which George Bungay rented from the rector and churchwardens is evidence of the departure of families from mud-walled dwellings which were left abandoned and derelict. (Flora Thompson attributed the abandonment of Sally and Dick's cottage in *Lark Rise* in part to a falling population.)

Another indication of the declining population of rural communities is provided by the Romsey Primitive Methodist Circuit Schedules which have survived from the years 1879 to 1889. Primitive Methodist congregations, which were for the most part drawn from the labouring classes and were particularly active in communities where there were a large number of residents dependent upon casual employment, were also susceptible to the effects of depression. The Circuit Schedules printed forms which asked a series of set questions, included a query about attendances at Sunday services. The figures provided seem in the larger congregations at least to have been estimated, and at the latter end of the ten years from 1879 begin to show a noticeable decrease. In 1882 the number attending Newtown Primitive Methodist Church was 120 but by 1889 it was 90, whilst the population of Lockerley was 608 in 1891 but by 1901 had declined to 531. Although no schedules survive from after 1889 it would appear that the drop in attendance at the Primitive Methodist chapel reflected a corresponding decline in the labouring population of the district. (In 1891 Awbridge had a population of 394 and in 1901 it was 301.) The turn of the twentieth century marked the lowest point in the number of inhabitants in both Lockerley and Awbridge. Between 1901 and 1911 the census showed a rise of thirty in the number living in the former and sixty-nine in the latter community, and as the occupants of mud-walled dwellings began to disappear from rural parishes another class of residents started to emerge there.

The name Canada Common is explained by at least two traditions, one suggesting that it was settled by inhabitants who had intended to emigrate but reached no further than West Wellow and another claiming that it was first described in this way because one of its earliest residents, Thomas Bennett, had lived for a time in Ontario. Neither seems particularly plausible, but the furthest end of the hamlet appears to have been settled by squatters whilst the lower part was sold by its owners George and James Penford (who had bought it for timber, which they had cleared) and purchased as building plots. The houses which were constructed were significantly different from the mud-walled dwellings erected by squatters, being brick-built villas with a more suburban character and with occupants typified by Thomas Bennett, who had a modest private income and could live in a manner which contrasted with that of the cottagers. The difference between the squatters and the newer inhabitants is illustrated by the presence of the Primitive Methodist chapel on the common itself, which was erected in 1867 and rebuilt in 1908, and the Anglican Mission Room, which had been built to provide Church of England services for the residents who found the distance to the parish church in East Wellow inconvenient. The Mission Room dated from 1884 but was substantially extended in 1889 by the Wesleyan Methodist builder William Newman Petty. The villas in Plantation Road, Canada Common, had their equivalent in other parishes. Marian Harding's grandfather, George Kendal, who had been employed on the travelling post office, the railway carriages adapted for the sorting of mail on the line from Waterloo to Exeter, retired to Landford where he bought a tract of glebe land on the common in 1895. Worthless for agriculture, it was regarded as a foolhardy purchase by the villagers but proved to be a worthwhile speculation, since it provided the site for several substantial houses which were let to a variety of tenants.

Further evidence of the changing character of rural communities is provided by Mrs Annie Jane Hawkesworth, the school inspector's wife whose bicycle was a contributing factor in the first fatal motor accident on the road from Salisbury to Southampton. She would have been regarded as a member of the lower middle classes and was living in Freemantle in Southampton, but had cycled to visit a friend, who would presumably have belonged to a similar social stratum, in Plantation Road. By 1911 the urban middle class was established in outlying rural parishes.

The labourers who left the land went in two directions. Many moved into the towns, and an examination of the enumerators' schedules for Southampton suburbs such as Shirley shows a high incidence of residents whose birthplace was in the country; whilst others went further afield, emigrating to Canada, Australia and New Zealand. The Romsey Primitive Methodist Circuit Schedules for 1889 included a note deeply regretting the need to report a decrease in members at the Newtown Chapel, but adding that 'this decrease is accounted for by thirteen credentialed removals[1] eight of whom including three local preachers went to West Queensland'.

By the turn of the twentieth century almost every edition of the *Romsey Advertiser* contained one or more advertisements offering colonial leases or freeholds to suitable applicants. In 1903 one such stated that the Canadian Farmers' Delegates were visiting Hampshire and inviting 'successful agriculturalists' to write to the Commissioner of Emigration for free particulars. The upper part of the insertion showed a pastoral scene with a sheaf of corn and a signpost pointing 'To Golden Canada', a board with the slogan '160 acre farms in Western Canada Free' printed on it, and in heavy type the heading 'Free Farms! No More Rent For Farmers'. In the same year another advertisement was placed by the Agent General for New Zealand, whose offices were next door to those of the Canadian Commissioner for Emigration. More specific in its details than the promise of free farms in Western Canada, it offered 2 million acres of farmland which could be leased for 990 years on easy terms or bought freehold, with assurances of a congenial climate, the lowest death rate on the globe and ideal conditions for rearing livestock and for arable farming ('highest return per acre in the world'). The advertisment was illustrated by drawings, with captions such as '80,000 acres of wheat, South Canterbury'. All of this was accessible through a reduced rate passage scheme.

In 1911 the States of Australia advertised for emigrants in the Romsey paper, appealing for farmers, agricultural labourers and domestic servants (with the offer of a free passage for a farmer's wife and family and for domestic servants if they were travelling to Queensland). In Tasmania there was the promise of a temperate climate and cheap living, for 'fruit growing, mining &c'.

The success of such advertising is shown by the names of men on village war memorials who served with the Anzacs and the Canadian Corps in the First World War, evidently having emigrated and returned with the colonial forces. Yet as the Australian advertisement indicates many emigrants found work in areas other than agriculture. Henry Bungay emigrated on the *Tortona* in 1911 and was employed in a foundry (volunteering for service with the Canadian forces in 1914, he was rejected for having flat feet), whilst an item printed in the *Romsey Advertiser* in May 1913 wrote of a fatal accident to an emigrant from the borders of West Wellow and Sherfield English. Frank Loader, who was twenty-eight, had only left for Canada the preceding September, and was working in the yard of the Grand Trunk Railway in Hamilton, Ontario, on New Year's Day 1913 when he was struck by a switching engine, which rolled him along the track and caused fatal injuries. News of his death had evidently reached his family but the details of the accident only became known with the arrival of the Canadian papers. (It is unclear who received these but the fact that they should have been taken and studied is evidence of the numbers who had emigrated and the interest which was felt in the colonies to which they had gone.)[2] The death of Frank Loader had an added poignancy since he was to have been married on 18 January: 'His fiancée is heart broken over the unfortunate affair and cannot be comforted.' She was 'Miss Bungay of Plaitford, who had previously journeyed to Canada for the purpose of being married, a feature which makes the fatality all the more sad'.

If the number and the character of the inhabitants of rural parishes were changing in the early twentieth century, the rapid developments in society at large were beginning to impinge upon rural communities. On Friday 6 May 1910 Edward VII died, and the next edition of the *Romsey Advertiser* appeared with black borders to every column. Some of the formalities which had been observed on the death of Queen Victoria were repeated. In Romsey itself flags were at half-mast, 'outfitters and drapers' showed 'windows of mourning apparel', and the Dead March from *Saul* was played at every church service although the organist at the Abbey, in a departure, also played Chopin's 'Funeral March' and the bells rang a muffled peal. At the same time there was evidence of the changes which were taking place in society. News of the King's death had reached the town early on Saturday morning, although it was only 'a few of the principal inhabitants' who had learned of the event at that time; for most residents 'it was left for one glance at the morning's paper posters to learn what had happened'. This detail is significant. The popular press had begun to emerge at the end of the nineteenth and beginning of the twentieth centuries. The *Daily Mail,* the first mass-circulation newspaper, began publication in 1896, whilst the *Daily Mirror* followed in 1903. It was probably the posters for publications such as these which made the people of Romsey aware of the King's demise (as they were later remembered to have been the means by which some members of the public learned that war had been declared in 1914).

The *Romsey Advertiser* gave considerable coverage to the response to the King's death in the town, but only recorded the reaction in two villages, Nursling and Mottisfont, where the knell was tolled at St Andrew's Church as soon as the news was received on Saturday morning (and it was heard in outlying parishes as soon as in Romsey), whilst the bells were muffled on the next day. It was, however, the rector's sermon which suggests that anxiety about the international situation was increasing, as he commented on Edward VII's role as a peacemaker: 'It was a peacemaker that the King would go down in history. He taught something new in the art of peace making. He left marks along the road for those who shall succeed him.' The vicar at Romsey Abbey took up the same theme in his address at the Sunday morning service: 'I would say that his name will go down in the annals of history as that of the greatest peacemaker of his own or almost any other time. These last nine years have witnessed an extraordinary improvement in our relations with every one of our national rivals. Edward VII of England has been called, with justice, "the corner stone of the peace of Europe".' The emphatic way in which the clergy impressed upon their congregations the extent to which the King had secured the peace in Europe suggests that they sensed that peace to be precarious.

The speed with which the news of Edward's death reached Romsey (and the end had come at 11.45pm) was indicative of the way in which communications were becoming increasingly rapid, and another story which the *Romsey Advertiser* covered in some detail illustrated the same development. During July 1910 the paper included reports on what it called 'The Cellar Crime' and the pursuit of its perpetrator, Hawley Harvey Crippen, and the woman with whom he had eloped, Ethel le Neve. Describing the events which led up to the arrest of Crippen, the newspaper followed the voyage of the *Laurentic* carrying Inspector Dew as he travelled to Canada to apprehend his prisoner, who with Ethel le Neve was trying to escape on the *Montrose*. Under the heading 'The Race Across the Ocean', the *Advertiser*, which must have acquired its material from a press agency, described how the *Laurentic* was drawing close to the *Montrose* and how the ships would be parallel, although 400 miles apart by the following day. The report continued: 'If necessary the "*Laurentic's*" course will be altered to enable Inspector Dew to speak by wireless with the "*Montrose*".' Wireless, which was a very recent innovation, was already permitting ships to communicate with one another and with the shore, and much of the interest in Crippen's case arose from the use which was made of it in securing the arrest.

Another more local means of communication was by the early twentieth century becoming increasingly widespread even in the rural parishes of south-west Hampshire and south-east Wiltshire. Dr Scallon, giving evidence at the inquest into the death of George Bungay as a result of a fall from a rick in 1912, stated that he had been summoned to attend the deceased both by telegraph and by telephone. It is not clear whose telephone was used to call the doctor. Landford had no exchange until the 1920s and before that lines were routed through Ower. The telegraph had been available in the village post office since the mid-1890s, but the phone, like the motor car, was the preserve of the affluent. Indeed, so unfamiliar was it and such was the suspicion which it aroused that the *Romsey Advertiser* gave an account in April 1912 of a bizarre experiment conducted at the instigation of the Post Master General by Dr Spitta, the bacteriologist to the King. This investigation was intended to establish whether tuberculosis could be transmitted on telephone receivers and involved Dr Spitta in examining telephones from what was described as a 'busy call office in London' which had not been specifically cleaned but proved to be free of the tuberculosis bacillus. The experiment then continued with an examination of telephones fitted in the wards of a sanatorium and used exclusively by consumptives at various stages of the disease. These too had been neither cleaned nor disinfected, and were again found to be free of infection. The report concluded by stating 'that the transmission of tuberculosis through the medium of the telephone mouthpiece is virtually impossible', adding reassuringly that 'These results are supported by other independent inquiries.'

Another innovation which, whilst it did not affect the lives of the villagers, was nonetheless attracting the attention of the local press was aviation. In the early years of the twentieth century airships aroused as much interest as aeroplanes. In October 1910 the *Romsey Advertiser* reported the flight of a young Welsh aeronaut, Mr E. Willows, who had established a British record for an airship by travelling 150 miles from

Cardiff to London in ten hours. In a detail which reflected the changing character of transport and with it the infrequency of motor cars, the newspaper report recorded that 'crossing the Bristol Channel, he sighted at Clevedon, an illuminated motor car, in which were his father and two mechanics. This was to act as his guide.' The twenty-one-year-old aviator lost sight of the car, though, and had to navigate by the lights of the towns over which he passed. Finally reaching London and attempting to land in the grounds of the Crystal Palace, he ran out of petrol and drifted across the capital until a gardener caught the rope and brought the airship down.

Airships briefly entered the experience of part of the population of Plaitford, Wellow and Sherfield English when in 1910 the military airship *Beta* made a forced landing near the boundaries of the three parishes, attracting a substantial crowd – among whom was Marian Harding's mother Ruth Curtis.

It is impossible to tell whether the readers of the *Romsey Advertiser* took news of aviation seriously, although it is hardy conceivable that they should have foreseen its future development. Whilst, if the response of the Romsey newspaper is accurate, there was universal grief at the death of Edward VII, it was 1912 which saw the event that caused the greatest impact both in the town and in the surrounding countryside. On Sunday 14 April 1912 the liner *Titanic* struck an iceberg and sank, and on the following Friday the *Romsey Advertiser* contained the first of a succession of reports describing the vessel's loss, the local reaction and the public enquiry into the disaster. The fact that lengthy articles dealing with the disaster were still being printed well into May was indicative of the impression it created. The long initial report, which again clearly derived its contents from press agency accounts, contained subheadings such as 'Hours of Heart Breaking Anguish, Struggle in the Darkness', 'S.O.S. the signal of Peril' (which had replaced the previous radio signal CQD, and was used by the ship's wireless operator) and 'Millionaire's Liner: 120,000 Capital Represented'. The article began with a summary of events and then continued: 'From the fact that most of the survivors are women and children, it is to be deduced that a noble heroism worthy of the best traditions of the sea was shown by those on board.' This is a view of the catastrophe which has tended to be taken ever since, although the 'List of Notable People on Board' which was subdivided into 'Among the Saved' and 'Among the Missing' included a large number of men in the former category, a reflection of the confusion which clearly prevailed at the time of the sinking and in its subsequent reporting.

The following week's edition of the *Advertiser* carried accounts of the local reaction to the disaster, beginning with a long account of the preaching at the town churches under the heading 'Pathetic Pulpit References at Romsey'. The vicar at the Abbey commented, in remarks which reflected the changing spirit of the age, 'The full details of the appalling night were withheld from us and he confessed he was one of those who hoped that they would never be made known. The morbid sensational appeal to that modern love of horror seemed to him quite the worst and most vulgar feature of present day journalism.' The vicar instead chose to make a theological point, claiming that those who had gone down with the ship should be seen 'as beginning to live, free from the limitations, intellectual, spiritual and moral that bound and clogged and weighed us down on earth' and now, having passed through the veil, 'would be face to face and know as they were known and sight and knowledge would bring them light and radiancy of life'. The Rev. Albert Bage, the minister at the Abbey Congregational Church, also used the disaster to make religious and moral points, arguing that in the ship's final moments there was no distinction between wealth and poverty (a claim which was without foundation: the great majority of survivors were from the first-class cabins), and that it was an indication that men and women should lead a life of faith and not rely upon a last minute conversion.

The pastor at the Baptist church also remarked that in such a crisis there was no distinction between classes or ranks (the equality of all men before God being a significant tenet in nonconformity) and used the opportunity to warn his congregation to be ready, for they knew not the day and the hour. The services at the Weslyan and Primitive Methodist churches were addressed by local preachers, and although they contained 'sympathetic allusions' to the disaster they were each dismissed in two or three sentences.

In the country churches memorial services were held for the victims of the sinking, and collections were taken for the Mayor of Southampton's appeal for those suffering distress because of the loss of the liner – while 'Nearer My God to Thee' was sung at most acts of worship. In one rural parish the disaster made a particular impact. In St Peter's Church, Bramshaw, a tablet commemorates seven young men from the village who went down with the ship. Five were from the hamlet of Fritham, and a plaque in the Free Church records their association with that place. Three were brothers, Lewis, Leonard and Stanley Hickman, who were sons of Herbert and Augusta Hickman, the postmistress. Tradition in the village claims that Lewis Hickman had emigrated to Canada and married. Returning home for a visit and leaving his wife behind, he persuaded two of his younger brothers to join him, all three taking steerage passage in the ill-fated liner with the result that they were all lost. An alternative and perhaps more plausible account suggests that Lewis Hickman had married in England and was going to Canada ahead of his bride, his younger brothers accompanying him; he was taking his wedding presents to help furnish their new home and these too were lost in the Atlantic. Leonard Hickman's body was reputedly recovered from the sea, but he was confused with his eldest brother whose overcoat he was wearing.

Much of the account of the sinking of the *Titanic* is surrounded with myth and confusion, and local accounts of involvement in the disaster have the same quality. Oral tradition claims that Briscoe Eyre paid the passage money of the victims whilst at least three separate accounts have been collected that refer to individuals or families who were to emigrate on the doomed liner but were prevented by unforeseen circumstances. Whatever the truth of these claims, the years immediately preceding 1914 were marked by increasingly accelerating change and with it an evident sense of apprehension. The great liner sailing towards the iceberg which was to send it and so many of its crew and passengers to the bottom seems to have aroused the anxieties which were increasingly being felt in society and the local community. The ill-fated ship seems to epitomise the old order, which was drifting towards a catastrophe of unprecedented magnitude and horror, and the Vicar of Romsey's remarks anticipate the attempts which many would make to reconcile themselves to the terrible losses to come.

Chapter XV
From Peace to War

O N 2 January 1914 the *Salisbury Times*,[1] which imitated its London namesake by printing advertisements on its front page, included an insertion announcing that Tamblings Christmas Club was open to subscribers. On the same page Pickfords, whose depot was in Fisherton Street, proclaimed that motor removals were a speciality, whilst a week later Rawlings of Silver Street began their sale by offering, among other lines, men's overcoats at 15s 6d, flannel shirts at 4s 6d, men's (as opposed to boys') trousers at 3s 11d, and gents' vests and pants at 1s. The Palace Theatre, which had begun to show moving pictures in 1910, was offering *Babes in the Wood*, although Elias Barker had already been advertising the bioscope,[2] with short topical films (which were presumably shown in halls and other public buildings) in 1901, and in January 1914 Smith's Music Store announced that they were stocking 'Pathescope, the home cinematograph [which] provides pictures for everyone'. Samuel Augustus Smith, whose shop was at 78 Fisherton Street, named his premises Handel House, in recognition of provincial musical taste, and was an enthusiastic motor-cyclist who advertised his premises on his machine.

In Redlynch it was announced that there was to be 'A most interesting and instructive lecture on the Church in Wales at St Mary's Church Hall' the following Thursday week. St Mary's Church Hall was recently completed. The apparently obscure subject was probably chosen because the Welsh Church had been disestablished in 1904, and the effects of that development were to be explained.

The squirearchy still retained their prominent position. On 16 January 1914 the New Forest Liberal Association held a meeting at Cadnam with Briscoe Eyre in the chair, and at Redlynch St Mary's Church Sunday School enjoyed their Christmas treat at New House with a splendidly decorated tree and refreshments. Mrs Eyre Matcham (who was related by marriage to Briscoe Eyre) presided and Miss Eyre Matcham presented the prizes.

At the same time some bizarre incidents were taking place. In January 1914 a madman was given temporary accommodation in Romsey Workhouse (which should correctly have been called the Poor Law Institution). He climbed onto the roof, took off some tiles and hurled them at the people on the ground. Another episode which suggested mental instability on the part of the perpetrator also occurred early in 1914. A wealthy American, Lee Bond of Lyndhurst, ordered his chauffeur (who was much alarmed by the instruction) to drive out into the countryside. There, brandishing a revolver, Bond held up other motorists, demanded petrol and fired at the police when they attempted to apprehend him. Eventually taken into custody, he was brought a meal, with a spoon and fork, but produced a knife which he had concealed about his person and attempted to cut his throat. He was then taken to the Royal South Hants Hospital in Southampton, and by early March he was sufficiently recovered to be bound over to appear before the Quarter Sessions at Winchester, identified not as Lee Bond but as Lewis Knight Brook Bruce – without further information being provided.

Early in the year the *Salisbury Times* began a lengthy correspondence when a leader was published about 'The Problem of Human Destiny', a subject which seemed particularly apposite in the light of coming events. An appetite for the dramatic was suggested by a 'three hour performance night' staged at the New Theatre, which included *A Marriage for Mavis*, *A King Cup* and *The Dreadful Secret*, 'cinema productions which will appeal to all lovers of sensation and adventure'.

The increasing number of pictures and picture houses (and the first moving pictures had been seen less than twenty years earlier) were indicative of the increasing pace of change. The number of motor vehicles was also increasing. W.H. Hudson had complained in 1910 that his favourite walk out of Salisbury to Old Sarum had been spoiled by the frequency of motors passing along it. By 1914 the *Salisbury Times* was carrying advertisements placed by Readheads Garage ('All makes of cars overhauled') and Longmans Motor Garage, who offered two-stroke Triumph motor-cycles for £42 and a four horsepower machine from the same manufacturer at a cost of £60.

At the same time the hazards of flying were made apparent by the three fatal accidents involving members of the Royal Flying Corps which took place in a fortnight in late February and early March. Heavier than air machines seem to have been taking a more prominent role, since all the fatalities occurred in these, with, in the final case, two junior officers killed when their plane broke down in mid-air and fell 2,000 feet.

The presence of the military on Salisbury Plain and in the vicinity of Salisbury may have made the local press and the community at large aware of their activities, and there was evident apprehension that war was approaching. The editorial printed in the *Salisbury Times* on 2 January 1914 was headed 'The Desirability of Peace'. Noting that in 1914 Britain would celebrate a century of peace with the United States, that 1915 would mark the centenary of the last conflict between Britain and France, and that there had not been hostilities between the country and Germany, the leader writer went on to claim that 'we are getting on but will war ever pass? Yes, because the fittest all survive and militarism cannot produce the fittest either physically, morally or spiritually.' By 1914 Germany was the greatest military power in Europe and the editorial, by claiming that survival of the fittest would eliminate future hostilities, seems to have been making a somewhat desperate attempt to persuade its readers that war would not occur. A more realistic proposal was debated by the Downton branch of the Church of England Men's Society on 7 January. The issue which was discussed was 'That war with Germany is inevitable and that there is an urgent need for the immediate introduction of conscription'. The Rev. Wilfred Clayton proposed the motion and it was opposed by Mr H.C. Spratling 'in an able speech'. Mr Spratling was supported by Colonel Marriott Smith, 'who joined in the negative discussion with a most interesting speech'. In the event two votes were taken on the motion, the first agreeing that war was unavoidable and the second rejecting conscription, results which anticipated events – since the regulars, territorials and reservists were augmented during 1914 and 1915 by a flood of volunteers, with conscription first introduced in May 1916, when the number volunteering proved insufficient to make good the ever-increasing losses.[4] The *Salisbury Times* reported the debate at Downton and, despite the gravity of the subject, claimed that it had made for 'a very pleasant evening'.[5] Far more serious were the dispatches sent in the aftermath of the second Balkan War of 1913 by Miss Edith Durham who wrote: '. . . is there anything more terrible than war? I reply emphatically, the time that follows immediately afterwards' – a time which is 'a wilderness of misery, hunger and disease'. In printing Miss Durham's report the *Salisbury Times* was perhaps expressing anxiety about the prospect of war even as it had sought to reassure its readers of the inevitability of peace in the editorial of 2 January.

Nor was it only the local newspapers which were mindful of the prospect of hostilities. In April 1914 the branch of the Band of Hope at Fritham Free Church gave presentations in which the musical items included 'The Temperance Host are Coming Now', 'The Tread of Mighty Armies' and 'The Gospel Temperance Battle Song', whilst on another occasion in the same month the children sang 'The War Drums are Beating'.

Evidence of change continued as the spring of 1914 advanced. In March, as the *Salisbury Times* reassuringly printed a table showing the relative strengths of the battle fleets of the nations, which demonstrated the numerical superiority of the Royal Navy over all its rivals, Salisbury City Council improved the surface of the Market Square to make it more suitable for motor vehicles.

In April Downton Parish Council considered the possibility of installing street lights and investigated two systems, both of which were potentially hazardous. One used acetylene gas and the other a mixture of petrol vapour and air; the latter, which had been installed at Fritham Free Church in 1904 and in the Sunday School Hall in 1912, was adopted. Petrol lighting, also used in domestic establishments, gave a particularly brilliant illumination.

On 10 June 1914 the managers of Landford Elementary School met and decided that the summer holidays (whose dates they set) should be from 31 July to 8 September. On the day that the Landford children broke up the *Salisbury Times* printed its last issue before the British declaration of war. Austria had declared war on Serbia a day earlier, Sir Edward Grey, the Foreign Secretary, had refused to give Germany a guarantee of British neutrality, Austria and Russia had mobilised and Austrian guns had bombarded Belgrade. In Salisbury Foster Brothers, an outfitters whose slogan was 'We cater principally for the working classes', advertised their summer sale, whilst the *Salisbury Times* printed a long article describing the contents of lectures given by Mr George Grey [Harold St George Gray] on 'The Prehistoric Monuments of Wessex' and Mr Heywood Sumner on 'The Excavations at Cranborne Chase'. A column entitled 'Suggestions for Gardeners' advised that 'Antirrhinums can be obtained in a variety of handsome colours' and that 'Water Cress may be grown in a shady position by the side of a wall facing north'. H.M. Livens, in his capacity as local secretary of the Selborne Society, had a letter published, complaining that he had been given two young cuckoos which had been misguidedly shot – as the bird was a friend to both the gardener and the grower.

The *Salisbury Times* printed a disclaimer denying that it had any connection with a bogus sales ploy. Packets of notepaper and envelopes had been hawked around Salisbury, Wilton and district, stamped with a number and the instruction that if it was sent to the *Times* a payment of 5s would be forthcoming. The *Salisbury Times* dissociated itself from this stratagem, as had the national newspaper.

The summer was very hot and fine, and on a beautiful day in late July the Downton branch of the Band of Hope enjoyed their summer treat in Breamore Park.

On 1 August France, Belgium and Germany mobilised and declared war on Russia. It being a Saturday, the *Salisbury Journal* was printed, giving indications of alarm which had been absent from the pages of its counterpart on the previous day. Under the headlines 'The European Crisis' and 'Grave News From Germany' it devoted several columns to what it now recognised as the inevitable approach of war, whilst an item noting that the Bishop of Salisbury had asked that prayers for the peace of Europe should be offered in the churches of the diocese may, with the *Journal* articles, be an indication of the way in which residents in outlying villages received the news that war was imminent.

On the next day German troops entered Poland, Luxemburg and France, and on 3 August invaded Belgium. This day was Bank Holiday Monday in Britain. The British government, demanding that German troops should withdraw from Belgian territory, received no reply, and on the following day declared war on Germany. The *Salisbury Times* was the first of the local newspapers to be published after hostilities began, and its edition of 7 August 1914 was a strange mixture of news of peace and war. The final two days of Rawlings' summer sale were advertised, whilst a match between Redlynch and Breamore Cricket Clubs, the last of the peace, was reported, together with the results of several other fixtures. In the same edition many columns were printed under the headline 'The Great European War', although they largely comprised reports of debates in Parliament. Smaller items provided incidental details: readers were informed, as an instance, that the German Army was unique in having a corps of gravediggers.

Other pages gave extensive coverage of the Whiteparish Flower Show, with a list of the winners in each of the classes, whilst there was an advertisement for Birds Custard and another which showed a young woman in summer clothes, sitting in a deck-chair and looking over her shoulder with a carton in her hand. The caption insisted that no one who was going to the seaside should fail to equip themselves with an ample supply of Beecham's Pills. (It is a reflection of the importance of the local press that national companies should have advertised in its pages.) The random insertion of items of war news with details of peacetime activities suggests that the paper was prepared hastily. Accounts of the Bank Holiday fetes at Coombe Bissett and Quidhampton appeared beside paragraphs recording that Emily Yates of Boscombe had been fined 20s and costs for assisting a deserter, James Robinson, whilst under the heading 'Redlynch Qui Vive' the *Salisbury Times* printed: 'This parish is watching the course of events in Europe with great interest as there are several young parishioners in the army and navy whilst several reservists have been called up this week and others ordered to make themselves ready. On Sunday the Rev. W.H. Wilson (Vicar) offered special prayers and made a reference to the situation in his sermon.' At the county police court proceedings against an unnamed naval reservist charged with drunkenness were abandoned as the accused had been called up, and in Fisherton Street station there was a constant succession of troops passing through, some of whom had paraded in the Cathedral Close. Units of the Hampshire, Somerset and Dorset Regiments had been assembled in this way, to be followed by the Wiltshire Territorial Battalion, which paraded into the Close to the strains of 'The Vly be on the Termit', the regimental march. The commander, the Earl of Radnor, rode at the head, with other scions of the landed classes acting as company commanders or as commanders of the cyclist corps or the machine gun section.

The county ladies also sought to play their part. On the afternoon of Monday 10 August Mrs Robinson of Redlynch House called a meeting to organise classes for nursing, ambulance craft and needlework in connection with the Red Cross Society in Downton, Redlynch, Plaitford, Landford and Charlton, although it is unclear whether this was in expectation of the widely but implausibly anticipated German invasion or to send support to the forces at the front. The same uncertainty applied to the suggestion made by the Guardians of the Alderbury Union that the workhouse infirmary, which was very well appointed, should be offered as a military hospital.

Yet whatever their expectations, and it is clear that there was a recognition that there would be a major conflict, none of the readers of the *Salisbury Times* and *Journal* and none of the residents of the outlying parishes can have anticipated the terrible cost of the hostilities which were beginning, nor the way in which war would transform their world and their way of life for ever.

Epilogue

A FEW feet from the gate of St Peter's Churchyard in Plaitford is a headstone, weathered by over ninety years' exposure to frost, wind and rain, which commemorates Private Robert Vincent Bowles of the Duke of Cornwall's Light Infantry. Killed on a quiet sector on the Western Front on 18 May 1918, Bob Bowles, who was eighteen years old, had fallen victim to a stray shell which had struck his position. He was buried in France, but in erecting the headstone to his memory his parents Alfie and Sarah Bowles were expressing the sense of loss and bewilderment experienced by the generation who had lived through the war. They faced a world in which, whilst much remained familiar, nothing would ever be the same again. The hostilities had not initiated the changes which followed. Many of the influences which would transform rural life were already evident by 1914, and as Percy Hatch wryly remarked of the flood of urban residents into the villages which had first begun in the late nineteenth century but increased ever more rapidly during the twentieth century, until the traditional inhabitants had largely disappeared, 'They wouldn't have come if they had to go down the bottom of the garden.'

The war nonetheless accelerated change, broke down ancient relationships and ensured that, whilst vestiges of the old order in the countryside would linger for decades afterwards, the rural world which had its final flowering between the accession of Victoria and 1914 would vanish for ever.

Notes

Prologue
1. Livens was a Unitarian minister who arrived in Nomansland in 1909. His pamphlet originally appeared as a series of articles in the *Salisbury Times* and has been reprinted twice, once in facsimile in 1975 and subsequently as part of *Nomansland. Its Two Hundred Years of History'* by David H. Kerridge, which was published in 2002.

Chapter I
On the Forest Edge
1. It was transferred to Hampshire under the Local Government act of 1894.
2. Thomas Edward, *In Pursuit of Spring*.
3. George Matcham's note was dated 8 June 1839 and appeared in the *Modern History of South Wiltshire Volume 5* (1844).
4 Fox Strangways was the family name of the Earls of Ilchester.
5. Lea, Hermann, *Thomas Hardy's Wessex* (1913).
6. John Hurst, the husband of Martha Hurst was described as a dealer in the census of 1861 whilst George Moody was noted to have followed a similar occupation in the deed for the sale of the site of Newtown Chapel in 1864.
7. Richard Jefferies claimed in writing to *The Times* in 1872 that he knew of a labourer who had made £4 from the sale of apples and £3 10s 0d from a single pear tree, although in an exceptional season.
8. Heywood Summer noted that this was the case on Ibsley Common.
9. Quoted in Sutherland, John, *Is Heathcliff a Murderer?*

Chapter II
Master and Man
1. Wise, John, *The New Forest. Its History and Scenery*.
2. The picture is from a glass plate negative taken by Arthur Kemish, an amateur photographer from Bramshaw.
3. She lived with her niece, a seamstress, and having no other family would have of necessity to have employed labourers.
4. Dawkins, John and Kenish, Eric, *Distant Views of Wellow and Plaitford*.
5. The Sloan Stanleys claimed descent from Sir Hans Sloane, hence the Christian name.
6. George Edward Briscoe Eyre was universally known as Briscoe to distinguish

him from his grandfather George Eyre and his father George Edward Eyre.

7. The living was in the hands of the Dean of Salisbury, who had nonetheless acceded to the Eyres' desire to appoint their relation.

8. Kilvert, Rev. Francis, *Kilvert's Diary 1870–79*.

9. *Romsey Advertiser*, 6 February 1903.

10. She spoke briefly at the opening of the Landford Wood Mission Hall in June 1899, her words being reported in the Romsey edition of the *Andover Advertiser*.

11. *Kilvert's Diary*.

12. Jefferies, Richard, *Wildlife in a Southern County* (1879).

13. Edna G. Young in correspondence with the author.

Chapter III
The Labourer at Home

1. *Romsey Advertiser*, 28 June 1912.

2. 'The Labourer's Daily Life' appeared in *Fraser's Magazine* in 1874 and was subsequently included in 'The Toilers of the Field', a collection of Jefferies' articles gathered by his widow in 1892.

3. Reprinted in *The Toilers of the Field*.

4. Ibid.

5. Sawyer, Rex L., *The Broadchalke Parish Papers* (1989).

6. Flora Thompson in *Lark Rise* alludes to this practice.

7. Jefferies, Richard, *The Toilers of the Field*.

8. De Crespigny, Rose C. and Hutchinson, Horace G., *The New Forest, Its Traditions, Inhabitants and Customs* (1899).

9. Hardy, Thomas, *Jude the Obscure* (1895).

10. Jefferies, Richard, *The Toilers of the Field*.

11. Ibid.

12. Ibid.

13. Thomas Hardy had written in *Far from the Madding Crowd*, 'In Weatherbury . . . Five decades hardly modified the cut of a gaiter, the embroidery of a smock-frock by the breadth of a hair.'

14. Jefferies, Richard, *Hodge and his Masters* (1880).

15. Wise, John, *The New Forest. Its History and Scenery* (1862).

16. Hatch, Louis, *Hamptith, Memories of Hamptworth before the First World War*.

Chapter IV
Birth and Marriage

1. Jeffries, Richard, *The Toilers of the Field*.

2. Ibid.

3. Ibid.

4. *Romsey Advertiser*, 3 May 1907.

5. Hudson, W.H., *Nature in Downland* (1899).

6. Jefferies, Richard, *The Toilers of the Field*.

7. Sarah Hurst died in 1880 aged twenty-one, presumably having always lived with her grandparents.

8. Jefferies, Richard, *The Toilers of the Field*.
9. *Salisbury Journal*, 26 January 1901.
10. Alfred Gay had accepted voluntary responsibility for Nomansland.

Chapter V
Deaths
1. Summer, Heywood, *The Book of Gorley* (1910).
2. John Wells's Lords Prayer hangs in the north transept of St Peter's Church, Bramshaw.
3. *Salisbury Journal*, 6 April 1878.
4. The 1891 census for Redlynch shows James Beauchamp, who was then aged fifty-seven, to have been a general labourer occupying his cottage with his forty-three-year-old wife Amelia and their four-year-old son Harold, both of whom were natives of Bitterne in Southampton. (James Beauchamp had been born in Redlynch.) On the other hand, the recollection of the family's disapproval and the remembrance of a housekeeper rather than a wife may suggest some irregularity in the household.
5. According to the instructions issued to enumerators, Gertrude Ings should have been classified as an idiot. Imbeciles were aged persons suffering from senile decay.
6. *Salisbury Journal*, 15 December 1855.
7. *Salisbury Journal*, 23 April 1864.
8. *Salisbury Journal*, 17 September 1875.
9. *Salisbury Journal*, 15 November 1864.
10. Letter to a correspondent identified only by the initials J.N., 3 December 1863.
11. Jefferies, Richard, *Wildlife in a Southern County* (1879).

Chapter VI
Outdoor Relief, Charity and Self Help
1. The Speenhamland System was first introduced in Speen, a Berkshire parish, in the late eighteenth century and was widely adopted elsewhere, although there were variations in the manner which it was implemented. Under the system the parish subsidised agricultural wages in line with the price of bread, the subsidy increasing as the cost of a gallon loaf rose. In many instances farmers took advantage of this practice by cutting wages in the knowledge that they would be made up by the overseers. Where the roundsman system, which also dated from the eighteenth century, was adopted, paupers were sent from farm to farm to work. Farmers paid their wages to the vestry, which then provided them with subsistence.
2. Overall responsibility for the New Poor Law was given to the Poor Law Board from 1847 to 1871, and from 1871 to the Local Government Board. This in turn was superseded by the Ministry of Health in 1919.
3. A mantua was a loose gown which was fashionable in the late seventeenth and eighteenth centuries. By 1849 mantuas were no longer worn, and a mantua-maker was merely a dress-maker.

4. The New Forest Union Workhouse was built in 1836. Before that date there was no poor house to which Nomansland residents could be admitted.
5. See Chapter XIV.
6. In an essay entitled 'The Wiltshire Labourer', which appeared in 1887, the year of his death, Richard Jefferies wrote of the labourer: 'You may give him a better cottage, you may give him a large allotment, you may treat him as an equal, and all is of no avail. Circumstances – the push of world – forces him to ask you for wages.'
The income from an allotment was clearly insufficient to support the cottagers on Plaitford Common without additional means of subsistence which had ceased to be available.
7. 1 Timothy IV, 8.
8. *Salisbury Journal*, 20 April 1877.
9. Romans XV, 5.
10. In a column headed 'Coming Events' the *Romsey Advertiser* listed nine fetes and festivals taking place between 11 June and 18 July 1906, six of which were organised by friendly or benefit societies.
11. Higher case letters were used in the original in imitation of the national press.
12. *Romsey Advertiser*, 22 May 1903.
13. The disjointed character of the sentence suggests that it was transcribed directly from the reporter's note book
14. 'The Besieged Generation' is the heading of Chapter 6 of *Lark Rise*.

Chapter VII
The Workhouse – The Pauper's Daily Routine

1. The former workhouse is now Church House.
2. Hardy, Thomas, *Far From the Madding Crowd* (1874).
3. A Romsey butcher, T. Butt and Sons, advertising in the *Andover Advertiser* in 1901, offered prime ox beef and Southdown wether mutton at their shop in Middlebridge Street, a working-class neighbourhood. Superior cuts were available at their premises in Bell Street, a superior locality.
4. The provision of alcoholic liquor in workhouses had been prohibited by the Local Government Board in 1884, although Guardians seem to have allowed themselves some freedom in interpreting official directives.
5. The poor law inspector's findings on the Alderbury and Romsey Union Workhouses are reprinted on the workhouse website, www.workhouses. org.uk, an excellent starting point for any investigation of the subject.
6. De Crespigny, Rose C. and Hutchinson, Horace G., *The New Forest, Its Traditions, Inhabitants and Customs*.
7. A report of the meeting of the Salisbury (Alderbury) Board of Guardians printed in the *Romsey Advertiser* recorded a resolution authorising the master to set vagrants to work picking oakum, chopping wood and grinding at the mills.
8. Sturt, George, *Memoirs of a Surrey Labourer* (1907).

Chapter VIII
The Workhouse – Education, Health and Changing Attitudes
1. The punctuation is that of the original, the clerk (somewhat surprisingly) misplacing capital letters and using inverted commas incorrectly.
2. See Chapter VII, note 5.
3. Sturt, George, *Memoirs of a Surrey Labourer.*
4. Jefferies, Richard, *Hodge and His Masters.*
5. Sturt, George, *Memoirs of a Surrey Labourer.*
6. According to the instructions to enumerators first issued in 1871, this was incorrect (see Chapter V, note 5.)
7. Jefferies, Richard, *The Toilers of the Field.*
8. Romsey Advertiser, 2 January 1912.

Chapter IX
Work – Labour in the Fields
1. Sturt, George, *Memoirs of a Surrey Labourer.*
2. Jefferies, Richard, *The Toilers of the Field.*
3. Jefferies, Richard, *Wildlife in a Southern County.*
4. Jefferies, Richard, *The Toilers of the Field.*
5. Fog is either a fine grass or the grass which grows after the first cut of hay. The origin of Jefferies' (evidently dialect) word is not known.
6. Jefferies Richard, *The Toilers of the Field.*
7. Ibid
8. Ibid.
9. Ibid.
10. Ibid.
11. Jefferies, Richard, *Wildlife in a Southern County.*

Chapter X
Work – The Artisan, The Shopkeeper and The Servant
1. Jefferies, Richard, *Hodge and His Masters.*
2. *Romsey Advertiser.*

Chapter XI
Nonconformity
1. Chandler, J.H. (ed.), *Wiltshire Dissenters Meeting House Certificates and Registrations 1689–1852* (1985).
2. Connexion is the eighteenth-century spelling of the word.
3. The date on the original trust deed and the Ecclesiastical Census.
4. Jefferies, Richard, *Wildlife in a Southern County.*
5. Summer, Heywood, *The Book of Gorley.*
6. Ritchie.

Chapter XII
The Natural Result of the Spread of Education
1. There is some confusion here. Robert Duncome Shafto owned the Hamptworth Estate in 1865, whilst the founding of Nomansland School

has also been dated in 1869 and 1875.

2. Livens, H.M., *Nomansland A Village History* (1910).
3. Romsey Advertiser, June 1906.
4. Romsey Advertiser, 25 January 1901.
5. Jefferies, Richard, *The Toilers of the Field*.
6. Reported in the Romsey edition of the *Andover Advertiser*.

Chapter XIII
Mobility
1. The figure is quoted in Chandler, J.H., *Endless Street* (1983).
2. Dawkins, John and Kerish, Eric, *Distant Views of Wellow and Plaitford* (1998).
3. Landford School log book, 13 October 1863.

Chapter XIV
Transition
1. Credentialled removals means accredited members who had left the church for another place.
2. In 1915 Wills cigarettes produced two sets of cards depicting Canadian and Australian life, with the same object.

Chapter XV
From Peace to War
1. Much of the material which follows is derived from the *Salisbury Journal*. The files of the *Romsey Advertiser* for 1914 have been lost.
2. The bioscope was an early name for moving pictures.
3. The debate is also referred to in *Downton and the First World War* by Edward Green.

Index

acorning, 127
Alderbury Union Workhouse, 94, 98, 100, 102
Alsop, Harriet, 172
Andover Union Workhouse, 117-18; scandal, 95
Arney, William, 62
Ashburton, Louisa Caroline, Dowager Countess, 17-19, 149, 158

bakeries, 136-8
Band of Hope, 154, 167, 195
Barter, William, 154
Batten, Sarah, 53
Beauchamp, James, 61; Mary, 61
Bell, Sarah, 76
besom making, 133-4
Biddlecombe, Albert, 26
Blackiston, Rev. Peyton, 104
Boham, John, 50, 68
bootmakers, 136
Bourne, George; see Sturt, George
Bowditch, Reginald, 160-1
Bowler, Henry Alexander, *The Doubt. Can These Dry Bones Live?* 69
Bowles, Alfred, 81; Charles, 12; Robert Vincent, 199
Bramshaw, 6, 59, 86, 92; Wesleyans, 147, 152
Brewer William, 147-8
brick making, 135
British and Foreign School Society, 158
broadcast sowing, 129
Broderick, Rev. Allan, 44, 156, 157
Budd, James, 21, 22, 23, 24, 169
Bungay Ellen, 34; Florence, 34; George, 29, 34, 189; Henry, 20, 21, 22, 23, 34, 36, 170; Hubert, 34

camp meetings, 145
Canada Common, 6, 185
Canterton Manor. 11
carriers, 176, 177
cars, motor, 178-82, 194
carters, 122
Chalk, Agnes, 99
Churchill, Harry, 85, 127, 159
cinema, 194
clothing, 41
clotten houses, 2
Cocks, James, 172-3
Collins, Emily Elizabeth, 71; Samuel, 62-3, 71
concerts, 171
Cooper, Rev. Mark, ii, 15, 17, 50, 67, 94
cowmen, 123
Cox, Ada, 111
Crespigny, Rose de & Hutchinson Horace, *The New Forest, Its Traditions Inhabitants and Customs*, i, ii, 27, 134, 159, 163
Crossley, Maud Sally, 178-9
Cull, Daniel, 132-3
Curtis, Frank, 81; George, 46-155; Jessie Eliza, 68; Walter, 46; William, 46

Dalgety, Frederick, 20-1; Pauline Caroline, 21, 23
de Crespigny, Rose & Hutchinson Horace, *The New Forest, Its Traditions Inhabitants and Customs*, i, ii, 27, 134, 159, 163
depopulation, 184-5
Derby Court, Salisbury, 31, 32
Dibden, Emily, 64; James, 5, 7
Dibdin, Edward, 74
Dible, William Arthur, 110
Dickens, Charles, *Bleak House*, 162; *Oliver*

Twist, 95
domestic service, 140-3
Domoney, William, 19-20
Dovey, Charles, 120
drapers, 138-9
drinking water, 35, 36
drovers, 132-3

Education Act 1870, 158
Education Act 1902, 155
Edwards, Samuel, 173-174
Elkins, Alfred, 63; Margaret Annie, 58
emigration, 79-80, 107, 186-7
evening classes, 169
Eyre, George, 157; George Edward Briscoe, 6, 12, 14, 16, 19-20, 193; Rev. Henry, 157; Mary, 17, 19

faggotting, match, i, iii, 8
field women, 124-6, 129
Fielder, Isaac, 78-9
Fleming, Baldwin, 115
flower and produce shows, 169-170
folklore, 162-3
Ford, Sidney, 58
Fordingbridge Union Workhouse, 94, 98, 99, 112
forestry, 134
friendly societies, 83-90
Fry, Charles, 100; George, 79
Futcher Eliza, 12

Gambling, Tom, 22, 23
Gay, Rev. Alfred H., 1, 82, 171
Giddings, John Pile, 53-4
Girdlestone, Rev. Francis, 143, 157; Rev. Henry, 65
gleaning, 126
Godden, Rev. John Whitworth, 17, 64
Griffen, Joseph, 155
guardians of the poor, 73-4
Gwyer, Henry, 65

Harding, Marian, 29, 41, 46, 47, 61, 174, 190
Hardy, Thomas, *Far From the Madding Crowd*, 48, 101 122; *Tess of the D'Urbervilles*, 48, 101, 102; *The Curates Kindness*, 103; *The Woodlanders*, 3
Hart, Evelyn, *Before I Forget.* 177

Hatch, Henry, 24; Louis, *Hamptith*, 42, 129; Percy. 6, 12, 14, 17, 20, 24, 26, 56, 66, 69, 137, 139, 151, 154, 159
Hawley, W.H.T., 97, 98, 100, 102, 108
Hayter, George, 134, 151
headstones, 61-62
Henbest, William, 87-8
holdings, life, 3
Hookey, Henry, 110-11
Hudson, W.H., *A Shepherd's Life*, 78, 109, 128, 176, 194; *Nature in Downland*, 48
Humby, Henry, 31
hurdle making, 133
Hursley Union Workhouse, 97
Hurst, Elizabeth, 49; John, 33; Martha, 1, 6, 33, 44, 50; Sarah, 49-50
Hutchings, James, 13; John, 62; Mary, 62
Hutchinson, Horace; *see* de Crespigny, Rose
Ilchester, Earls of, 2, 3
illegitimacy, 49-54
infant mortality, 45-7
Ings, Elizabeth (Bessie), 38; Ellen (Nellie), 38, 41; Frederick, 132; Florence Mary, 60-1, 140-1, 176; Gertrude, 61; James, 39; Sarah, 39; William, 39

Jefferies, Richard, 24, 48, 49, 51, 54, 66, 121, 140, 150-1, 168; *Green Feme Farm*, 129; *Hodge and his Masters*, 37, 51, 55, 68-9, 74, 76, 77, 82, 101, 102, 103, 127, 163; *The Open Air*, 120-1; *The Toilers of the Field*, 32, 33, 35, 44, 45, 125

Kendal, George, 185-186; Oliver, 57
Kilvert Rev. Francis, *Diary*, 16, 19
King, Henry. 86; J.W., 155; Willis, 155

lace making, 38
Landford National School, 159
Lea, Hermann, *Thomas Hardy's Wessex*, 4
Legge, George, 56-8
Levi, John, 112
life holdings, 3
Light, George, 151
literacy. 161-2
Livens, Herbert Mann, *Nomansland, A Village History*, i, 8, 40, 81, 147, 152
Loader, Frank 187
Lockerley. 3, 88-90, 161; Hall, 21. 22, 23

lunatics, pauper, 110-11
Lymington Parish Work House, 104

Macey, Edward, ii, 62
magic lantern, 167-8
Maidment, Edith, 88; Frederick Charles, 88-90; Wilfred, 88
Mangan, Rev. Samuel Waring, 24
marriage, 54-8
match faggotting, i, iii, 8
Matthews, George, 28
Meech, James, 88
Melchet Court, 11, 169, 171
Merson, Elizabeth, *Once There Was A Village School*, 19, 128, 159, 161
milkers, 122-5
Minstead, 10, 49
Moody, Anne, 36; Daniel, 134; Reuben, 135, 154; Silas, 135
motor cars, 178-82, 194
Mowlem, Francis, 158, 171

National Society, 51, 157
Nelson, Frances Elizabeth, Dowager Countess, 60, 157; Hon. Henry, 66
Newey, John, 160
New Forest Union Workhouse, 93, 94, 106, 107, 115
newspapers, 162-7
Newtown Primitive Methodist Church, 3, 140
Nomansland, i, ii, 1, 32, 36, 39, 80-1, 147-8, 149, 155
nonconformist burial grounds, 70
Nunn, George, 6, 63

Old Tame, 59, 151-2

Page, Samuel, 178
Parsons, Mary Ann, 53-4
pauper lunatics, 110-11
Penny, Elizabeth, 76
Permain, Charles, 131
pig keeping, 39
pit sawing, 135
Plaitford, 1, 2, 45, 56, 59, 148, 184
Pointer, John, 136
poor, guardians of the, 73-4
Poor Law Amendment Act, 1834, 73
poor rate, 80-1

population decline, 184-5
post offices, 138
preaching, 149-51
Price, Joseph, 79-80
privies, 35

railways, 176
reading rooms, 168-9
Redlynch, 32, 84-5, 193
relieving officers, 77-9
Reynolds, Edward Charles, 64-5, 109
Rigg, Rev. T.C .. 63
roads, turnpike, 174-5
Romsey Union Workhouse, 95, 97, 98, 101, 102, 103
Russell, Caroline, 50; Hannah, 75

Salisbury Infirmary, 109
sawing, pit, 135
Scallon, Dr. E.O., 30, 189
school boards, 158
Scultze Gunpowder Company, 28
Scout Motors, 181-2
Scovell, William, 64
settlements, 109
Sherfield English, 59, 139
Shergold, John, 1
Shoe Inn, Plaitford, 172-4
Sillence, Hannah, 151
Snellgrove, George, 75; Mary, 75
sowing, broadcast, 129
squoyling, 42
stage coaches, 172-4
Stockbridge Union Workhouse, 116-17
Sturt, George (George Boume), *Memoirs of A Surrey Labourer*, 30, 36, 102, 108-9, 120
suicide, 62-3
Sullivan, Douglas, 179-80
Sumner, Heywood, 59, 151

Tate, W.E., *The Parish Chest*, 47
temperance movement, 153
Thomas, Edward, *In Pursuit of Spring*, 1, 181-2
Thompson, Flora, *Lark Rise*, 10, 29, 34, 35, 48, 55, 121, 149, 160, 184
Thorne, Annie, 141-3
Thwaites, Rev. Edgar Nembhard, 183
Tidridge, Mary, 159

Titanic disaster, 190-2
Turbury, 37
turnpike roads, 174-5
Tutt, Edwin, 63; John, 131; William, 131

vagrancy, 112-114

Walke, Rev. Nicholas, 179; William Coope,
   179-80
water, drinking, 35, 36
Wellow (West and East), 24-25, 49, 85-6,
   158, 169

Wells, James, 59; John, 59-60; Sarah, 59
wheelwrights, 132
Whiteparish, 55, 132, 133, 134, 138;
   Horticultural Society, 169-70
Wise, John, *The New Forest, Its History and
   Scenery*, i, ii, 10, 41, 162, 163
women, field, 124-6, 129
Wood, Mrs Henry, East Lynne. 142
workhouse: christmas, 116-118; dietaries,
   95-7, 113; infirmary, 108-9; schools,
   104-6; *see also* individual workhouses
   by name

Lightning Source UK Ltd.
Milton Keynes UK
02 December 2010

163737UK00003B/16/P